Ship Otago

AGREEMENT No. 5

Amount of Wages per Week, Calendar Month, Share, or Voyage. 11	Amount of Wages advanced on Entry. 12	Amount of Weekly or Monthly Allotment. 13	Signature or Initials of Superintendent, Consul, or Officer of Customs. 14	PARTICULARS OF DISCHARGE, &c. To be filled in by the Master upon the Discharge, Death, or Desertion of any Member of his Crew. Date, Place, and Cause of leaving this Ship, or of Death. Date. 15	Place. 16	Cause.* 17	Balance of Wages paid on Discharge. 18	RELEASE (late M). We, the undersigned Members of the Crew of this Ship, do hereby release this Ship, and the Master and Owner or Owners thereof, from all Claims for Wages or otherwise in respect of this Voyage. Signatures of Crew (each to be on the Line on which he signed in Col. 1). 19	Signature or Initials of Superintendent, Consul, or Officer of Customs before whom the Balance of Wages was paid and Balance signed. 20	Reference No.
6 . .	—			[illegible]				[illegible]	A. W. Stringer	21
3 10 -	—			as the ... was ... discharged from his former ship and is now sick in hospital					A. W. Stringer	22
3 10 -	Nil		[illegible]							23
3 10 -	"		[illegible]	17/3/88	Sydney	Dis		Thomas Smith		24
3 10 -	"		[illegible]							25
3 10 -	"		[illegible]							26
3 10 -	"		[illegible]	failed to join						27
3 10 -	Nil		J. C. Hoskens Master	This man engaged as substitute for Edward Gaden and signed on board, the shipping office being closed and ship going to sea at once.						28
As per Agreement			[illegible]							29
4	Discharged in New Zealand		[illegible]							30
4			[illegible]							31
4			[illegible]							32
3			[illegible]							33
			[illegible]							34
4 .			[illegible]							35
5 . To the ...			[illegible]							36
										37
										38
										39
										40

* ... the Ship," thus "H.M.S. Revenge"; and the other Causes of leaving the Ship should be ...

[Twelve Pages.]

CONRAD'S EASTERN WORLD

The real is only the base. But it is the base

WALLACE STEVENS

CONRAD'S EASTERN WORLD

NORMAN SHERRY

Lecturer in English, University of Singapore

CAMBRIDGE
AT THE UNIVERSITY PRESS
1966

PUBLISHED BY
THE SYNDICS OF THE CAMBRIDGE UNIVERSITY PRESS

Bentley House, 200 Euston Road, London, N.W. 1
American Branch: 32 East 57th Street, New York, N.Y. 10022
West African Office: P.M.B. 5181, Ibadan, Nigeria

Printed in Great Britain at the University Printing House, Cambridge
(*Brooke Crutchley, University Printer*)

LIBRARY OF CONGRESS CATALOGUE
CARD NUMBER: 66–11282

CONTENTS

Contents

ILLUSTRATIONS

PLATES

Between pages 332 *and* 333

ACKNOWLEDGEMENTS

I should like to acknowledge the help I have received from a number of individuals and institutions in carrying out this study of the sources of Joseph Conrad's Eastern novels. It is impossible to list them all, but I wish to express my gratitude to all those who have helped me.

Miss Jean Waller, the Librarian of the University of Singapore, and her staff were invaluable in obtaining books and microfilms for me. The Australian and New Zealand authorities were extremely helpful in supplying me with copies of relevant material, especially G. L. Fischer, Archivist, Public Library of South Australia; the City Librarian, City of Sydney Public Library; the Secretary, Marine Board of Victoria; the City Librarian, Newcastle, New South Wales; the Principal Archivist of New South Wales; the Town Clerk of Dunedin; and the Librarian of Auckland Public Libraries. I am also indebted to the India Office Records and the Principal Civil Hydrographer in England; the Town Clerk of Bundoran, County Donegal, Ireland; the Master-Attendant of Shipping, the Registrar of Births and Deaths, Mr Wee the deputy Editor and Mr Quek the Librarian of the *Straits Times*, the Librarian of the National Library, all in Singapore; the Registrar of Shipping and Seamen in Wales; Mark Shideler, former editor of the *Bangkok World*, in Bangkok; Peter Martin in Sourabaya, and Clifford Hill, Karim Namazie, René Eber, Mrs Patricia Lim, and Charlie Ng in Singapore. I am indebted to the scholarship of Ifor B. Powell of Cardiff and the late Dr C. Gibson-Hill.

I am particularly grateful to the relatives and descendants of those men Conrad used as originals for his characters who have answered my numerous inquiries with great patience.

Acknowledgements

I must not omit J. I. M. Stewart and Professor Ian Watt who read the manuscript at an earlier stage. Finally, I should like to acknowledge the inspiration provided by Professor Peter Ure who started me off, the encouragement of Professor Edward Shils which came when I most needed it, and the assistance of the editorial staff of the Cambridge University Press whose suggestions saw me through the final stages.

I am indebted to Yale University Library for permission to quote from Conrad's manuscripts.

Some parts of this study have appeared in *Review of English Studies*, *Notes and Queries*, *Modern Philology*, *Modern Language Review*, *Publications of the Modern Language Association of America*, *Philological Quarterly*, *Review of English Literature*, and *Nineteenth Century Fiction*.

N. S.

NOTE

The superior figures in the text relate to the references starting on p. 323

For my Mother and Father

Conrad's Eastern World

I

INTRODUCTION: THE CONDITIONS OF CONRAD'S ACTIVE LIFE

Between the years 1883 and 1888, Joseph Conrad sailed for a time in Eastern waters as a British merchant seaman; when he began to write, it was to the East that he turned especially for inspiration. The East not only provided him with the initial creative impetus—he wrote in *A Personal Record*, 'If I had not got to know Almayer pretty well it is almost certain there would never have been a line of mine in print'[1]—but it also remained a constant source for him. Of *The Shadow-Line* he said in the Author's Note: 'As to locality, it belongs to that part of the Eastern Seas from which I have carried away into my writing life the greatest number of suggestions.'[2] The dates of those works concerned in some way with the Eastern Seas show the thread of this influence from the beginning to the end of his life as a writer: *Almayer's Folly* (1895), *An Outcast of the Islands* (1896), 'Karain' and 'The Lagoon' (1898), *Lord Jim* (1900), 'Youth' and 'The End of the Tether' (1902), *Typhoon* and 'Falk' (1903), 'A Smile of Fortune', 'The Secret Sharer', and 'Freya of the Seven Isles' (1912), *Victory* (1915), *The Shadow-Line* (1917), and *The Rescue* (1920).

Conrad's period in the East was, therefore, of great importance to him, yet very little is known of Conrad's experiences at that time. The account of these years takes up only 51 out of the 687 pages of Jean-Aubry's biography of Conrad,[3] and about 30 of the 451 pages of Jocelyn Baines's biography.[4] Apart from the briefness of the period Conrad spent in the East (it amounted to only a few months), the nature of his life there—that of a mariner—accounts for the meagre amount of biographical detail in existence about it. 'Landfall and Departure mark the rhythmical swing of a seaman's life and of a ship's career. From land to land is the most concise definition of a ship's earthly fate', he wrote in *The Mirror of the Sea*,[5] and it was this rhythmical swing of the seaman's life, with all that it implies of brief contacts with lands and peoples, that formed the conditions of his life as a seaman in the East. Except for the names of ships he sailed in, dates of voyages and destinations of ships, names of captains and crews, there would seem to be little more which could be discovered about this period. We do know that in Borneo Conrad came into contact with a certain trader named Charles Olmeijer who was to become the Almayer of *Almayer's Folly*; and that the Captain Lingard of *Almayer's Folly*, *An Outcast of the Islands*, and *The Rescue*, and the Captain Ellis of *The Shadow-Line* were based upon an actual Captain Lingard and an actual Captain Ellis.[6] Captain Lingard was a trader and free-booter in the Eastern seas, and Captain Ellis was the Master-Attendant at Singapore who gave Conrad his first command. Yet little is known about these men, apart from their names and occupations, and, as I shall show, not all the information we have about them is correct. Certainly what has been discovered would hardly account for Conrad's acknowledging such a profound debt to the Eastern seas. He must have found there a much wider experience than has yet been suspected.

*

It has frequently been concluded that Conrad's life as a seaman must, by its nature, have provided him personally with the experiences he required for his fiction; it has been accepted that such a life was necessarily out of the ordinary, filled with adventure and excitement. Henry James, writing to Conrad about *The Mirror of the Sea*, commented: 'But the book itself is a wonder to me really—for its so bringing home the prodigy of your past experiences: bringing it home to me more personally and directly, I mean, the immense treasure and the inexhaustible adventures. No one has *known*—for intellectual use—the things you know...'[7]

No doubt Conrad's life was adventurous. He had his share of dangerous experiences in Eastern waters, and we learn something of them from 'Youth' and *The Shadow-Line*. Certainly, a Conrad who had not been to sea would not have been the same writer at all, but there is another side to Conrad's sea-life which suggests that we should not exaggerate the adventurous aspect and its influence on his fiction. Edward Garnett recalls a significant remark of Conrad's in this connection:

> On one occasion, in describing to him a terrible family tragedy of which I had been an eye-witness, Conrad became visibly ill-humored and at last cried out with exasperation, 'Nothing of the kind has ever come my way! I have spent half my life knocking about in ships, only getting ashore between voyages. I know nothing, nothing! except from the outside. I have to guess at everything!'[8]

Garnett also recalled that Conrad 'deplored the lack of opportunities for intimate observation that a sailor's life had offered him'. Conrad himself admitted in the Author's Note to *Within the Tides*: '...my life as a matter of fact was far from being adventurous in itself. Even now when I look back on it...its colouring wears the sober hue of hard work and exacting calls of duty, things which in themselves are not much charged with a feeling of romance.'[9] 'I have had some impressions, some sensations—in my time—impressions and sensations of common things', he claimed.[10]

Allowing here for a change in perspective due to the passage of time, it must still be conceded that his life as a sailor was bound to include long stretches of dull routine and hard work. The 'sober hue' of such a life he ascribes to the experience of Captain Whalley in the *Sofala* in 'The End of the Tether':

> He knew it well, too, this monotonous huckster's round, up and down the Straits; he knew its order and its sights and its people. Malacca to begin with, in at daylight and out at dusk...At noon the three palms of the next place of call, up a sluggish river...Sixty miles farther on there was another place of call, a deep bay with only a couple of houses on the beach. And so on, in and out, picking up coastwise cargo here and there, and finishing with a hundred miles' steady steaming through the maze of an archipelago of small islands up to a large native town at the end of the beat. There was a three days' rest for the old ship before he started her again in inverse order, seeing the same shores from another bearing, hearing the same voices in the same places, back again to the *Sofala's* port of registry on the great highway of the East, where he would take up a berth nearly opposite the big stone pile of the harbour office till it was time to start again on the old round of 1,600 miles and thirty days. Not a very enterprising life...(pp. 203–4).

And between voyages there would be days or weeks in a foreign port, staying either on board ship or at a Sailors' Home. At times these must have been periods of idleness for Conrad, spent hanging about the dock area of the port. His first visit to Singapore after the loss of the *Palestine* was probably one of these periods, and other instances are suggested in his works. There is the description of Lord Jim associating 'with the men of his calling in the port' while waiting for a berth,[11] and the feelings of the narrator in *The Shadow-Line* while he is staying at the Sailors' Home: 'I had never in my life felt more detached from all earthly goings on. Freed from the sea for a time, I preserved the sailor's consciousness of complete independence from all land affairs.'[12] Conrad describes in *The Mirror of the Sea* the 'lonely officer' left on duty on board ship in an Australian port, listening for hours to the 'voice of a man crying "Hot saveloys!"', falling into conversation with casual visitors to the docks, or overhearing the 'impolite stories' told by the cabmen who had come to meet a passenger-boat, 'every word of which reached me distinctly over the bulwarks as I sat smoking on the main-hatch', the ship's crew having melted swiftly away into the town.[13] On other occasions, Conrad must have been frantically occupied with commercial matters, interviewing charterers, getting together a cargo, taking on the full complement of crew. This was certainly the case during his stay in Bangkok, as the following passage from 'Falk' suggests: 'The crew was sickly, the cargo was coming very slow; I foresaw I would have lots of trouble with the charterers, and doubted whether they would advance me enough money for the ship's expenses. Their attitude towards me was unfriendly. Altogether I was not getting on' (p. 178).

Such a life might well cause Conrad, in retrospect, to complain that he knew nothing except from the outside. He was unlikely to get to know people or places in the East with any degree of intimacy. In a letter to J. M. Dent, his publisher, he wrote: 'But indeed I knew very little of and about shore-people. I was chief mate of the S.S. *Vidar* and very busy whenever in harbour. And anyway I would not have cared to form social connections, even if I had had time and opportunity.'[14] He emphasized this absence of contact with the society of the places he visited in the East, in a letter to W. G. St Clair (see Appendix E, p. 317, below). St Clair, formerly editor of the *Singapore Free Press*, had corresponded with Conrad about his Eastern experiences and published two letters from Conrad, which I recently discovered, in an article in the *Malay Mail*, 2 September 1924. In his first letter, Conrad indicated the extent of his contact with men in the East. Specifically he stated: 'As you may guess we had no social shore connections. You know it isn't very practicable for a seaman.'

My researches show, I think, that this is not entirely true. Conrad certainly formed some significant social shore connections in Singapore. But we must keep in mind that the fact that he knew the East as a seaman posits a special relationship between him and the Eastern world which provided his source material. Primarily he must have been limited to seagoing society and mariners' talk both on the sea and ashore. Moreover, what he observed was only what a seaman could observe in port; mostly trivial, certainly impersonal. What his outburst to Garnett shows is a sense of not having been involved in the life of the feelings, the things which a settled or social existence would bring.

One can say further that, while the common experiences or disasters of the sea were part of Conrad's lot, the outstanding sea-events fell to the lot of others, such as the officers of the pilgrim ship *Jeddah* in 1880 who abandoned their ship with almost a thousand pilgrims on board, and the mate and captain of the *Cutty Sark* who were involved in a murder—events which were famous scandals of their day. The men concerned in these scandals betrayed 'a tradition...as imperative as any guide on earth could be'.[15] Conrad, who appears never to have 'failed' in this sense, was aware of the possibility of failure—'I always suspected that I might be no good'[16]—and he had experienced situations in which one might fail. Perhaps it was this consciousness of the very real possibility of failure which caused him in his fiction to connect famous sea-crimes with his own knowledge of the conditions of 'moral isolation' in which man's weaknesses could take control.

But however specialized Conrad's contact with the Eastern world of the 1880's was, in many ways that world was a fascinating locality for any future novelist because of its thriving trade, its mixture of sophistication and primitiveness, its sense of adventure and its adventurers, and especially perhaps its intimacy—the intimacy of a small society of white men in an alien setting—which served to throw up gossip and scandal and to cause certain men to stand out in sharp relief. And even though Conrad was not in any sense committed to this society, certainly the 'suggestions' he referred to lay there and can be rediscovered. Once the search is begun, one discovers that the information obtainable is of a wide scope. It allows us to date his movements at this time with greater accuracy, to discover something of his experiences as a seaman, of the people he met, the things he saw, and the places he visited.

This book is an attempt to recreate the world Conrad knew as a seaman in the East of the 1880's, in order to discover what those 'suggestions' were which he claimed to have carried away with him, and to follow the processes of creation such 'suggestions' went through in becoming the completed works. In trying to find the inspiration for any particular work, it is not sufficient to trace *one man* or *one incident* in the East, for Conrad drew upon the whole of the Eastern world he knew, however superficially he knew it, and reproduced many aspects of it with remarkable fidelity. Research into the sources of specific works only reveals the complexity of the world he had known—a small world with its centre in the small island of Singapore—and the complexity of his method as a writer.

*

The search for Conrad's source material in the East demands also a consideration of the way such material came to him. The sources of Conrad's Eastern novels were fourfold—hearsay, observation, personal experience, and reading.[17] Conrad drew upon all these reserves of source material for his Eastern fiction, but I have found that inquiry along the lines of Conrad's possible personal experience, hearsay, and observation has been most fruitful in providing information about the source material that came his way in the East. He said that *The Shadow-Line* was 'exact autobiography', and I have attempted to discover those personal experiences as master of the *Otago* which formed the basis of this story. On the other hand, two scandals of the Eastern seas form the sources of the first part of *Lord Jim* and of 'The Secret Sharer', and these came to Conrad primarily through hearsay and observation. Personal observation plays a large part in 'The End of the Tether', while reading appears to be an important source for those novels set in the Bornean jungle—*Almayer's Folly*, *An Outcast of the Islands* and the second part of *Lord Jim*. Most studies of Conrad's sources have concentrated upon his reading, but so far as his Eastern novels are concerned, the influence of Conrad's reading was a specialized one, as I shall show, providing him not so much with suggestions for plots, themes, or ideas as with information about the East which, because of his short stay there, he could not have obtained at first hand.[18]

We can rarely rely upon Conrad's own statements about his sources. Ford Madox Ford, though he is not always a reliable witness, gives us some indication of Conrad's attitude to revealing his sources. In the Author's Note to *The Secret Agent*, Conrad relates how a friend had given him the subject of the novel 'in the shape of a few words'. The friend was Ford, who states:

> And the writer knew—and Conrad knew that the writer knew—a great many anarchists of the Goodge Street group, as well as a great many of the police who watched them. The writer had provided Conrad with Anarchist literature, with memoirs, with introductions... But Conrad, when he met the writer after the publication of the *Secret Agent* with preface in 1920, remarked almost at once and solicitiously: 'You know... The preface to the *Secret Agent*...I did not give you away too much... I was very cautious.'...He had wished politely to throw a veil of eternal respectability over the writer.[19]

What Conrad meant in this case by not giving Ford away too much, was in fact a denial that Ford knew anything about anarchists. He writes: 'I am sure that if he [Ford] had seen once in his life the back of an anarchist that must have been the whole extent of his connection with the underworld.'[20] Ford, speaking from personal experience, added: 'And of course few men in self-revelations and prefaces have ever so contrived under an aspect of lucidity to throw over themselves veils of confusion.'[21]

But though Conrad may be cautious in giving information as to his sources, he does give several examples of these sources 'at work', as it were. In other words, he gives examples of the kind of hearsay, observation, and personal experience which provided him with his source material. There are his explanations of how he met the 'flesh and blood' individuals who stand behind his fictional characters, for instance, his description of how he came to know Charles Olmeijer (the original of Almayer):

I had seen him for the first time some four years before from the bridge of a steamer moored to a rickety little wharf forty miles up, more or less, a Bornean river....He stepped upon the jetty. He was clad simply in flapping pyjamas of cretonne pattern (enormous flowers with yellow petals on a disagreeable blue ground) and a thin cotton singlet with short sleeves. His arms, bare to the elbows, were crossed on his chest. His black hair looked as if it had not been cut for a very long time...I had heard of him at Singapore...I had heard of him in a place called Pulo Laut...in a place called Dongola, in the Island of Celebes, when the Rajah of that little-known sea-port...came on board in a friendly way with only two attendants, and drank bottle after bottle of soda-water...That morning, seeing the figure in pyjamas moving in the mist, I said to myself: 'That's the man.'[22]

And then there is his meeting with the original of Mr Jones of *Victory*:

Mr Jones (or whatever his name was) did not drift away from me. He turned his back on me and walked out of the room. It was in a little hotel in the island of St Thomas in the West Indies (in the year '75) where we found him one hot afternoon extended on three chairs, all alone in the loud buzzing of flies to which his immobility and his cadaverous aspect gave a most gruesome significance. Our invasion must have displeased him because he got off the chairs brusquely and walked out, leaving with me an indelibly weird impression of his thin shanks.[23]

This is one kind of personal experience, involving confrontations of varying intensity with the men he was to write about.

Then there is the special nature of the hearsay which was another source. 'Men', Conrad writes in his Author's Note to *Lord Jim*, 'have been known, both in the tropics and in the temperate zone, to sit up half the night "swapping yarns".'[24] And again in the Author's Note to *Typhoon* he refers to that source of a seaman writer, seamen's yarns, or 'marine shore-talk' as he also called it: 'Years before I had heard it [the *Typhoon* anecdote] being talked about in the East as a recent occurrence. It was for us merely one subject of conversation amongst many others of the kind. Men earning their bread in any very specialised occupation will talk shop...'[25] In the section of *The Mirror of the Sea* entitled 'Initiation', Conrad gives a particular example of 'marine shore-talk'. He has been speaking earlier of ports and docks and the shipping that fills them—sights which must have been familiar to him at every landfall and departure. Then he tells of the elderly seaman who 'gave [him] a glance to make sure of [their] fellowship in the craft and mystery of the sea'. The old seaman had just been taken on as quartermaster on the *Hyperion*, and in reply to the question, 'What sort of a name has she got?' he says:

Just now...he had heard that this very voyage...she broke her sheer, struck adrift, and lost an anchor and chain...this looked as though she were pretty hard on her ground-tackle. Didn't it? She seemed a heavy ship to handle, anyway. For the rest, as she had a new captain and a new mate this voyage...one couldn't say how she would turn out...

In such marine shore-talk as this [Conrad goes on] is the name of a ship slowly established, her fame made for her, the tale of her qualities and of her defects kept, her idiosyncrasies commented upon with the zest of personal gossip, her achievements made much of, her faults glossed over as things that, being without remedy in our imperfect world, should not be dwelt upon too much by men who, with the help of ships, wrest out a bitter living from the rough grasp of the sea.[26]

And Conrad refers to a further example of such marine shore-talk in a letter to the Dowager Ranee Margaret of Sarawak:

> For all my admiration for and mental familiarity with the Great Rajah the only concrete object I ever saw connected with him was the old steamer 'Royalist', which was still in 1887 running between Kuching and Singapore. She was a venerable relic of the past and the legend, I don't know how far true, amongst all the officers in the Port of Singapore was that she had been presented to Rajah Brooke by some great lady in London.[27]

These quotations give valuable clues to the nature of some of Conrad's sources and of his contact with them, revealing an extension of his 'hearsay' into visual terms, for the actual presence of ships connected with well or locally known people and incidents must have provided a concrete background to sailors' stories.

And this kind of exchange among seamen, concerning the reputations of ships and the reputations of the men who sail them, frequently appears in his fiction as a dramatic method of narration. Examples of seamen's gossip occur in at least two places in *Lord Jim*, and must reflect the common pool of interest which Conrad found in all ports and in all ships and which consisted of sea stories, factual and fictional. One example is the sea captains' gossip about the *Patna* incident in the ship-chandler's parlour in 'an Eastern port' (chapter XVIII), and the other is Marlow's discussion of the same incident with the French naval lieutenant in an Australian port (chapters XII and XIII). *Lord Jim* depends more than any other novel upon marine shore-talk for both content and method, and I shall consider this in more detail later. But an example from *The Shadow-Line* shows how naturally, yet dramatically, the method of communication among seamen has become a method of narration of the novelist. It is a passage from the narrator's first interview with his mate, Mr Burns:

I fell back on a question which had been in my thoughts for a long time—the most natural question on the lips of any seaman whatever joining a ship...

'I suppose she can travel—what?'

Now a question like this might have been answered normally, either in accents of apologetic sorrow or with a visibly suppressed pride, in a 'I don't want to boast, but you shall see' sort of tone. There are sailors, too, who would have been roughly outspoken: 'Lazy brute', or openly delighted: 'She's a flyer'. Two ways, if four manners.

But Mr Burns found another way, a way of his own which had, at all events, the merit of saving his breath, if no other.

Again he did not say anything. He only frowned. And it was an angry frown. I waited. Nothing more came.

'What's the matter?...Can't you tell after being nearly two years in the ship?' I addressed him sharply.

He looked as startled for a moment as though he had discovered my presence only that very moment...He said that a ship needed, just like a man, the chance to show the best she could do, and that this ship had never had a chance since he had been on board of her. Not that he could remember. The last captain...He paused (pp. 68–9).

Conrad's interest in the ships he once knew continued after he had left the sea. He traced their fate through newspaper reports and *Shipping Gazettes* and this must also have been a means of recalling for him stories he had heard about them:

Often I turn with melancholy eagerness to the space reserved in the newspapers under the general heading of 'Shipping Intelligence'. I meet there the names of ships I have known. Every year some of these names disappear—the names of old friends.[28]

And again:

The unholy fascination of dread dwells in the thought of the last moments of a ship reported as 'missing' in the columns of the *Shipping Gazette*.[29]

In looking for those experiences in Eastern waters which Conrad used in his fiction, it is this specialized kind of hearsay and observation that we must keep in mind, as well as his personal experience and reading.

*

The Conditions of Conrad's Active Life

The search for the sources of Conrad's novels has gone on for many years. As early as 1917 Conrad received a letter from a clerk in an Australian shipping firm—the firm that employed Conrad in his first command—who had been trying to discover the sources of Conrad's novels in the East. I have discovered two previously unknown letters from Conrad to this clerk, A. T. Saunders. Saunders's limited success in his search was, nevertheless, sufficient for Conrad to write to him: 'You are a terror for tracking people out! It strikes me that if I had done something involving penal servitude I wouldn't have liked to have you after me' (see Appendix A, p. 295, below). But this letter of Conrad's to Saunders is interesting because of what Conrad has to say about his attitude to the facts he used as source material:

> I need not point out that I had to *make* material from my own life's incidents arranged, combined, coloured for artistic purposes. I don't think there's anything reprehensible in that. After all I *am* a writer of fiction; and it is not what actually happened, but the manner of presenting it that settles the literary and even the moral value of my work. My little vol: of autobiography of course is absolutely genuine. The rest is a more or less close approximation to facts and suggestions. What I claim as true are my mental and emotional reactions to life, to men, to their affairs and their passions as I have seen them. I have in that sense kept always true to myself.

Conrad is here stating his own conviction of what is involved in the creative process so far as the writer is concerned and I hope by revealing the sources of Conrad's Eastern fiction to be able to examine this process more closely. In describing how his story *Typhoon* developed, Conrad writes:

> From the first the mere anecdote, the mere statement I might say, that such a thing had happened on the high seas, appeared to me a sufficient subject for meditation. Yet it was but a bit of a sea yarn after all. I felt that to bring out its deeper significance which was quite apparent to me, something other, something more was required; a leading motive that would harmonise all these violent noises, and a point of view that would put all that elemental fury into its proper place.[30]

When we trace Conrad's source materials—'the mere anecdote'—in some detail, it becomes possible to see how he brought out the deeper significance of the original, what changes he thought necessary, what leading motives arose from the contemplation of the source material, how, in short, his creative intelligence went to work.

And fortunately Conrad's method of work as a novelist makes this search for his original sources a less impossible task than it appears at first, for he was a novelist who found it necessary to deal in fact to a large extent, as he stated a number of times:

> I am not a facile inventor. I have some imagination,—but that's another thing.[31]

> As for the story ['An Outpost of Progress'] itself it is true enough in its essentials. The sustained invention of a really telling lie demands a talent which I do not possess.[32]

> ...the mere fact of dealing with matters outside the general run of everyday experience laid me under the obligation of a more scrupulous fidelity to the truth of my own sensations.[33]

Because Conrad was scrupulous in recalling the details of his inspiration, we can trace the origin of this inspiration fairly accurately in many cases. There are documents relating to the ships he *sailed in* and the ships he *saw*: there are newspaper accounts of events with which he must have been familiar and which he made use of; there are descendants still alive of men he used as subjects for his novels. By conducting research along these lines I have been able to reconstruct some of the 'conditions' of life in the East with which he was familiar, and to rediscover the gossip, the yarns, and the environment to which he refers.

For the purpose of this study I shall consider only that part of Conrad's 'active' life which brought him into contact with the Eastern seas, taking the 'East' in this sense to be those parts of the South-east Asian archipelago which he knew, with a digression on his contact with Australia where this is relevant. I shall deal first with the biographical aspect of Conrad's stay in the East and secondly, and more exhaustively, with the 'nature of the knowledge, suggestions, or hints' he found there and upon which so much of his later imaginative work depended, and finally with the relationship between source material and completed works.

2

BIOGRAPHY: THE EASTERN SEAS

Conrad's contact with the East came primarily through the agency of three ships—the barque *Palestine*, the S.S. *Vidar* and the barque *Otago*. It was as second mate of the *Palestine*, first mate of the *Vidar*, and master of the *Otago* that he came into contact with the people and places which were to provide him with inspiration. The experience connected with each of the three ships—*Palestine*, *Vidar*, and *Otago*—was to become the basis of at least one individual story—'Youth', 'The End of the Tether' and *The Shadow-Line*, respectively. And because of his berths in these ships he was to become acquainted with three different parts of the East, three strictly limited geographical areas, to which he was to return repeatedly in his writing—Singapore, Tandjong Redeb on the river Berau on the east coast of Borneo, and Bangkok.

On 19 September 1881, when he was twenty-four years old, Conrad found a berth as second mate in the barque *Palestine*, 425 tons, commanded by Captain Beard and bound ultimately for Bangkok. Conrad describes his experience in the *Palestine* in the story 'Youth', which he calls 'a feat of memory...a record of experience...'.[1] To a large extent this is what it was, and Conrad seems to have kept to the facts of the *Palestine*'s journey to Bangkok.

The *Palestine* was an old ship, built at Sunderland in 1857. She was owned by John Wilson of South Hackney, the man described by Conrad's uncle, Tadeusz Bobrowski, as 'your ship-owner...a rascal who risks the lives of ten men for the sake of a blackguardly profit'.[2] Conrad disguised the name of the ship, changing *Palestine* to *Judea* in the story, but kept the name of the master and mate unaltered, though he made Captain *Elijah* Beard into Captain *John* Beard.*

The *Palestine* met with nothing but trouble on her voyage to Bangkok. She 'took sixteen days in all to get from London to the Tyne'[3] because she got into a gale. And, according to 'Youth', on leaving the Tyne she was rammed by a steamer and consequently delayed three weeks, though the Newcastle upon Tyne newspapers do not contain any report of this incident. On 24 December 1881 she was forced to put back to Falmouth due to gales she encountered. At Falmouth she had, again according to 'Youth', to take on several changes of crew because the men refused duty. The Agreement and Account of Crew of the *Palestine* confirms this, for it shows that thirty ordinary seamen either deserted or were discharged between North Shields and Falmouth.

It was not until 17 September 1882 that she began what was to be her last voyage, carrying a cargo of West Hartley coal. Her journey was both slow and disastrous, as the following extract from the report of the Court of Inquiry held in Singapore into her loss shows:

On the 17th September 1882 the 'Palestine' sailed from Falmouth with a complement of 13 hands all told, and proceeded on her voyage to Bang Kok. The passage was tedious owing to persistent light winds, but nothing unusual occurred until noon of the 11th March, when a strong smell resembling paraffin oil was perceived; at this time the vessel's position was lat. 2 36 S and long. 105 45 E. Banca Strait. Next day smoke was discovered issuing from the coals on the port side of main hatch. Water was thrown over them until the smoke abated, the boats were lowered, water placed in them. On the 13th some coals were thrown over-

* Elijah Beard's Application to be Examined for a Certificate of Competency as Master. Conrad writes in 'Youth', 'Poor old Captain Beard looked like the ghost of a Geordie skipper' (p. 16). Beard was born in Essex but he asked for his Certificate to be sent to him care of the Mercantile Marine Office, South Shields. Thus, in a way, he could be called a 'Geordie skipper'. Jean-Aubry describes him as 'an old, bent man' (*Life & Letters*, I, 66) and I have no evidence that he was not bent, but he was not so very old. He was born on 2 May 1824 and was, therefore, fifty-seven at the start of the *Palestine's* voyage.

board, about 4 tons, and more water poured down the hold. On the 14th, the hatches being on but not battened down, the decks blew up fore and aft as far as the poop. The boats were then provisioned and the vessel headed for the Sumatra shore. About 3 p.m. the S.S. 'Somerset' came alongside in answer to signals and about 6 p.m. she took the vessel in tow. Shortly afterwards the fire rapidly increased and the master of the 'Palestine' requested the master of the 'Somerset' to tow the barque on shore. This being refused, the tow-rope was slipped and about 11 p.m. the vessel was a mass of fire, and all hands got into the boats, 3 in number. The mate and 4 seamen in one boat, the 2nd mate [Conrad] with three hands in another and the master in the long boat with 3 men. The boats remained by the vessel until 8.30 a.m. on the 15th. She was still above water, but inside appeared a mass of fire.*

Sometimes the changes Conrad makes when turning his experience into fiction are difficult to account for, unless one puts them down to a lapse of memory. As the report shows, Conrad was placed in charge of a boat with three hands, but in 'Youth' he reduces the number by one: 'I had two men with me.'[4] It was after a thirteen-and-a-half-hours' journey in an open boat that Conrad first saw the East and its people, though, as he describes it in 'Youth', his narrator Marlow 'steered many days'[5] before the 'boat's nose' ran 'against the end of a jutting wharf'.[6] Conrad landed at Muntok on the island of Banka, off the coast of Sumatra. From there, the officers and crew of the *Palestine* were taken on to Singapore in the S.S. *Sissie*, arriving on 22 March 1883: 'The boats arrived at Mintok [*sic*] at 10 p.m. on the 15th, and the master reported the casualty to the harbour master. The officers and crew came on to Singapore in the British steamer "Sissie" arriving on 22nd March' (Report of the Court of Inquiry). A certificate in my possession shows that Conrad was discharged at Singapore on 3 April 1883 and paid $171.12.†

* See Appendix B, pp. 297–8, below.

† 'Certificates of Indorsements made by Consuls' included in the crew list of the *Palestine*. Eleven others, along with Conrad, received discharge and wages. Mahon, the first mate, described by Conrad in 'Youth' as having a 'Roman nose, a snow-white, long beard' received only $110.92.

'Youth' ends on a romantic note, with the young Marlow meeting the East and its people for the first time:

> ...I see it always from a small boat, a high outline of mountains, blue and afar in the morning...I have the feel of the oar in my hand, the vision of a scorching blue sea in my eyes...We drag at the oars with aching arms, and suddenly a puff of wind...comes out of the still night—the first sigh of the East on my face (p. 43–4).
>
> And then I saw the men of the East—they were looking at me. The whole length of the jetty was full of people. I saw brown, bronze, yellow faces, the black eyes, the glitter, the colour of an Eastern crowd. And all these beings stared without a murmur, without a sigh, without a movement. They stared down at the boats, at the sleeping men who at night had come to them from the sea (p. 48).

This is the East which Marlow in 'Youth' finds 'impalpable and enslaving, like a charm, like a whispered promise of mysterious delight'[7] but the final scene of the drama was different for Conrad—at Singapore the Inquiry was held into the loss of the *Palestine*. Although Conrad did not include this part of his experience in 'Youth', he recalled it when he dealt with the Court of Inquiry into the desertion of the pilgrim ship *Patna* in *Lord Jim*.*

This was the future novelist's first contact with Singapore, the Eastern port which was to be important to him both as a seaman and as a writer. He spent a month there on this occasion and he was then an insignificant deck officer, but it was to be in Singapore that he reached the peak of his career as a seaman with promotion to the command of the *Otago*.

His impressions of Singapore appear in many of his stories, the most extended description being in 'The End of the Tether'. Singapore was a thriving port with a busy harbour, a city containing a vivid mixture of races, as it does today. It had already become what its founder, Sir Stamford Raffles, hoped it would: 'If no untimely fate awaits it, Singapore promises to become the emporium and pride of the East.'

* See Chapter 3, below.

There Conrad would associate with other seamen, meeting those like 'the dozing stranger' in *The Shadow-Line*—'Both his eyes were partly opened now, but they did not seem to see anything. He was supine'[8]—who had succumbed to the easy life of the East, and the merchant adventurers like Captain Lingard who were little rajahs in their own sphere. This latter type fascinated the young Conrad and he refers to them early in his novel *Lord Jim*:

> Some, very few and seen there [in Singapore] but seldom, led mysterious lives, had preserved an undefaced energy with the temper of buccaneers and the eyes of dreamers. They appeared to live in a crazy maze of plans, hopes, dangers, enterprises, ahead of civilisation, in the dark places of the sea; and their death was the only event of their fantastic existence that seemed to have a reasonable certitude of achievement (p. 13).

He would have found a city of contrasts, from the fine post office and cathedral and the modern cable cars, to the noise and confusion of the Chinese quarter. He would observe the gharry drivers and the Malay seamen, and the Governor driving past in his carriage in the cool of the evening. And he would hear the local gossip from the other seamen—gossip of the sea and of the shore.

On this occasion he may well have stayed at the Sailors' Home in Singapore, a place he was to refer to in *Lord Jim* and which he described more extensively in *The Shadow-Line*. No official records concerning the Home have survived to prove that Conrad stayed there. It is possible that they were destroyed when the Home was pulled down in 1922 to make room for the cinema which stands on the site today. In *The Shadow-Line*, the narrator says to the Chief Steward of the Home, 'Can you give me the one [room] I had before?'[9] which may indicate that Conrad stayed there on at least two of his visits to Singapore. He almost certainly—then or later—dined at the Hotel de l'Europe, the hotel which he refers to, though not by name, in *Lord Jim*. We can be certain that on his first visit he became acquainted with the quayside area of the port. Conrad does not in his work reveal any extensive knowledge of the rest of the town but only of that part with which any sailor would become acquainted.

One source of 'marine shore-talk' in Singapore for Conrad, on this and later occasions, must have been certain tiffin-rooms where he undoubtedly could have associated with the men of his calling. There is a specific reference to these tiffin-rooms in the MS of *The Rescue*[10] when Shaw is telling Captain Lingard how he heard him being discussed by some of the seafaring population during a visit to Singapore—the name of the port is actually given:

> When we were the two days in Singapore you told me to have a run ashore if I liked, and so I took a day off...I had a walk in the morning and about noon I sighted some tiffin-rooms—on the quay there, near the harbour-office...The tiffin was good though it cost more than I am used to pay for my food...By-and bye [*sic*] some gentlemen came in from a kind of bar-like place...They spoke to me most aff..ably... (p. 41).

We cannot know to what extent Conrad is drawing upon an actual experience of his own, but the tiffin-rooms he describes existed in Singapore and were popular among sailors. J. H. Drysdale, at one time an engineer on the *Vidar*, though at a date earlier than Conrad's service on her, refers to this restaurant, which was known as Emmerson's Tiffin Rooms, and testifies that the actual Captain Lingard patronized them:

> On the site of Whiteaway's Building there stood in olden times a long rambling building—the home of old-established firms such as Motion and Co...McAlister and Co., C. Gaggino and Co., and the then famous restaurant and tiffin-rooms which were a regular haunt of all and sundry, from the Tuan Besar down to the seafaring class. In those old times there was more of the 'hail fellow well met' feeling throughout the whole community of Singapore, and when the captain-owners of the pioneer trading vessels, such as Ross and Lingard, met, there was quite an air of joviality, and conversation all round became of a more rollicking nature than one can find at present![11]

The 'long rambling building—the home of old-established firms...' and the 'famous restaurant and tiffin-rooms' stood opposite the Harbour Office, beside Cavenagh Bridge (Plate 14*a*). This whole area appears several times in Conrad's work.

The 'air of joviality' and the 'rollicking nature' of the conversation as well as the discussion of the affairs of men known well locally, such as Lingard, are reflected further in this passage from the MS of *The Rescue*:

'Just so, Shaw', interrupted Lingard. 'Did they speak of me?'

'They said many things—I take it—in a joc..ular way sir. They ended by being noisy too having—as I said—a good deal of cargo on board... Yes, they spoke of you. They said you were a friend of them there Malays—and thick with some prince...I recollect one of them saying you had a hand in some troubles with the natives in Celebes...and that if the Dutch got hold of you it would be all over with you...Another contradicted him and kept shouting "There's no proof! There's no proof!"...One of them—an old chap with eye-glasses said that the existence of men like you was a diss..grace to ci-vi-li-zation...' (pp. 42–3).

McAlister and Company, a firm of ship-chandlers, was situated in the same building as the tiffin-rooms, as Drysdale points out, and it is almost certain that Conrad knew the firm and its premises and made them the originals for the firm and premises of Egström and Blake (also ship-chandlers) in *Lord Jim*. McAlister's was 'a vast and cavern-like shop' (p. 1). Taking into account this fact and the tiffin-room conversation recorded in the MS of *The Rescue*, it would appear likely that Conrad transferred a conversation heard in the tiffin-rooms to the parlour of Egström and Blake. The 'old chap with eye-glasses' who said that the existence of men like Lingard was 'a disgrace to civilization', is reminiscent of 'large, noisy, old Captain O'Brien' in *Lord Jim* who shouts, with reference to the *Patna* affair, 'It's a disgrace to human natur'.'[12]

Emmerson's Tiffin Rooms, McAlister and Company, ship-chandlers, the Harbour Office, the Post Office which stood next to it, the Sailors' Home were all buildings likely to be the haunt of seamen and all were situated within a small area of Singapore. Taken together, they form the nucleus of Conrad's Singapore and the source for much of the information he gleaned about the area. The view from the tiffin-rooms and McAlisters and the Post and Harbour Offices, was the harbour of Singapore, and ships connected with the men of the East that Conrad heard discussed.

Conrad's first visit to the East ended in May 1883 and had lasted almost six weeks. Jocelyn Baines tells us that 'at the beginning of May [Conrad] took a passage for Liverpool on a passenger steamer'.[13] No evidence is given for this statement but, if his information is reliable, Conrad must have travelled on 1 May 1883, since the *Singapore Free Press* reports in its Departure of Shipping Lists only one vessel (Spanish) leaving for Liverpool at this time: '1 May, Leon XIII, Sp. Str. Capt. Lopez for Liverpool.'

*

On his return to England, Conrad went off to meet his uncle and guardian, Tadeusz Bobrowski. They stayed together a month, first at Marienbad and then at Töplitz. A photograph taken at this time shows Conrad the young seaman after his first experience of the Eastern world (Plate 1). Back in England he was quick to return to sea and on 10 September 1883 he embarked as mate in the *Riversdale*, a sailing ship of 1,500 tons, bound for the East. Conrad did not, on this occasion, sail in Malayan waters. When the vessel arrived at Madras he left her and returned to England on another sailing ship, the *Narcissus*, which he joined at Bombay. Conrad's experience on that ship provided him with material for *The Nigger of the 'Narcissus'*. He spent the winter in England and on 3 December took his first mate's examination. He did not return to the East until he joined the *Tilkhurst*, which sailed from Hull on 24 April 1885. Thus it was over two years before Conrad again saw Singapore. According to the *Straits Times*, 23 September

1885, the *Tilkhurst* arrived on 22 September: 'Arr. 22nd Sept. *Tilkhurst*, Blake, Brit. St., 1527 tons from Cardiff' and she departed, with Conrad on board, for Calcutta on 19 October 1885.*

We do not know what Conrad did during this month in Singapore, but some letters have survived which he wrote from that port to his friend Spiridion Kliszczewski and these letters are important because they are the earliest known pieces of writing in English by Conrad.[14] Although the letters give us no help in reconstructing Conrad's experiences in the East at this time, they do suggest that he was unsettled and unhappy. In one of them he puts forward his plan to go in for whale-fishing, and to take out an insurance policy on which money could be raised for this project, but the scheme was soon abandoned. At the same time, he was considering, as an alternative, going into commerce. His reason for wishing to leave the mercantile marine service was 'to work for myself. I am sick and tired of sailing about for little money and less consideration.'[15]

It is strange that these letters reflect nothing of the Eastern surroundings in which they were written. In 'Youth' he described the East as 'impalpable and enslaving', but there is no indication that in 1885 he had felt this charm. It is probable that in spite of what he wrote in 'Youth' he had not at this time consciously come under the spell of the East. But three important events were to take place in the following year and these may have made him more open to the influence of the East on his third and last visit.

After leaving the *Tilkhurst* on 17 June at Dundee, Conrad obtained his master's certificate (11 November 1886), and on 19 August of the same year he became a British subject. More significantly, he seems to have written his first short

* Jean-Aubry wrongly states: 'After remaining about a month at Singapore (25 September to 25 October), the *Tilkhurst* weighed anchor for Calcutta' (I, 86).

story at this time. There is some doubt about this latter event. The story in question was 'The Black Mate', published in the *London Magazine* in 1908. Conrad was not too pleased at the prospect of having it included in his collected works since, as he wrote to Pinker, his agent, '...it would complicate my literary history in a sort of futile way. I don't remember whether I told you that I wrote that thing in '86 for a prize competition, started, I think, by *Tit-Bits*. It is an extraneous phenomenon. My literary life began privately in 1890 and publicly in 1895 with *Almayer's Folly*.'[16] His wife Jessie denied that 'The Black Mate' was the *Tit-Bits* story, and Conrad seemed to prefer that *Almayer's Folly* should be considered his first piece of fiction. His letter to Pinker shows this, and he emphasizes the fact in *A Personal Record*. But Baines points out[17] that, in May 1886, *Tit-Bits* offered a 'Special Prize for Sailors' in one of its competitions, and also that 'The Black Mate' could have been written for such a competition.

One cannot be certain that this was Conrad's first story. Apart from the conflicting statements given above, we have a direct contradiction in Conrad's description of how he came to begin his writing life with the story of Almayer in the autumn of 1889, when he returned to London after resigning as commander of the *Otago*:

> ...my first novel was begun in idleness—a holiday task...It was not the outcome of a need...The necessity which impelled me was a hidden, obscure necessity, a completely masked and unaccountable phenomenon ...Till I began to write that novel I had written nothing but letters, and not very many of these. I never made a note of a fact, of an impression or of an anecdote in my life. The conception of a planned book was entirely outside my mental range when I sat down to write; the ambition of being an author had never turned up...yet it stands clear as the sun at noonday that from the moment I had done blackening over the first manuscript page of 'Almayer's Folly'...had, in the simplicity of my heart and the amazing ignorance of my mind, written that page the die was cast.[18]

This is rather an abrupt beginning to a writing life and seems to be linked with Conrad's concern not to 'complicate' his literary history. It is much more likely that the desire to write came upon him gradually, finding its first expression in the *Tit-Bits* story. If this supposition is acceptable, it would also help to account for the fact that he prolonged his third visit to the East, taking first a berth as mate in the *Vidar*, and then the command of the *Otago*. He may have felt that the East could be an important source for his writing and have wished to extend his experience of it. It might merely have been, of course, that with his naturalization and master's certificate he felt more secure and could take the risk of staying for some time in the East. But I think we can conclude that he was more open to the influence of the East on his third visit.

This took place in 1887. It was the longest period he spent there, and it ended with his engagement as master of the *Otago*, a command that took him away from the East forever.

The exact date on which Conrad arrived in port on this occasion has not been known, but we do know the circumstances under which he arrived. He joined the sailing ship, the *Highland Forest*, at Amsterdam on 16 February. The ship was bound for Samarang, Java, and her master was Captain McWhirr, whose name Conrad used for the commander of the *Nan-Shan* in his story *Typhoon*. In *The Mirror of the Sea*, he describes something of this journey, during which he was injured by a falling spar:

> A piece of one of the minor spars that did carry away flew against the chief mate's back, and sent him sliding on his face for quite a considerable distance along the main deck. Thereupon followed various and unpleasant consequences of a physical order...inexplicable periods of powerlessness, sudden accesses of mysterious pain;...the Dutch doctor who took the case up in Samarang...said...'Ah, friend, you are young yet; it may be very serious for your whole life. You must leave your ship...' In a great airy ward of a Far Eastern hospital, lying on my back, I had plenty of leisure to remember the dreadful cold and snow of Amsterdam...(pp. 54–5).

Conrad was discharged from the *Highland Forest* at Samarang on 1 July 1887, and on the advice of a doctor went into hospital in Singapore. Apart from the date of his discharge, the events of the next month are vague, but I have been able to establish some of them more definitely. The *Highland Forest* is not reported in the newspaper as docking in Singapore, and therefore Conrad must have travelled from Samarang to Singapore on some other ship. During July and August of that year I could discover only one ship arriving in Singapore from Samarang—this was the *Celestial*, and she left Samarang on 2 July 1887, docking at Singapore on 6 July 1887: 'Arr. 6 July, Celestial, Br. Str. 640, Captain Follett, Samarang, July 2' (*Straits Times*, 13 July 1887). Since Conrad was discharged from the *Highland Forest* on 1 July, it is almost certain that he came to Singapore in this ship. This is interesting because, at the end of 'Youth', the castaway Marlow is picked up by the *Celestial*. Her master says, 'This is the *Celestial*, from Singapore on her return trip.'[19] If Conrad had kept exactly to the facts of his experience at this point in 'Youth', Marlow would have been picked up by the *Sissie*, for this was the ship that took the stranded Conrad from Muntok to Singapore after the loss of the *Palestine* in 1883. For some reason, Conrad substituted the name of the ship that carried him from the islands of the archipelago to Singapore on the second occasion in 1887.

But the *Celestial* is interesting for another reason, for she leads us directly to the acquaintances Conrad made in the East. In the letter to W. G. St Clair which I have previously referred to, Conrad qualifies his statement that he made 'no social shore connections' by naming certain men with whom he became acquainted in Singapore. The exceptions are of extreme significance where his writing is concerned:

The only man I chummed with was Brooksbanks, then chief officer of the S.S. *Celestial* and later, as I've heard, Manager of the Dock at Tan-Jong

Pagar. I've heard of course a lot about the men you mention....I knew slightly both his nephews [Captain Lingard's] Jim and Jos, of whom the latter was then officer on board the King of Siam's yacht.*

What Conrad does not mention here is that chief officer Brooksbank of the *Celestial* was married to the daughter of Captain Lingard, the original of Conrad's hero, Captain Tom Lingard, who appears in *Almayer's Folly*, *An Outcast of the Islands*, and *The Rescue*; and that Jim Lingard, his nephew, was already at that time established with Olmeijer at the trading post at Berau. Undoubtedly, Brooksbank was an important source of information for Conrad and it must have been in this third and final period in the East that he made these sea connections which were to be so fruitful for him.

Like Conrad, Jim in *Lord Jim* is 'disabled by a falling spar' and is put into 'the white man's ward' of the hospital:

The hospital stood on a hill, and a gentle breeze entering through the windows...brought into the bare room the softness of the sky...Jim looked every day over the thickets of gardens, beyond the roofs of the town, over the fronds of palms growing on the shore, at that roadstead which is the thoroughfare to the East—at the roadstead dotted by garlanded islets, lighted by festal sunshine, its ships like toys, its brilliant activity resembling a holiday pageant, with the eternal serenity of the Eastern sky overhead and the smiling peace of the Eastern seas possessing the space as far as the horizon (pp. 12–13).

This is clearly a description of Singapore harbour, and a map of the city made in 1884 shows a European Hospital situated just behind and slightly to the right of the General Hospital. The European Hospital is no longer in existence, but the General Hospital is still standing and has been extended on

* Appendix E, p. 317, below. Joshua Lingard would seem to appear as a background figure in several of Conrad's stories in a way which suggests that he may have 'succumbed to the East' and that Conrad's relationship with him was an equivocal one. It will be recalled that in *Lord Jim*, Jim hears the talk of the sailors in the Eastern port and 'how ...that one was doing well in the Siamese navy' (p. 14). And in Bangkok it is a 'cross-eyed Dane...first lieutenant in the Royal Siamese Navy' whom Jim throws over the verandah of Schomberg's hotel into the Meinam river (p. 243). He may also be the 'supine stranger', 'an officer of some Rajah's yacht', who had been 'seeing life' in *The Shadow-Line* (pp. 14–15).

the same site. It is some distance from the harbour, and is situated on a slope. In spite of the sky-scrapers that have been built around it, one can still see from the third floor of the building a view of the 'ships like toys' anchored in the roadstead.

Conrad entered hospital most likely on the 6 or 7 July 1887, since the *Celestial* docked on 6 July; presumably during the next month 'directly he could walk without a stick', he, like Lord Jim, 'descended into the town to look for some opportunity to get home. Nothing offered just then, and, while waiting, he associated naturally with the men of his calling in the port.'[20] His discharge from hospital took place before 22 August, for by that date he had changed his mind about finding a passage to England and had signed on as mate of the *Vidar*. The *Vidar* was a local ship, trading among the islands of the South-east Asian archipelago. Jean-Aubry describes her course as: '... from Singapore through Carimata Strait, from South Borneo to Banjarmassim, then between the Isle of Pulo Laut and the coast of Borneo. She coaled at Pulo Laut, touched at Dongala on the western coast of the Celebes, returned to Coti Broeuw, and finally reached Bulungan [returning by] the same route to Singapore.'[21] (See map facing p. 1.)

Captain Craig, master of the *Vidar*, later told Jean-Aubry that the first time he met Conrad was 'at the Shipping Office of Singapore about the middle of August 1887'.[22] The local newspapers show that the *Vidar* arrived in Singapore on 19 August and she sailed again on 22 August. Conrad must certainly have met Craig between 19 and 22 August.

There seems to be no doubt about the length of time Conrad sailed in the *Vidar*. He joined her on 22 August 1887 and left on 4 January 1888*—a period of four and a half months. But there is some doubt about the number of voyages

* Jean-Aubry is a day out here (*Life & Letters*, I, 101).

he made. Jean-Aubry states that Conrad travelled five or six times from Singapore to Bulungan (and Berau) in Borneo, each trip lasting, as a rule, three weeks. I have traced the voyages of the S.S. *Vidar* during Conrad's period of service in her, through the records of arrivals and departures of shipping in the *Singapore Free Press*, and these show that Conrad must have made only four journeys.* These are remarkably few, given the influence of the Bornean scene on his work.

The importance of 'sea connections' between Conrad and his source material is apparent, and certainly existed in Brooksbank of the *Celestial* and Joshua Lingard, but Conrad had such connections in the *Vidar* also, and in this case they formed a link for him with Berau. The *Vidar*'s most important calls, from Conrad's point of view, were made at the settlement on the river Berau where the Lingard trading post was established and where Olmeijer and Jim Lingard were trading. Conrad's intimacy with these two men could not have been great, given the limited time he spent at Berau; yet while his experience of the archipelago as a whole was of importance, his contact with the Berau trading post was crucial. From it came *Almayer's Folly*, *An Outcast of the Islands*, the second part of *Lord Jim*, and *The Rescue*. During his four short visits to the settlement he met Charles Olmeijer, whose character and home were the inspiration for Conrad's first novel. At Berau also he saw physical evidence of Captain Lingard's

* The *Vidar* was cleared for 'Bulungan' on 22 August 1887 and returned to Singapore from Berau on 26 September. She left again for Berau on 30 September and returned on 31 October. After five days in Singapore harbour, she left for Berau on 4 November, returning on 1 December. I was not able to trace the next clearance, but the *Vidar* returned to the port of Singapore on 2 January 1888, thus concluding Conrad's last voyage in her. He gave up his berth two days later and on 5 January the ship was again cleared for Berau.

The *Vidar's* journeys lasted from twenty-seven to thirty-five days each, with a period of about four days in the port of Singapore between voyages. The *Sofala's* voyages in 'The End of the Tether' which last thirty days are, therefore, closer to the facts of Conrad's experience than Jean-Aubry's three weeks.

pioneering efforts in the existence of that trading centre in 'one of the lost, forgotten, unknown places of the earth'. And he met also Lingard's nephew, Jim Lingard, who, I hope to show, was an important influence in the second part of *Lord Jim*.

Though Conrad's own contact with these men was superficial, there were members of the *Vidar*'s crew no doubt better acquainted with the Europeans at the settlement. James Allen and John Niven, first and second engineers on the *Vidar*, had been travelling through the archipelago in her for at least four years before Conrad joined the ship. The *Singapore and Straits Directory* for 1883 (p. 96), gives the following information:

Name	*Rank*	*Vessel*	*Trade*
A. A. Vincent	Master	S.S. *Vidar*	Java
John Anderson	Mate	,,	,,
John Allan [*sic*]	1st Eng.	,,	,,
John Nevin [*sic*]	2nd Eng.	,,	,,

Allen and Niven appear in *The Shadow-Line*. Allen is the young man 'with a mist of fluffy beard all round his haggard face', a 'confirmed dyspeptic',[23] and Niven is the 'fierce misogynist'.[24] Jean-Aubry states that it was from these two men, and from Captain Craig, master of the *Vidar*, that Conrad 'got all the information he could about these people [at Berau]: their antecedents, morals, intimacies, and intrigues'.[25] But Allen and Niven must have been able to give Conrad more information about the trading settlement at Berau than Captain Craig, who became master of the *Vidar*, as I have discovered, only a year before Conrad joined her (May 1886).

*

If we are to believe *The Shadow-Line*, Conrad gave up his berth in the *Vidar*, although he was happy in her, because of an unexplained restlessness and dissatisfaction. It is likely that he found the regular journeys of the trading ship monotonous and boring once the novelty of what was new and strange had worn off. Perhaps he was aware of the lack of future prospects in such an existence, and the possibility of settling into the kind of rut in the East that he writes of as a danger to the white man in *Lord Jim*. It would appear, in any case, that having left the *Vidar* he intended to return to Europe, and no doubt he stayed at the Sailors' Home while waiting for a passage.

It was at this time that he was offered his first and only command (on a sea-going ship) by the Master-Attendant of Singapore, Henry Ellis, another man who was to appear in Conrad's stories. Conrad left Singapore on the *Melita*, as he records in *The Shadow-Line*, to take over the command of the *Otago* at Bangkok.

His stay in Bangkok was extremely short—he arrived on 24 January and left on 9 February—and yet it was to be almost as fruitful a source for his future fiction as was Berau. Neither of Conrad's biographers, Jean-Aubry and Baines, has any information about Conrad's visit, apart from what is given in two letters, one from the *Otago*'s owners, the other from the Legation doctor in Bangkok. These letters seem to confirm that in *The Shadow-Line* and 'Falk' Conrad was keeping to the facts of his experience. But I have discovered information about the Bangkok period which shows that even *The Shadow-Line*, the story closest to Conrad's experience, is not 'exact autobiography', and I shall deal with this in detail in the section on *The Shadow-Line*.

Conrad's first command was not an easy one. He took over a fever-ridden ship, and seems also to have had difficulty over cargo and replacement of crew. When he took the *Otago* out of the Meinam river, she had a slow uncertain journey through the Gulf of Siam because of the calms she encountered.

He reached Singapore and obtained medical aid there, although, according to the Singapore newspapers, the *Otago* remained outside harbour limits. The press makes no mention of the *Otago*'s departure and certainly her arrival was much less noticed than has been believed.

This period in the *Otago* is, perhaps, the most difficult of all Conrad's time in the East to reconstruct, especially as three weeks of it were spent in travelling through the Gulf, and no official record of this journey has survived. The log book of the *Otago*, had it been preserved, would have been invaluable. As it is, I have collected the crew lists of the ship for this period and these throw fresh light on Conrad's experiences at this time. Also, I did find a short account of Conrad's journey from Bangkok to Sydney, in the *Sydney Morning Herald*:

> The iron barque *Otago* arrived in port yesterday from Bangkok, with a full cargo of teak. Her captain reports that light winds were had down the Gulf of Siam, with light winds and airs through the China and Java Seas. Passed through the Straits of Sunda on March 15. The S.E. trades were very light and were carried to 26 S. Passed Cape Lewin on April 15, when a very heavy gale from the west was encountered. The gale continued with unabated fury for two days ere it moderated. The barque behaved herself exceedingly well, and beyond plenty of water finding its way on board no damage was sustained. Cape Otway was abeam at 3 a.m. on the 28th ultimo. Wilson's promontory was passed on the 2nd instant. Experienced N.N.E. winds through the Bass's Straits. On Friday and Saturday last a very heavy gale from the westward, the wind going round to the S.S.W., was encountered; the vessel laboured heavily and kept her decks full. The Hornby light was sighted at 8 p.m. on Sunday and the Heads were entered at 9 a.m. yesterday in tow of the *Irresistible*. The *Otago* anchored off Elizabeth Bay.

Here is Conrad's first report as master of the barque *Otago*—a report which has lain unnoticed in an Australian newspaper for almost eighty years. Its intrinsic interest lies in the fact that it is a report in the colourless language of the log book of a journey which was to receive artistic treatment in *The Shadow-*

Line. The two together reveal the contrast between Conrad the seaman and Conrad the novelist. Without dealing at this point with the authenticity of much of the so-called biographical detail of *The Shadow-Line*, or with the malign influence of Conrad's predecessor buried, as he is reported to be in Conrad's story, in the Gulf of Siam, we can see that the light winds and calms encountered by the ship in *The Shadow-Line* were based on those encountered by the *Otago* in the Gulf of Siam.

This was Conrad's third and last period in the East. It had been his longest, and, in terms of his fiction, the most influential, extending in all from 1 July 1887 to 3 March 1888, a period of eight months. During this time, he renewed his acquaintance with Singapore, made four visits to Tandjong Redeb on the river Berau and visited Thailand's capital, Bangkok. He went on then to Australia, commanded the *Otago* for two more years, and finally returned to Europe.

*

Conrad arrived in Australia, according to the *Sydney Morning Herald*, on 7 May: 'Arrivals—May 7, Otago, barque, 345 tons, Captain Konkorzentowski [*sic*] from Bangkok, February 9' (8 May 1888).* In the Imports section of the newspaper, the *Otago*'s cargo is given as teak: 'Otago, from Bangkok, 220,000 ft. teak.'

Her next voyage was to Mauritius. The *Sydney Morning Herald* reported in its Departure of Shipping Lists: 'August 7, Otago, barque, for Mauritius.' Two days previously it had listed the cargo that Conrad took to Mauritius: 'Otago, for Mauritius: 853 casks, 1,093 bags sulphate ammonia, 1,180 bags fertiliser, 600 boxes soap, 7 casks tallow.'

Conrad got permission to take the *Otago* by way of the Torres Straits, and his story 'A Smile of Fortune' deals in

* Two days after the date given by Jean-Aubry, *Life & Letters*, I, 110.

part with his journey to Mauritius, his stay there, and his return to Melbourne. The narrator in the story stresses that he had been at sea 'sixty-one days',[26] but the actual journey took fifty-four days. Conrad spent just over three weeks in Mauritius, leaving, according to a Melbourne newspaper, on 23 November 1888, and arriving in Melbourne on 5 January 1889.*

Conrad did not remain master of the barque *Otago* for much longer. Jean-Aubry tells us that during 'February and March he navigated the *Otago* between Melbourne, Sydney, and Port Adelaide, and at the end of March...he resigned his command...'[27] Baines adds that in February Conrad took the *Otago* from Melbourne to Port Minlacowie in South Australia where he picked up a cargo of grain for Adelaide.[28] Conrad in fact spent one month in Melbourne (5 January to 4 February) and then one month in Minlacowie (22 February to 21 March).[29] Recalling this time, Conrad wrote to A. T. Saunders, the clerk already referred to in the now defunct firm of Henry Simpson and Co., owners of the *Otago*: 'I did go to Minlacowie. The farmers around were very nice to me, and I gave their wives (on a never-to-be-forgotten day) a tea-party on board the dear old "Otago" then lying alongside the God-forsaken jetty there.'† The *Otago* arrived in Port Adelaide on 26 March: 'Arrived Coastwise: Tuesday, March 26, Otago barque, 346 tons, C. Korzienowski [*sic*], master from Port Minlacowie' (*South Australian Register*, 27 March 1889).

It was then that Conrad resigned his command. On 4 April the same newspaper briefly reports: 'The Otago has changed masters—Captain Trivett [*sic*] having received the appointment.' A letter sent by Henry Simpson and Co.

* According to Jean-Aubry, Conrad left Mauritius for Port Adelaide on 18 November (*Life & Letters*, I, 113), whilst Baines, closer to the truth, says that 'on 22 November the *Otago* sailed for Melbourne' (p. 99).

† See Appendix A, p. 295, below.

to Conrad on 2 April 1889 confirms that Conrad had resigned:

> Referring to your resignation of the command...of our bark *Otago*, we now have much pleasure in stating that this early severance from our employ is entirely at your own desire, with a view to visiting Europe, and that we entertain a high opinion of your ability in the capacity you now vacate, of your attainments generally...[30]

Several reasons have been put forward for Conrad's resignation. 'A Smile of Fortune' implies that he resigned because of a love affair in Mauritius. It has also been suggested that he resigned because he wished to see his uncle who was in poor health. But there was a change of plan regarding the *Otago*'s next journey which can be discovered from Saunders' letter and from newspapers, and which may have accounted for Conrad's resignation of his command.

A. T. Saunders wrote in a letter which he sent to the *Advertiser*, 10 November 1932, that Conrad 'loaded wheat at Minlacowie for a foreign port [Port Elizabeth, Africa] but owing to marked alterations he was directed to bring the *Otago* to Port Adelaide'. The *South Australian Register*, 27 March 1889, carries a report which also indicates a change of intention on the part of the owners:

> The *Otago*, barque, which belongs to this port, made a good voyage from Melbourne to Minlacowie, one of the outports in Spencer's Gulf (South Australia), where she loaded a cargo of wheat and cleared out for Guam with intent to proceed to Port Elizabeth in East [*sic*] Africa. Shortly before sailing she had orders to proceed to Port Adelaide, and having sailed on March 21, arrived here on Tuesday evening, when she came to anchor to await a tug on the following morning's tide.

Conrad's next journey was to the Congo, and both Jean-Aubry and Baines have stressed that Conrad probably decided to go to the Congo because of a wish formed in childhood.[31] This may well be true; and since Conrad had hoped to take the *Otago* to Africa, and then found that plans had been altered, he may have left Australia for Europe with the determination to fulfil his hopes by some other means.

The date on which Conrad left Australia for Europe has not been known exactly. Jean-Aubry states that 'there is no document which gives us the exact date of Conrad's return to Europe', and Baines simply says that 'he took a passage to England by steamship'.[32] But there is documentary evidence of the date of Conrad's return to Europe.

He left Adelaide for Europe on 3 April 1889 in the S.S. *Nurnberg*. His departure is recorded in one of the outward passenger lists held in the Archives of the Public Library of South Australia. He is listed as 'Captain Conrad, aged 35 [*sic*], destination Southampton'. This is the first time he is referred to as Captain Conrad rather than Captain Korzeniowski. It is not surprising that Conrad dropped his surname when he became a novelist. I have yet to find the name Korzeniowski spelt correctly in early Singapore, Bangkok, and Australian newspapers.

Conrad, then, left Australia on 3 April 1889 with, whether he was aware of it or not, the material and inspiration for a great number of stories already at his disposal.

'LORD JIM'

THE FIRST PART

3
THAT SCANDAL OF THE EASTERN SEAS

As a subject for source study *Lord Jim* is unique among Conrad's works, since it reflects so accurately what were for him two most important aspects of his experience of the East. Both the world of Singapore and the world of Berau are singularly mirrored in the novel. And in addition, linked appropriately with each setting is the experience of two kinds of men—the seaman, and the adventurous trader and pioneer of the period.

One of the most famous scandals in the East of the 1880's was the case of the pilgrim ship *Jeddah*. It was Conrad's meeting with this scandal in Singapore, and the forceful way in which the story was brought to his attention, that resulted in the first part of *Lord Jim*. Conrad refers to the pilgrim ship episode in his Author's Note to the novel of 1917, and makes it plain that the original conception lay in this: '...my first thought was of a short story, concerned only with the pilgrim ship episode; nothing more. And that was a legitimate conception. [It was only later that he] perceived that the pilgrim ship episode was a good starting-point for a free and wandering tale...' (p. viii). Yet the connection between the *Jeddah* case and the novel was not suspected until twenty-three years after *Lord Jim* had been published. Sir Frank Swettenham, in a letter to *The Times Literary Supplement*, 6 September 1923, was the first to suggest that Conrad had based his story of the desertion of the pilgrim ship *Patna* upon the desertion of the pilgrim ship *Jeddah* by her European master and officers.

A study of the two incidents—the fictional one of the *Patna* and the actual one of the *Jeddah*—throws some interesting light on Conrad's use of his source. His retention and rejection of detail from the original incident shows him adapting it creatively to his purpose. Further, it enables us to discover why the *Jeddah* case appealed to Conrad and became the inspiration for what is probably his best-known novel.

The story of the *Patna* is basically a simple one. The young sailor, Jim, romantic and dreaming of heroic adventures, but who had never been 'tested by those events of the sea that show in the light of day the inner worth of a man',[1] takes a berth as mate in the *Patna*. The *Patna*, 'a local steamer as old as the hills...eaten up with rust worse than a condemned water-tank'[2] was a pilgrim ship and, before she left the 'Eastern port' for Jeddah, 'eight hundred pilgrims (more or less)...streamed aboard over three gangways...spread on all sides over the deck'.[3] The *Patna* cast off and backed away from the wharf. 'She cleared the Strait, crossed the bay, continued on her way through the "One-degree"[4] passage. She held on straight for the Red Sea under a serene sky.' In the 'marvellous stillness' that 'pervaded the world' Jim, on the bridge, his thoughts full of valorous deeds, did not see 'the shadow of the coming event'.[5]

In the midst of the calm there was a mysterious collision: 'The sharp hull driving on its way seemed to rise a few inches in succession through its whole length, as though it had become pliable, and settled down again rigidly to its work of cleaving the smooth surface of the sea.'[6] Sent below to assess the damage, Jim sees the bulkhead bulge—'a flake of rust as big as the palm of [his] hand' falls off.[7] Convinced that the ship would sink, he could think only of the sleeping pilgrims—'Eight hundred people and seven boats—and no time!'[8] The captain and officers desert the ship, and, last of all, Jim jumps into the boat with them. They are picked up by the *Avondale* and give a false report which Jim, in spite of his conscience, does not deny—'As the first boat was lowered ship went down in a squall. Sank like lead.'[9] But the *Patna* had in fact survived, and when the deserters reached 'an Eastern port' and prepared to report her loss, it was to be told, 'The *Patna*... French gunboat...towed successfully to Aden...Investigation...'[10] The captain and officers, in one way or another, evade the subsequent Inquiry, and Jim alone stays to face it out.

This story, providing as it does an extreme instance of a highly dramatic situation involving moral responsibilities in which men could be tested, is in its essentials and in the issues involved the story of the actual pilgrim ship, the *Jeddah*.

The *Jeddah* was employed in carrying Muslim pilgrims from Singapore to Jeddah. She left Singapore on 17 July 1880 on one of these trips, and after a stormy passage, during which her boilers gave trouble and she began to leak, she was abandoned off Cape Guardafui at 2 a.m. on 8 August 1880 by her captain and her European officers. They were later picked up by the steamship *Scindia* and taken to Aden where they reported that the *Jeddah* was lost with all her passengers. The appearance of the *Jeddah* at Aden a day later with the pilgrims on board, towed in by the S.S. *Antenor*, caused a great scandal both in London and Singapore, and the incident was the subject of an inquiry at Aden, an action for salvage at Singapore, a debate in the Singapore Legislative Assembly, and a question in the House of Commons.

The incident of the pilgrim ship must have attracted Conrad because of two important circumstances. The first was the predicament of the captain and officers when the *Jeddah*'s sinking became an imminent danger. The main complication was, of course, the inadequacy of the ship's boats to take off the 900-odd pilgrims. Only a small number of those on board the *Jeddah* could hope to be saved. This classic situation of the sea-story would, romantically, demand that the captain should go down with his ship, having seen that those who could escape did so. In the *Jeddah* case this first code of the sea is dishonoured; yet the strains inherent in the position of the captain and officers must have been very apparent to Conrad—indeed to any one—and it is this crucial involvement that so bothers Jim later, and causes him to ask Marlow: 'What would you have done? You are sure of yourself—aren't you? What would you do if you felt now—this minute—the house here move, just move a little under your chair? Leap! By heavens! you would take one spring from where you sit and land in that clump of bushes yonder' (pp. 129–30).

The second complication, inherent in the actual incident, was that the ship did not sink. This not only reflected further on the action of her officers, but removed any possibility of their concealing the original act of cowardice. It must have seemed to Conrad that the story of the pilgrim ship revealed his favourite 'Chance' at work in the lives of men. First the situation which showed 'in the light of day the inner worth of a man, the edge of his temper, and the fibre of his stuff; that reveal[s] the quality of his resistance and the secret truth of his pretences',[11]—a situation in which the choices were absolute; and then the twist of fate which determined that the consequences of the choice should not be escaped, either publicly or privately.

Writing of *Typhoon*, which also derived from a sea yarn, Conrad 'felt that to bring out its deeper significance which was quite apparent to me, something other, something more was required; a leading motive...'.[12] In the case of *Typhoon* that something was McWhirr. In the case of *Lord Jim* the requirement was Jim himself, the man to whom the initial situation should be the kind of heroic test he had always dreamed of, and the final irony of fate the kind of truth he would always try to escape. Conrad's selection of details from the case of the *Jeddah* to create the case of the *Patna* were determined by his conception of the character of Jim, and no doubt it was this conception which lengthened the tale of the pilgrim ship into a full-length novel. He must often have mused on the state of mind of the deserters of the *Jeddah* both when they abandoned her and later, when the full truth of their action was known. But generally speaking, the changes Conrad makes to the original story are all in the direction of developing the character and predicament of his hero Jim.

There is another minor source in Conrad's own experiences in the *Palestine*, and some changes are made with a view to using these experiences in the interpretation of motive, feeling, and individual situation.

*

Conrad calls his pilgrim ship the *Patna*, and the name has attracted some attention. Czeslaw Milosz speculates that *Patna* might mean '*Patria*'[13] and Gustav Morf firmly believes that '*the sinking ship is Poland.* The very names are similar. *Patna* is the name of the ship, and *Polska* the (Polish) name of Poland.'[14] Such speculations need not detain us long. On 17 January 1888 a steamer of 1,149 tons came into Singapore harbour. It was called the *Patna* (*Straits Times*, 18 January 1888). During this time, Conrad was staying at the Sailors' Home, Singapore (4 January to 19 January 1888) before leaving on the S.S. *Melita* for Bangkok in order to take over command of the barque *Otago*. He obviously made use of this name.

Conrad strongly emphasizes the age of the *Patna*: 'The *Patna* was a local steamer as old as the hills, lean like a greyhound, and eaten up with rust worse than a condemned water-tank.' The engineer grumbles about the state of her engines: 'The durned, compound, surface-condensing, rotten scrap-heap rattled and banged down there...the refuse of a breaking-up yard.'[15] Sir Frank Swettenham, J. D. Gordan, and Jocelyn Baines[16] all state that the *Jeddah* was an old ship. They are probably arguing here from the fictional *Patna*, for the *Jeddah* was not an old ship. Conrad must have known the condition of the *Jeddah* at the time of the disaster (I shall show that he saw her in port in Singapore), and therefore he deliberately altered his source. According to the *Jeddah*'s registration, held at the Master-Attendant's office, Singapore, the *Jeddah* was only eight years old in 1880.* No doubt Conrad made the *Patna* an old ship to increase the sense of inevitable disaster felt by Jim when, after the *Patna*'s mysterious collision, he examines the bulkhead; but it enabled him also to draw upon his own experience of sailing in an old ship. In terms of age, the *Palestine* fits the *Patna*. According to the transcript of her registration, the *Palestine* was twenty-six years old when Conrad sailed in her on her last voyage. The *Judea* in 'Youth', which is based on the *Palestine*, is described in these terms: 'The ship...was old...She had been laid up in Shadwell basin for ever so long. You may imagine her state. She was all rust, dust, grime...[17], 'the old barque... heavy with her age...'[18], and she 'wallowed on the Atlantic like an old candle-box',[19] 'a something hooker that wanted pumping eight hours out of the twenty-four'.[20]

The *Jeddah* was owned by the Singapore Steamship Company and the *Singapore and Straits Directory*, 1876, shows that Syed Muhammad Alsagoff was Managing Director of this company. Swettenham tells us that the boat was 'heavily insured', that Alsagoff was 'principal owner', and that the master of the ship was 'part owner'. The ship was certainly

* She was built at Dumbarton in 1872, and first registered in Glasgow, and then in Singapore on 7 November 1876. She was in Eastern waters earlier than this, however, for there is a reference to her in the *Straits Observer* in 1875.

heavily insured. Before she left on her fateful journey, the *Jeddah* was insured for the large sum of £30,000,[21] but I have found no support for Swettenham's suggestion that her master was 'part owner', or Gordan's that the master and Alsagoff 'wished to collect on her' and that the motive for the abandonment of the *Jeddah* was 'a fraudulent insurance scheme'.[22]

The master of the *Jeddah* was a Captain Joseph Lucas Clark, a man of forty-four at the time of the *Jeddah* incident, according to his Application for Renewal of his Master's Certificate in 1895. Clark, as early as 1871, was carrying pilgrims to Jeddah in the *Sumfoo*, a ship owned by the same company. The *Straits Times*, 7 March 1874, reported that Clark took the *Sumfoo* through the Torres Straits and that he was the first master of a steamer to do this journey. It was a dangerous journey and he was praised for making it. Conrad was later to make the same journey as commander of the sailing ship *Otago* and it is extremely likely, therefore, that he knew of Clark both in this connection and in connection with the *Jeddah*. Yet Conrad did not make use of this knowledge in writing of the master of the *Patna*. The *Patna* is commanded by 'a sort of renegade New South Wales German' of enormous size, a grotesque and particularly unpleasant character. He is 'the fattest man in the whole blessed tropical belt',[23] 'a trained baby elephant walking on hind legs'.[24]

There is an important dramatic reason for this change. The captain of the *Patna* and the other members of the crew were to arouse no sympathy in the reader and were to form a contrast with Jim so that he should be seen to be of a different nature. It is in this way that Marlow views them as they stand outside the harbour office: '...I saw his monstrous bulk descend in haste...his large purple cheeks quivered...The other three chaps that had landed with him made a little group waiting at some distance...The third was an upstanding, broad-shouldered youth' (p. 47).*

We can reconstruct the details of the *Jeddah*'s fateful journey in July 1880 from two accounts—her Captain's report, published in the *Straits Times Overland Journal*, 8 September 1880, and the report of the Findings of the Court of Inquiry into her abandonment held at Aden.

Captain Clark states:

> I left Penang† on 20th July with a crew of 50 men, 5 European officers and 953 adult pilgrims bound to Jeddah. The weather was heavy and threatening, strong head winds and high sea up to the '1½ degree channel', for two days only we had fine weather. After this (29th July) the weather became very heavy the wind increasing almost to hurricane force at times with a very high cross sea, the ship rolling, pitching and straining heavily.‡

Three facts are of interest here—the number of pilgrims given as 953, the weather conditions, and the route taken by the *Jeddah*. Conrad is not concerned in his novel about the actual number of pilgrims on board the *Patna*—he gives the number as 'eight hundred pilgrims (more or less)'[25]—but he is at pains to represent them vividly as a human flood filling up the *Patna*, 'like water filling a cistern, like water flowing into crevices and crannies, like water rising silently even with the rim'[26] and emphasizes their silence, faith, and helplessness as they trust themselves to the skill of 'unbelievers'. This is much more to his purpose than exactness in number; moreover Conrad most probably witnessed pilgrims filling up the

* But there may have been other influences at work on Conrad which resulted in a German captain rather than one of any other nationality. There was considerable annoyance among traders in Singapore in the 1880's who felt that the Germans were being too successful in business, and Conrad may be reflecting something of this. Conrad has 'good' Germans in his fiction—Stein in *Lord Jim*, Hermann in 'Falk'—but he was not averse to making fun of them and in stories such as 'The End of the Tether' he is giving expression to a recognized attitude in Singapore during the 1880's: 'Doesn't seem to be so much room on it [the island of Singapore]', growled the Master-Attendant, 'since these Germans came along shouldering us at every turn' (p. 254).

† Having previously left Singapore on 17 July.

‡ See Appendix C, p. 309, below.

Jeddah at a later date when he himself was in Singapore. I have seen pilgrims in Singapore boarding a pilgrim ship, and Conrad's description of the event still holds good today. But the route of the *Patna*, on Jim's first journey in her, is that of the *Jeddah*, and it is given with sufficiently exact detail: 'She cleared the Strait, crossed the bay, continued on her way through the "One-degree" passage. She held on straight for the Red Sea...'[27]

Unlike the *Jeddah*, however, the *Patna*'s journey takes place in calm weather. The silence, the sun, and the stillness are emphasized:

> She held on straight for the Red Sea under a serene sky, under a sky scorching and unclouded, enveloped in a fulgor of sunshine that killed all thought...And under the sinister splendour of that sky the sea, blue and profound, remained still, without a stir, without a ripple, without a wrinkle—viscous, stagnant, dead. The *Patna*, with a slight hiss, passed over that plain, luminous and smooth, unrolled a black ribbon of smoke across the sky (p. 17).

This change is obviously more effective in the story, preparing the way for the contrast between calmness and sudden calamity, but probably Conrad was making use of his own experience in the *Palestine* which he describes in 'Youth'. The *Judea* (*Palestine*) encountered her difficulties in the midst of the same calmness of the elements:

> And she crawled on...in the serene weather. The sky was a miracle of purity, a miracle of azure. The sea was polished, was blue, was pellucid, was sparkling like a precious stone, extending on all sides, all round to the horizon...And on the lustre of the great calm waters the *Judea* glided imperceptibly, enveloped in languid and unclean vapours, in a lazy cloud ...defiling the splendour of sea and sky (p. 23).

There are several similarities between these two passages in choice of detail, ordering of detail, and effect; they suggest that Conrad was not only making use of the same basic experience but was working with the text of 'Youth' in mind. In both, the ship is first described in motion—'she held on', 'she crawled on'; the sky is next described—'serene', 'scorching', 'unclouded', 'a miracle of purity, a miracle of azure'. The calmness of the sea is emphasized next—'blue and profound, remained still, without a stir, without a ripple', 'polished', 'blue', 'pellucid', 'the lustre of the great calm waters'. Finally, the ship is seen as if at a distance, the only moving object and one which defiles, in some way, the sea and the sky—'unrolled a black ribbon of smoke across the sky', 'enveloped in languid and unclean vapours'.

As a result of the gale she encountered, the *Jeddah*'s boilers came adrift. Captain Clark stated:

> The gale continued with unabating fury and the ship labouring and straining so heavily caused the boilers to break adrift from their fastenings on the 6th August...The water rose in the ship very rapidly and the steam pumping power was rendered useless. The deck pumps were all at work and the Hadjis and firemen were bailing the water out of the engine room in buckets. Notwithstanding, the water gained about an inch per hour, and on the 7th, the water still increasing, all the boats were ordered to be prepared and provisioned.*

Though Conrad most probably knew these details of the *Jeddah* disaster—the treacherous seas, the boilers coming adrift, the shipping of water, and the fact that these conditions were spread over several days—, in the case of the *Patna* he introduces instead the mysteriousness of the event—'She went over whatever it was as easy as a snake crawling over a stick'[28]—and its suddenness. Although he describes vividly the strange effect of the mysterious collision, he does not explain what the collision was:

> He [the junior engineer] let go the rail and made ample gestures as if demonstrating in the air the shape and extent of his valour; his thin voice darted in prolonged squeaks upon the sea, he tiptoed back and forth for the better emphasis of utterance, and suddenly pitched down head first as though he had been clubbed from behind...an instant of silence

* See p. 309, below.

followed upon his screeching: Jim and the skipper staggered forward by common accord, and, catching themselves up, stood very stiff and still gazing, amazed, at the undisturbed level of the sea...What had happened? ...Had the earth been checked in her course? They could not understand; and suddenly the calm sea, the sky without a cloud, appeared formidably insecure in their immobility...The engineer rebounded vertically full length... (p. 30).

In 'Youth' he describes a similar incident, though in the case of the *Judea* it is the result of an explosion. But the effect of the incident is almost the same:

About ten, the mate being on the poop, I stepped down on the main-deck for a moment. The carpenter's bench stood abaft the main-mast: I leaned against it sucking at my pipe, and the carpenter...came to talk to me. He remarked, 'I think we have done very well, haven't we?' and then I perceived with annoyance the fool was trying to tilt the bench. I said curtly, 'Don't, Chips', and immediately became aware of a queer sensation, of an absurd delusion—I seemed somehow to be in the air. I heard all round me like a pent-up breath released...and felt a dull concussion which made my ribs ache suddenly. No doubt about it—I was in the air, and my body was describing a short parabola...I was sprawling full length on the cargo. I picked myself up and scrambled out. It was quick like a rebound (pp. 25–6).

Marlow is amazed to see the ship still afloat: 'Also the peace of the sky and the serenity of the sea were distinctly surprising.'[29]

There are parallels between these two situations. First there is the calmness, the suggestion of the ordinary life on board going on as usual, then the sudden jolt, which throws the engineer in *Lord Jim* and Marlow in 'Youth' to the ground, followed by the return of silence, calmness of sea and sky, as though nothing had happened. The same words 'rebound', 'full length' are used in both passages to describe the way the man was thrown off his feet and leaped up again. There is the same feeling of inconsequence in the incident on the *Patna* and the *Judea*, of a strange suspension of time for a few moments.

Conrad alters other details of the *Jeddah* incident, which he must have known of, in order to remove all possible excuse for Jim's action in joining the deserters, and, at the same time, to isolate him from them. There were certain circumstances in the case of the *Jeddah* which might be thought to have lessened the offence of the captain and officers in deserting her, for they were likely to arouse panic. Conrad does not give the master of the *Patna* the excuse of having his wife on board, as had the master of the *Jeddah*. The Assessor and Port Officer at Aden, W. K. Thynne, stated in his report, 'I am of opinion had the master's wife not been on board the master would not have deserted his ship' (see Appendix C, p. 309, below). Moreover, on the *Jeddah*, there was fighting between the pilgrims and the European officers:

> ...On the night of the 7th there was a great difference in the demeanour of the pilgrims, they armed themselves with knives and clubs. About 400 were clustered all around my cabin on deck and I was informed it was their deliberate intention to murder my wife...At midnight they refused to take the pumps, saying that they would sooner die than pump. I passed my wife through the window of my cabin and got one of the officers to put her in one of the boats. Immediately after this, when starting to lower the boat, a general rush was made by the pilgrims and I was pushed into the boat during which I received several serious blows.*

A. P. Williams, the chief officer, had his hand wounded and was flung into the sea by the pilgrims, being picked up by the captain. But there is no panic among the pilgrims in the novel. They are not even aware of trouble, though Jim is concerned about them: 'Do you suppose,' he said, 'that I was thinking of myself, with a hundred and sixty people at my back, all fast asleep in that fore-'tween-deck alone...knowing nothing about it...'[30] The removal of these two aspects emphasizes the fact that, in *Lord Jim*, the 'white men were about to leave the ship through fear of death'.[31]

* Captain Clark's report. See p. 310, below.

Perhaps there is some reflection of Conrad's knowledge of the reaction of the pilgrims of the *Jeddah* in Jim's encounter with the pilgrim who wanted water. This is especially noticeable in the manuscript version. In the published text Jim, after he has discovered the bulging, rust-eaten plates which he expected would give way at any moment, begins to run unsteadily back to the bridge. A pilgrim speaks to him suddenly and clutches him:

> The beggar clung to me like a drowning man...He was stopping me, time was pressing, other men began to stir; I wanted time—time to cut the boats adrift. He got hold of my hand now, and I felt that he would begin to shout. It flashed upon me it was enough to start a panic, and I hauled off with my free arm and slung the lamp in his face. The glass jingled, the light went out, but the blow made him let go, and I ran off—I wanted to get at the boats... (p. 109).

In the manuscript we can see what Conrad decided to excise.

> The glass jingled, the light went out, but there were other lamps hanging under the fore-derrick and I could see a great stir below the awnings. They were getting up and chattering all about me. The blow made the man let go. Somebody called out my name from the bridge and yelled 'Keep them back.' I ran off—I wanted to get at the boats....[32]

But the shortage of boats on the *Patna*—'three times as many [passengers] as there were boats for, even if there had been time'[33]—was true also of the *Jeddah*, and was the subject of a letter printed in the *Straits Times Overland Journal*, 20 September 1880. The writer argued that there was no security for pilgrims travelling on pilgrim vessels and referred to the *Jeddah* case:

> When a steamer of 993 tons register is allowed to leave port with over one thousand adults on board without including infants or young children, and provided with no other means for saving life than six ordinary ship's boats; then it becomes painfully apparent that any surveys which she may have undergone are worse than useless, because they are delusive.

He goes on to add, what was ignored by many of the critics of the deserters:

...a fourth of the people on board would have loaded every boat to the gunwale, even supposing that the work of embarking the passengers had been carried out in the most orderly manner, and but a little food and water taken. Where there are so few boats a great desire naturally exists on the part of those on board to get speedily into them, and this too often results in the boat getting swamped by a rush taking place, becoming overcrowded, and all in it drowned.

*

A most dramatic moment in the desertion of the *Patna* is the death of the engineer, George, whose place Jim eventually takes in the boat with the other deserters. His death, from a heart attack, is one of the vivid impressions Jim retains of that moment when he stood 'glued to the planks' waiting for the ship to sink:

He didn't exactly fall, he only slid gently into a sitting posture, all hunched up and with his shoulders propped against the side of the engine-room skylight...'Weak heart. The man had been complaining of being out of sorts for some time before...[He'd] been fooled into killing himself... if he had only told them to go to the devil when they came to rush him out of his bunk because the ship was sinking!' (pp. 130–1).

This incident was certainly not taken by Conrad from the *Jeddah* case, since it was the second officer of the *Jeddah* who died and he was drowned when one of the ship's boats sank:

...it appears that the passengers tried to prevent the second officer leaving the ship, which he appears to have attempted, by leaving the captain's boats and going over to the port-side to the boat to which he was appointed, and which was manned and ready for lowering. Two of the passengers, Lojis, and an Arab, appear also to have got into this boat. On the pilgrims ordering the people to come out of the boats, and on their refusal, some of the pilgrims (it cannot be ascertained who) cut the falls, and it fell into the sea bow first from the fore fall being cut first, and all in it appear to have perished.*

* See Appendix C, p. 300, below.

The whole incident of Jim's paralysis in the face of danger, the death of George, and Jim's sudden leap into the boat is an instance of the kind of imaginative reworking of the original story that Conrad was capable of. The deserters' journey in the ship's boat until they are picked up by the *Antenor* again shows Conrad at work imaginatively transforming his source, though there may be something here of his own experience in the *Palestine*'s boat before he reached Muntok.

The *Jeddah* and *Patna* stories run parallel again in the fate of the ship after the desertion, and here Conrad seems at times to be consciously using the *Jeddah* and also to be incorporating some of his experiences on the *Palestine*.

The real hero of the *Jeddah* incident was a Mr Campbell, first officer of the *Antenor*, the ship which towed the *Jeddah* to Aden: 'Though taking the *Jeddah* in tow was accomplished after considerable difficulty, and with the exercise of much patience, skill, and ingenuity, the Chief Officer steered the *Jeddah* himself until he had taught two of the crew of the *Jeddah* to steer...'[34] The towing of the *Jeddah* was a dangerous business. Captain Worsley, master of the telegraph ship *Sherard Osborne*, said, 'I think the *Antenor* ran considerable risk; even in smooth water there is risk of collision in a large steamer going alongside another near enough to take a hawser on board...The darkness would enhance the risk...If the *Antenor* had snapped her rope and fouled her screw she would have been in danger.'[35] Conrad must have known of Mr Campbell's actions, for the lieutenant of the French gunboat which towed in the *Patna* acts in a remarkably similar way, although he is heavily disguised as a Frenchman. In the Report on the Action for Salvage it was stated:

The [first] officer return[ed] [t]o the *Jeddah* with t[he] [boatswain] and 4 of the crew, after arranging signals with the Captain to be used in case of the *Jeddah* sinking, so as to take them off in time. The boatswain and crew returned to the *Antenor* at 10 p.m. but from that time until the

Jeddah was successfully towed into Aden, the Chief Officer never left her...Whilst the Chief Officer was thus engaged on board the *Jeddah*, the Captain and 2nd Officer of the *Antenor* kept alternate watches on board the *Antenor* and were in constant communication with the Chief Officer by means of a board on the bridge of the *Antenor*.[36]

The French lieutenant tells Marlow:

'There was a good deal of noise, too, round the two officers...They got two hawsers on board promptly (*en toute hâte*) and took the *Patna* in tow ...Luckily...the sea was level...and there was no...wind...we had two quartermasters stationed with axes by the hawsers, to cut us clear of our tow in case she...' He fluttered downwards his heavy eyelids, making his meaning as plain as possible...'Two quartermasters—thirty hours—always there...It is droll how one forgets. I stayed on that ship thirty hours...It was judged proper...that one of the officers should remain to keep an eye open...and for communicating by signals with the towing ship—do you see?...We made our boats ready to drop over—and I also on that ship took measures...' (pp. 170–3).

Taking into account the differences in tone that arise as a result of Conrad's need to create and present the character of the French officer by means of his speech, there are at least two distinct similarities between the fictional *Patna* and actual *Jeddah*. In both cases, arrangements are made for constant communication between ships so as to allow for the escape of the boarding officer in case the towed ship should sink. And in both cases, great emphasis is placed on the fact that the boarding officer remained with the derelict ship until it was finally towed into Aden harbour. But Conrad would seem to be introducing something of his own experience also, for the *Palestine* was towed for a time by the S.S. *Somerset* and Conrad has it in 'Youth' that Mahon and Marlow crawled forward to cut the tow-rope with an axe, thus recalling the two quartermasters in *Lord Jim*.

A further circumstance suggests that Conrad is using his own experience in the case of the *Patna*. The report on the action for salvage which Alfred Holt, owners of the *Antenor* which towed the *Jeddah* into Aden, brought against the *Jeddah*, states that when some of the *Antenor*'s crew went on board the *Jeddah* they found 'everything on board was in confusion, and all persons on board were panic stricken'.[37] On board the *Patna*, however, 'the cooks were preparing the food in the cooking-boxes forward as usual'.[38] The similarity here is again with 'Youth'. When Marlow returns to the *burning Judea* to see why the crew have not taken to the boats he finds 'they were sitting on deck right aft, round an open case, eating bread and cheese and drinking bottled stout'.[39]

*

Marlow in *Lord Jim* refers to that mysterious cable message from Aden which first announced the news of the *Patna*'s desertion and started 'us all cackling'.[40] For 'a couple of weeks or more', 'the whole waterside talked of nothing else...[and] every confounded loafer in the town came in for a harvest of drinks over this affair: you heard of it in the harbour office, at every ship-broker's, at your agent's, from whites, from natives, from half-castes, from the very boatmen squatting half naked on the stone steps as you went up'.[41] The announcement of the *Jeddah* disaster was made in Singapore by means of not one but two cables. On 12 August 1880, the *Singapore Daily Times* carried the following report:

> The following are textual copies of the telegrams received by the [Singapore Steamship] Company here which have kindly been furnished us by the Managing Director.
>
> 1. To Alsagoff, Singapore.
> Aden, 10th August 8.20 p.m.
> *Jeddah* foundered. Self, wife, Syed Omar, 18 others saved.
> Clark.
>
> 2. To Alsagoff, Singapore.
> Aden, 11th August 9.15 p.m.
> *Antenor* towed down here *Jeddah* full of water. All life saved, now in charge of Government. Telegraph further particulars tomorrow. Omar gone Jeddah last night.

These telegrams, arriving as they did in Singapore within twenty-four hours of each other, were published together and certainly must have been mysterious enough to set the whole of Singapore talking. In fact, in the following month, 13 September 1880, the *Straits Times* reported: 'Public excitement has risen to fever heat here in surveying the conduct of Captain Clark, who is well known here, and his officers and engineers in deserting the S.S. *Jeddah*.'

But Conrad made certain changes in the story where the deserters were concerned. The officers of the *Jeddah* were picked up at 10 a.m. on the day of the desertion by the steamship *Scindia* and taken to Aden. Alsagoff's Agent in Aden listed them in a letter published in the *Straits Times Overland Journal*, 13 September 1880: '...he [Clark]...and his wife, Syed Omar [Alsagoff], 1st Mate, 1st Engineer and 21 others arrived per S.S. *Scindia*.' After the Inquiry at Aden, Captain Clark and his chief officer returned to Singapore. Alsagoff's Agent wrote: 'Captain Clark has got leave to proceed on, and he is going to-day to Singapore with his wife per M.M. Co's steamer. He has Rs. 710 to pay to the Captain of the *Scindia* who brought them, which we have debited to the Company.' And in the same issue of the newspaper was the comment: 'The fame of Captain Clark, who, we believe, is realising his property here with the object of leaving for England, has preceded him.'

The chief officer of the *Jeddah*, A. P. Williams, arrived in Singapore on Wednesday 15 September 1880 (reported *Straits Times Overland Journal*, 20 September 1880), in the S.S. *Naples* from Aden. A. P. Williams, who was to be the only member of the *Jeddah* crew to remain in Singapore, arrived one day after the Legislative Council had debated a motion to have the master of the *Jeddah* arrested and re-tried.*

* There is no doubt that if the Governor or the Secretary of State could have taken criminal action against Captain Clark and Chief Officer Williams they would have done

Apart from Captain Clark and Chief Officer Williams, no other member of the crew of the *Jeddah* appears to have returned to Singapore. A letter from Baldwin, chief engineer of the *Jeddah*, to a private resident in Singapore, was published in the *Straits Times Overland Journal*, 2 October 1880, in which he stated:

> ...the whole affair was bad enough to make me decide to have no more to do with the *Jeddah*, and so I told the Agent in Aden, who telegraphed for another Chief, and last Tuesday Mr J. C. Anderson arrived here with Capt. Craig and the mates...I leave this to-morrow or next day for home. The *Jeddah* is also going to London, and the Agent has offered me a free passage, but I prefer paying my way in another steamer.*

These happenings are compressed effectively by Conrad in his handling of the story. The *Patna*, like the *Jeddah*, is towed into Aden, but her officers are taken, in ignorance of her fate, to 'an Eastern port' which is certainly not Aden and which I believe to have been Singapore.

Their arrival becomes a dramatic event which Marlow witnesses: 'There they were, sure enough, three of them as large as life, and one much larger of girth than any living man has a right to be, just landed with a good breakfast inside of them from an outward-bound Dale Line steamer that had come in about an hour after sunrise' (p. 43).

so. In a Straits Settlement Dispatch from Governor Weld (22 September 1880), there is a reference to the indignation felt in Singapore at 'the dastardly conduct of the Captain and the greater part at least of his officers', but Weld admits that for want of witnesses they are unable to prosecute. The Board of Trade held the same view, and the sentence—suspension of certificate for three years for Captain Clark and a reprimand for Chief Officer Williams—seemed to them to be totally inadequate: 'The misconduct of the Master in deserting his ship with 1,000 lives on board, and not only taking no step to send them assistance, but, on the contrary, reporting falsely that she "had foundered, and that the second engineer had been murdered", deserves the severest punishment which could be inflicted by law, and even if the Authorities at Aden had no power to take steps for the criminal prosecution of Mr. Joseph Lucas Clark, there can be no doubt that the Court should by cancelling his Certificate, have done all in their power to prevent him from again having command of a British ship' (Board of Trade to Under Secretary of State, India Office, Register of Letters Written for 1881 M.T. 4/300 no. 2777).

* See Appendix C, p. 311, below.

The two Inquiries into the *Jeddah* case—the Aden Inquiry and that held in Singapore later—become one in the novel, and are set against a background which is obviously Singapore (see Chapter 8).

The concentration Conrad achieved by this means is enhanced by the fact that only Jim stays to stand trial, the other deserters disappearing from the scene of action.

The Court of Inquiry, as it is presented in *Lord Jim*, has an air of authenticity. This is due partly, I think, to the fact that Conrad is recalling his own experience during his first visit to Singapore. In describing the officials of the Court of Inquiry in *Lord Jim*, Conrad says:

> Their business was to come down upon the consequences, and frankly, a casual police magistrate and two nautical assessors are not much good for anything else...The magistrate was very patient. One of the assessors was a sailing-ship skipper with a reddish beard, and of a pious disposition. Brierly was the other...Big Brierly—the captain of the crack ship of the Blue Star line (p. 68).

Conrad must have made use of his own Court of Inquiry, and not the Aden Inquiry or the Singapore case for salvage on the *Jeddah*, when he came to write the fictional inquiry in *Lord Jim*. He had, for one thing, just concluded 'Youth', in which he stopped short before the Inquiry into the abandonment of the *Palestine* and was, therefore, likely to have had it in mind. Moreover, the report of the Aden Court of Inquiry was signed by one session Judge, G. R. Goodfellow, and one nautical assessor, W. K. Thynne, whilst the case for salvage held in Singapore on the *Jeddah* was a much more full-dress affair held before the Chief Justice, Sir Thomas Sidgreaves. In the case of the Inquiries into the fictional *Patna* and the actual *Palestine* there is one 'police magistrate and two nautical assessors'.*

* See Appendix B, p. 297, below.

Conrad's 'police court of an Eastern port', where the official Inquiry into the loss of the *Palestine* was held, is no longer standing in Singapore and it is not possible, therefore, to verify the exactness of Conrad's description of it in *Lord Jim*. This is not important, because his remarks are of a general kind giving the sort of detail that would fit, during Conrad's day, any large police court in the East—that is, the 'cool lofty room', the 'big framework of punkahs', 'narrow benches'—but at least one assessor described by Conrad in *Lord Jim* approximates in appearance to one of the assessors who sat in judgment over Captain Beard and Conrad in the case of the *Palestine*. ' "Did you think it likely from the force of the blow?" asked the assessor sitting to the left. He had a thin horseshoe beard, salient cheek-bones, and with both elbows on the desk clasped his rugged hands before his face ...' (p. 33). This is the same assessor described above as a 'sailing-ship skipper with a reddish beard' and a 'pious disposition'. I have a photograph in my possession of John Blair, one of the nautical assessors in the *Palestine* Inquiry. He is a man of strong appearance, noticeable cheekbones and a thin horseshoe beard. Blair was not, at the time of the *Palestine* Court of Inquiry, a 'sailing-ship skipper' but he had been some six years previously, before his vessel was wrecked off Raffles Lighthouse, Singapore.

*

How Conrad came upon the *Jeddah* story is an important question, since to some extent his manner of retelling the story depended upon the nature of his contact with his source.

Conrad must have read the reports of the *Jeddah* incident in the London newspapers in 1880. At that time he was staying in London before embarking on the *Loch Etive* for Sydney on 21 August 1880. There were vivid accounts to be read in *The Globe*, the *Daily Chronicle*, *The Times*, and the *Daily News*.

The Globe published its first report with the headlines: DREADFUL DISASTER AT SEA. LOSS OF NEARLY 1000 (11 August 1880), for it was understood at first, because of the report of the *Jeddah*'s captain at Aden, that the ship and her pilgrims were lost. And on the following day, 12 August 1880, when it was discovered that it was a false alarm and that Captain Clark, the chief officer, the chief engineer, the assistant engineer, the captain's wife and sixteen natives had abandoned the ship and her passengers, the newspapers were extremely critical:

> That she should thus have been abandoned and her living freight left to their fate is one of the most dastardly circumstances we have ever heard of in connection with the perils of the deep...It is to be feared that pilgrim ships are officered by unprincipled and cowardly men who disgrace the traditions of seamanship. We sincerely trust that no Englishman was amongst the boatload of cowards who left the *Jeddah* and her thousand passengers to shift for themselves. (*Daily Chronicle*)

> ...even if the *Jeddah* had afterwards foundered there would have remained an indelible stain of discredit upon the men who had thus run away at the moment of peril. But the fact that the ship was not in any extremity of peril is clearly proved by her eventual safety and the charge becomes thus one of over-timidity as well as simple *lâches*...
> (Evening issue of *The Globe*)

> ...There was something very unpleasant in the facts thus stated; for, to the honour of sailors, nothing is more rare than that, in a disaster at sea, the Captain and the principal officers of the vessel should be the chief or sole survivors... (*The Times*)

> The relief which is felt at the safety of the pilgrims will be modified by a feeling of indignation and horror at what seems the cowardly desertion of their post and trust by the master and seamen of the ship.
> (*Daily News*)

Conrad's reference to the steamer *Royalist* in his letter to the Dowager Ranee of Sarawak—his having seen the ship and heard officers' tales about her—reminds us of the importance of shipping in port and on the high seas as events of interest in the lives of seamen. And it was by this means that, three years later, Conrad came again upon the *Jeddah* story. A day before he arrived in Singapore for the first time, the *Straits Times* recorded the arrival of the S.S. *Jeddah* (21 March 1883). The sight of the *Jeddah* in harbour, together with sailors' gossip about her—in the very port from which she had sailed and where the impact of the incident was most strongly felt—must have recalled the newspaper reports to Conrad's mind. And he must have found further interest in the case since, just as *he* was then involved in the Inquiry into the loss of the *Palestine*, so the captain and officers of the *Jeddah* had undergone a much more sensational inquiry in Aden three years earlier.

The story of the *Jeddah* was not allowed to slip from Conrad's memory, for he was able to observe something of her later history. During his *second visit* to Singapore, the following advertisement appeared in the *Straits Times*:

For Sale—The A.I. Steamer 'Diamond' of 1,035 nett register carrying about 27,000 piculs dead weight. Engine of 200 horse power, speed 10 knots, with a consumption of 14 tons Cardiff. Built by Wm. Denny & Bros. of Dumbarton. For further particulars apply to M. Alsagoff, Manager, Singapore (8 September 1885).

This advertisement must have occasioned a great deal of 'marine shore-talk' in Singapore, and Conrad could hardly have avoided hearing it, for the *Diamond* was the *Jeddah* in disguise. She had not returned to Singapore until 25 July 1881—a year after the 1880 desertion. As the *Jeddah* she had then continued on the pilgrim run to Jeddah, but it would seem that Conrad was right in speaking of 'that scandal of the Eastern seas' which 'would not die out',[42] for she often lay unused in harbour. Captain Clark had had his certificate suspended for three years, but at the end of this period he returned to Singapore and was listed in the newspaper on one occasion as her commander. However, the owners must have thought it unwise to retain him, for before the ship left port

Clark had been replaced. During 1884 and 1885 the *Jeddah* was almost entirely disengaged. Returning from Jeddah on 7 November 1884, she was put up for sale. It appears that the owners at this point employed a ruse to get rid of the ship's bad reputation. She was not sold, but her name dropped out of the 'Shipping in Harbour' column of the *Straits Times* on 28 February 1885, although she was not listed as having been cleared from the harbour. Significantly, however, the S.S. *Diamond* of the same tonnage and with the same commander, a Captain Geary, was cleared for Palalangan. A check of the Register of Shipping, Harbour Office, Singapore, showed that the *Diamond* was indeed the *Jeddah*, for the date and place of her origin and all other particulars were the same. The *Diamond* was then sold to Lee Phee Yaow of Penang. She returned to the pilgrim trade and seems to have continued in this trade until she was sold to a Japanese subject on 24 December 1894.

This then was the 'pilgrim ship episode', and the use Conrad made of it—'an event...which could conceivably colour the whole "sentiment of existence" in a simple and sensitive character'.[43] It remains to consider the origin of this 'simple and sensitive character', Jim himself.

4
THE FLESH AND BLOOD INDIVIDUAL

It has been thought that Conrad found his inspiration for the character of Jim in one of the *Jeddah*'s officers. Again Sir Frank Swettenham was the first to suggest that the source for Conrad's hero might be the second officer of the pilgrim ship *Jeddah*:

> ...the master and all the officers except one, *I think the second mate*, [my italics] abandoned her in the darkness of the night and left the pilgrims to their fate. The one officer left behind—Lord Jim of Mr Conrad's story —was so left because he was not quick enough to get into the boat or boats with the other deserters...'Jim', the hero of the story, was taken to Singapore where he found work in a ship chandler's store, grew fat and prospered. That was how he really 'worked out his salvation'.[1]

Swettenham admitted that he was 'far from any means of reference to books and documents' and that he was 'trusting to his memory' when he wrote this, but J. D. Gordan, following this, naturally concluded: 'Conrad made a striking change in the character and adventures of the one officer of the *Jeddah* who did not leave the ship.'[2] And Jocelyn Baines went further: 'None of the crew, as far as is known, played the role which Conrad gave to Jim.'[3]

But 'that scandal of the Eastern seas' caught Conrad's imagination and had to be used by him precisely because of one man who did leave the ship. Moreover, research into Conrad's sources suggests that he was unlikely to make such a striking change as to turn a man who did not leave into a fictional character who did. It would seem more logical, given Conrad's reliance on fact, to consider Jim's counterpart, the first mate of the *Jeddah*, as the possible inspiration for Lord Jim.

The first mate of the *Jeddah* at the time of the desertion was a man called Augustine Podmore Williams. All that I have been able to discover about him from his descendants and from official and unofficial documents suggests that he was Conrad's inspiration for the whole of the first part of the novel. Williams, like Jim, was from a parsonage, he was the last officer to leave the *Jeddah*, he figured prominently in the subsequent Inquiry, and he afterwards, like Jim, became a ship-chandler's water-clerk in Singapore. Unlike Jim, he worked out his salvation in this way, growing fat and prospering.

Conrad builds up his brief description of Lord Jim's background by means of such precise detail that some kind of factual source is suggested, and, indeed, I discovered that Williams's background was identical with that of Lord Jim. Conrad writes:

> Originally he [Jim] came from a parsonage. Many commanders of fine merchant-ships come from these abodes of piety and peace...The little church on a hill had the mossy greyness of a rock seen through a ragged screen of leaves. It had stood there for centuries, but the trees around probably remembered the laying of the first stone. Below, the red front of the rectory gleamed with a warm tint in the midst of grass-plots, flower-beds, and fir-trees, with an orchard at the back, a paved stable-yard to the left, and the sloping grass [*sic*] of greenhouses tacked along a wall of bricks. The living had belonged to the family for generations; but Jim was one of five sons, and when after a course of light holiday literature his vocation for the sea had declared itself, he was sent at once to a 'training-ship for officers of the mercantile marine' (pp. 3–4).

Later in the story, Brierly, one of the members of the Court of Inquiry which Jim had to face, says, 'The old man's a parson, and I remember now I met him once when staying with my cousin in Essex last year. If I am not mistaken, the old chap seemed rather to fancy his sailor son' (p. 82). A. P. Williams did come from a parsonage and was one of five sons. His daughter, Mrs Norah Thornett of Sussex, confirms this: 'My father was from a parsonage as mentioned in *Lord Jim* & was one of five sons. He was born at Porthleven,* Cornwall on 22 May 1852' (letter of 13 July 1962). The parsonage at Porthleven was centuries old, and Conrad has given a fairly accurate description of it. The present vicar of Porthleven had this to say about the parsonage in a letter of 7 September 1962:

> I should say that, allowing for a certain amount of 'writer's licence', the description of the rectory in *Lord Jim* is of Porthleven Vicarage, as one can see from the garden through the trees, Breage Church (very ancient) standing out on a hill about 2 miles away. The Vicarage here is a mixture of brick and stone/or granite—mostly granite blocks. The lawn slopes steeply in the front and there is a belt of fir trees, with a small stable and orchard at the back. Of course, the garden is much altered now and there are no greenhouses; but the description, on the whole, tallies with Porthleven Vicarage.

According to Miss Nancy Williams of Penzance, the fir trees were planted by her grandfather, A. P. Williams's father. But the living had not 'belonged to the family for generations'.† So far as I know A. P. Williams's father was the first of the Williams family to hold it. 'The old parson' was not so very old at the time of the *Jeddah* disaster. He was born at Bath on 31 January 1823 and was therefore fifty-seven years of age.‡

Though his daughters knew nothing of his early life, it

* Conrad probably placed the vicarage in Essex because he was living at Stanford-le-Hope, Essex, when he began to write *Lord Jim*.

† Williams's father certainly held the living for a long time. Miss Williams says of him, 'He died aged 95 in (I think) 1919 and was for over 30 years Vicar of Porthleven.' Mrs Thornett gives a more definite date: 'My grandfather died on 2 April 1919 at the age of 97.' This means that he outlived his son by some three years.

‡ He took holy orders, was ordained Deacon on 30 May 1847, and Priest on 18 June 1848. According to his grand-daughter, Mrs G. A. Neill of Dunedin, New Zealand, he was a Fellow of Trinity College, Cambridge, and later Professor of Greek at King's College, Aberdeen. Miss Williams adds: He was a notable High Churchman, friend of Keble and a very commanding personality. He had 15 children of whom...the last, Fabian, died two years ago, being the last of his generation (letter of 25 September 1962).

seems likely that Williams went to a 'training ship for officers of the mercantile marine,' as did Lord Jim. His brother Robert, younger than he by a year, was educated at St John's, Leatherhead, Surrey, a public school for the sons of clergymen. This school has no record of A. P. Williams as a pupil though its records go back to the foundation of the school in 1851. I have, however, some evidence in support of his being at a training-ship in a photograph dated 1868 which was sent to me by Mrs Neill (Plate 2). 'This antique', she writes, 'shows my grandfather and his family.' The photograph appears to have been taken at the back of the rectory and probably in the orchard. A. P. Williams, who was then sixteen, is on the extreme right of the family group. He is wearing a uniform of some kind which, with its brass buttons and cap, could be the uniform of a cadet officer of a training-ship.

On 2 July 1880, when he was twenty-eight years old, A. P. Williams was taken on at Singapore as first mate of the *Jeddah*. It was not his first appointment as an officer in a ship in the East.* Before this date he had been first mate on the S.S. *Dale* from 4 April 1879, though only for four months. He had had his first chance as chief officer on the S.S. *Washi* (registered at Hong Kong) for one year, from July 1877 until 3 August 1878. The earliest date I can trace for his arrival in the East is when he served on the S.S. *Thales* as second mate 3 October 1876. He was then very young, only twenty-four, and this is close to the age of Lord Jim—'not yet four-and-twenty'.[4] Williams could not have suspected when he joined the *Jeddah* as first mate, on 2 July 1880, that this would be his first and last journey in the pilgrim ship, and that his whole career as a seaman was to be blighted.

* Mrs Thornett did not know when her father came out East but she thought it was 'long before 1880' and that he 'was very young' (letter of 13 July 1962). I have been able to obtain a copy of Williams's Application for a copy of his first mate's certificate. He applied for this in 1915 when he was living in Singapore, and his application gives some information about the ships in which he served.

A. P. Williams, like Jim, was the last officer to leave the pilgrim ship, though he did not jump but was thrown overboard. Captain Clark reported: '...the Chief Mate who was in the ship, was hurled overboard and every effort was made to sink my boat...I picked up the first officer and took him into my boat.'* The report of the Aden Court of Inquiry on the *Jeddah* as published in the *Straits Times Overland Journal* gives us further information:

> When the boat was lowered, the pilgrims commenced to throw boxes, pots, and pans and anything they could lay hands on onto the boat and pulled the First Officer, who was lowering the boat, off the rails...The 3rd Engineer had...got into the boat and the First Officer found himself in the water and was taken into it and the boat was then cut adrift... (*Straits Times Overland Journal*, 13 September, 1880).

But the Report in Document no. 896 has some additional comments:

> Failing in preventing the lowering of the boat, the pilgrims proceeded to endeavour to swamp her; two pistol shots were fired in the direction of the pilgrims from the boat by the first officer, and these appear to have prevented any further attempts to swamp the boat, which then was cast off and away from the ship.†

Just as, in *Lord Jim*, Jim takes physical action by dashing a lamp in the face of a pilgrim, so A. P. Williams took physical action by firing the shots in the direction of the pilgrims; but generally speaking, Williams's part in the desertion was much more active than Jim's.

A. P. Williams himself wrote in a letter to the *Straits Times*, 20 September 1880, '...I was thrown overboard by the Hadjis after a severe wound was inflicted on my hand...' (see p. 74, below). The reference to 'a severe wound' inflicted on his hand might of course be an exaggeration on Williams's part, but Miss Williams stated in a letter written to me on 20

* Captain Clark's statement. See p. 310, below.

† See Appendix C, p. 303, below.

November 1962: 'I have just been staying with my brother and he thinks Uncle Austin *did* have a scar on his hand.' Assuming that Conrad met Williams in Singapore (and I believe he did), and assuming that Williams had a scarred hand, Conrad must have noticed it. Although he does not transfer the wound or the scar to Lord Jim, he perhaps transferred it to another character, the French officer whom Captain Marlow meets and who guided the deserted *Patna* back to port:

> It gave me the opportunity to 'note' a starred scar on the back of his hand... (p. 172). I perceived that the three last fingers of his wounded hand were stiff and could not move independently of each other, so that he took up his tumbler with an ungainly clutch (pp. 178–9).

It is obvious that Conrad changed the details of the desertion of the *Jeddah* radically in writing *Lord Jim*—Jim was not attacked and wounded by the pilgrims nor was he thrown overboard—for Conrad did not wish Jim's desertion of the *Patna* to be in any way justified. It had to be 'abominable funk (*un trac épouvantable*)'.[5] At the moment of crisis, Jim, though profoundly aware of the helplessness of the 800 sleeping pilgrims on what he believes to be a sinking ship, is completely ineffectual and in fact deliberately isolated from events until he jumps. The jump is clearly an instinctive reaction, after a period of immobility, in response to the calls of the deserters.

> 'With the first hiss of rain, and the first gust of wind, they screamed, "Jump, George! We'll catch you! Jump!" The ship began a slow plunge; the rain swept over her like a broken sea; my cap flew off my head; my breath was driven back into my throat. I heard as if I had been on the top of a tower another wild screech, "Geo-o-o-orge! Oh, jump!" She was going down, down, head first under me...I had jumped...' he checked himself, averted his gaze...'it seems,' he added...'I knew nothing about it till I looked up...' It had happened somehow...He had landed partly on somebody and fallen across a thwart. He felt as though all his ribs on his left side must be broken... (p. 135).

The criticism of A. P. Williams in the Report of the Court of Inquiry at Aden was severe, and we cannot but conclude that he had a very strong character and he certainly played a leading part in the desertion. This is the more surprising when we consider that Williams, like Jim, was a very young man at the time and Captain Clark was forty-four.[6]

Before concluding, the Court consider it necessary to place on record their disapprobation of the conduct of the first officer of the 'Jeddah', Mr Williams, who may be said to have more than aided and abetted the master in the abandonment of his vessel. The Court consider it very probable that, but for Mr Williams's officious behaviour and unseamanlike conduct, the master would...have probably done his duty by remaining on the ship.*

The Assessor stated:

The first mate of the 'Jeddah', according to his own statement, is greatly to blame in doing what he could to demoralize the master, by advising him to leave the ship, telling him his life was in danger, also his wife's life; that he, the master, was sure to be killed if he remained on board; and that he, the first mate, did thrust the master into the boat. The mate worked on the fears of the master for the safety of his wife, and by so doing hurried the master into leaving the ship.†

Whereas Williams acted *with* the captain and officers of the *Jeddah*, Conrad emphasizes the isolation of Jim and deliberately makes a distinction between him and the other officers of the *Patna*. When the rest of the officers discover that it is Jim who is with them in the boat and not George, the third engineer, they threaten him—'What's to prevent us three from firing you overboard?'[7]—so that the next morning finds Jim still on guard against them.

And the rising sun found him just as he had jumped up first in the bows of the boat...He had been holding the tiller in his hand, too, all the night ...Six hours more or less on the defensive; six hours of alert immobility while the boat drove slowly or floated arrested, according to the caprice of the wind... (p. 149).

* See Appendix C, pp. 304–5, below. † See Appendix C, pp. 307–8, below.

Jim's attitude towards the other officers is one of loathing—'I loathed them. I hated them'[8]—and when the deserters are picked up, Jim refuses to add to their story. ' "The *Avondale* picked us up just before sunset...They told their story..." "You said nothing," I whispered. "What could I say?" he asked, in the same low tone...' (p. 163). The changes Conrad made to his source have, therefore, a twofold effect. They make Jim's action unjustifiable, but at the same time reveal him as being of a different moral character from the other deserters; so they gain some sympathy for a man who had acted directly against a sailor's faith, and his loyalty to his ship.

*

What must have struck Conrad most forcibly if he met Williams in Singapore was that here was no ordinary coward. Williams returned to Singapore, after leaving the *Jeddah*, on the S.S. *Naples* and his return was announced in the *Straits Times Overland Journal*, 20 September 1880: 'Mr Williams, late Chief Officer of the S.S. *Jeddah*, and whose name has been so frequently mentioned in the findings of the Court of Inquiry at Aden, arrived here this morning by the S.S. *Naples* from Aden' (from *Daily Times*, 15 September 1880). He did not return home as he might have done, for his certificate, unlike that of the master of the *Jeddah*, and of Lord Jim[9] was not suspended. In spite of the severe censure he had received both in the report of the Court of Inquiry at Aden (which was also published in the Singapore papers), and in the Singapore Legislative Council,[10] Williams returned to a Singapore buzzing with news of the desertion: 'Public excitement has risen to fever heat' (*Straits Times*, 13 September 1880). In those days mercantile society in Singapore was very small and there would be no chance of Williams losing himself in anonymity, even if he had wished to. This aspect of facing it out is referred to again and again in the novel, and Conrad may emphasize it because it was this action of Williams in particular that forced itself upon his consciousness. Brierly suggests that Lord Jim should 'creep twenty feet underground and stay there',[11] and Marlow replies: 'There is a kind of courage in facing it out as he does, knowing very well that if he went away nobody would trouble to run after him.'[12] Of course, Conrad is referring in the novel to the fact that Jim alone faced up to the Court of Inquiry—another distinction between him and the rest of the officers of the *Patna*. But if we replace the facing up to the Inquiry with the notion of facing up to people Williams knew intimately in Singapore, the Harbour Office employees, the ship-brokers, the shipping agents, the seamen, then Conrad's remarks can be taken as revealing why he was so impressed by Williams: '... I became positive in my mind that the inquiry was a severe punishment to that Jim, and that his facing it—practically of his own free will—was a redeeming feature in his abominable case' (pp. 82–3). When Jim speaks to Marlow outside the Courtroom thinking he has called him 'cur', he says, 'That's all right...I am going through with that. Only...I won't let any man call me names outside this court' (p. 86). Marlow catches up with Jim in the street and taxes him with running away and Jim answers, 'From no man—from not a single man on earth.'[13] This attitude he reiterates: 'But I knew the truth, and I would live it down—alone, with myself,'[14] and: 'I won't shirk any of it ...I am bound to fight this thing down—I am fighting it *now*.'[15] Although Conrad emphasizes so strongly Jim's feeling that he must 'stick it out', Jim does not in fact do so in the novel—apart from 'sticking out' the Inquiry: 'He retreated in good order towards the rising sun.'[16] I think this is an instance of Conrad not entirely adapting his source to the fictional character, for Williams did indeed stick it out in Singapore.

Jim's determination to fight and to allow no man to call him names is foreshadowed in the letter from A.P. Williams to the *Daily News* on his return to Singapore, which was reprinted in the *Straits Times Overland Journal.* In this he aggressively insists that his critics at least keep to the facts, though the facts he refers to are of minor importance in the context of the desertion. He writes:

Sir,—In reading your Journal of yesterday's date giving a report of the debate in the Legislative Council regarding the *Jeddah*, I find in Mr Campbell's speech the following remarks:—'From the evidence adduced at the Court of Inquiry it would seem that his (Captain Clark's) fears were utterly unfounded. However he orders a boat to be lowered, in which he puts his wife, and into which he, with his Chief Officer and the Chief Engineer manage to get.'

I am the Chief Officer of the *Jeddah* referred to, and I beg to inform you Mr Campbell's statement, so far as it refers to me, is untrue. The evidence given before the Court of Inquiry will show that I was thrown overboard by the Hadjis after a severe wound was inflicted on my hand, and that I was afterwards picked up out of the water by Captain Clark and taken into his boat. In official discussions it would be advisable to keep to the facts.

I wish to say no more,

Yours obediently,

A. P. Williams,

Late S.S. *Jeddah*

This letter appears to provide further evidence that Williams was Conrad's source for Lord Jim. His blunt statement, 'I am the Chief Officer of the *Jeddah*' recalls a passage in *Lord Jim*: '"And where might you have come across him, captain, if it's fair to ask?" "He was the mate of the *Patna*..."' (p. 239). In the published text this statement is made by Marlow to Egström, Jim's employer, but in the manuscript[17] the form in which the statement is made is much closer to Williams's letter. In this case, it is Jim who says, 'I am the mate of the *Patna*', and he looks at Egström 'as if he wanted to swallow' him.

Gordan comments on Conrad's revision: 'Conrad must have seen at once...that it would never do for Jim to announce his past. It was entirely out of character; it also released the information too soon and destroyed the dramatic enlightenment of Egström.'[18] There is some justification for this suggestion that the change was made for the sake of dramatic effect, but in view of Williams's letter, we must recognize that the original writing of the scene would not have been entirely out of character so far as Williams was concerned. Conrad might be recalling the personal experience of hearing those words from Williams himself, and be attempting in his revision to make the necessary adjustment from Williams's character to that of Jim.

Apart from the necessity of sticking it out, Lord Jim felt that he could not return because his father, who thought so much of him, would have read of the scandal in the newspapers. 'He has seen it all in the home papers by this time,...I can never face the poor old chap...I could never explain. He wouldn't understand' (p. 96). This might also have been the reason why Williams stayed in Singapore, for his father would certainly have 'seen it all in the home papers'.* He must have known the strength of the criticisms that had appeared in the London papers, since extracts from them appeared in the *Straits Times Overland Journal*, 13 September 1880, two days before Williams returned to Singapore.

Linked with the attitude of not shirking and of 'fighting this thing down', is the ideal of the English gentleman. References to Jim's gentlemanliness are made constantly in the novel, and in this sense also he is distinguished from the rest of the deserters. It implies a special mode of speech and behaviour on Jim's part, and his action and his situation in the Inquiry become much worse because of his transgression of the gentleman's code. The engineer of the *Patna* says he is 'too much of a bloomin' gentleman'[19] and the little second whines, '...and you call yourself a gentleman...'.[20]

* See quotations from the London papers, p. 62, above.

It is this that disturbs Brierly during the Court of Inquiry and makes him willing to put up two hundred rupees if Marlow will put up another hundred and undertake to persuade Jim to 'clear out early to-morrow morning. The fellow's a gentleman...This infernal publicity is too shocking...'[21] Marlow is in some ways a cypher for Conrad himself and therefore it is interesting that Jim should link himself and Marlow on the grounds that they are both gentlemen: 'Of course I wouldn't have talked to you about all this if you had not been a gentleman. I ought to have known...I am—I am—a gentleman, too...'[22] Mrs Thornett writes: 'I should say my father was conscious of being a gentleman and in some ways a snob...I have the seal of gold with the crest and coat of arms which belonged to my father and I remember he always had this on his watch chain which hung on his waistcoat' (letter of 30 September 1962). What Mrs Thornett says about the seal is verified by two photographs of Williams (Plates 3 and 4).

Baines tells us that Conrad was 'a Nałęcz Korzeniowski, Nałęcz being the heraldic name of the family coat-of-arms'.[23] The Williams's family crest was of a lion passant bearing a broken chain and the motto 'Vinctus Sed Non Victus—chained but not conquered'. Ford Madox Ford says of Conrad, 'His ambition was to be taken for—to be!—an English country gentleman of the time of Lord Palmerston',[24] and it is not unlikely, therefore, that Conrad should be attracted to a 'gentleman sailor', a man only slightly older than himself, then working as a ship-chandler's water-clerk and earning probably about £5 a month.

The conception of what is appropriate to a gentleman probably accounts for the kind of language used by Jim on occasions, and particularly in chapters XVII and XXIII. '"Jove!" he gasped out. "It is noble of you!...What a bally ass I've been."'[25] Cornelius is referred to as 'the Johnnie who's going to get the sack', a 'principal man' as a 'big pot',[26] and Stein's hurried escape from Patusan after the death of his princely supporter is a 'beastly shame'.[27] The Malayan chieftain Doramin is that 'jolly old beggar', and conditions in Patusan are described in this way: 'There had been no news for more than a year; they were kicking up no end of an all-fired row amongst themselves, and the river was closed. Jolly awkward, this; but, no fear; he would manage to find a crack to get in' (p. 287). Here a civil war is reduced to 'an all-fired row' in schoolboy slang.

It has not been possible to discover whether this language was typical of A. P. Williams, though an old Singaporean* who knew him says he was 'very polished in speech—very good mannered'. Certainly Jim is given preparatory school language and enthusiasms which do not suit the man we have met earlier narrating the story of his disaster to Captain Marlow. No doubt Conrad was trying to reproduce the language of a young gentleman and we must take into account that preparatory school slang may have sounded less absurd then than it does now. But it may be Conrad's intention to offer in this way a submerged criticism of Lord Jim, indicating his fundamental immaturity. The inadequacy of Jim's response in terms of language at certain crucial moments suggests an ironic attitude to his hero on Conrad's part.

Physical likeness between a fictional character and his source is not an easy thing to prove, but I think that in this case there is sufficient evidence to establish the relationship, particularly since Lord Jim has certain outstanding physical features which are stressed by Conrad. Jim is described in these terms:

> He was an inch, perhaps two, under six feet, powerfully built, and he advanced straight at you with a slight stoop of the shoulders, head forward, and a fixed from-under stare which made you think of a charging

* The chief clerk of the firm of Rodyk and Davidson. The original Mr Davidson acted on behalf of the defendants in the action for salvage against the *Jeddah*.

> bull. His voice was deep, loud, and his manner displayed a kind of dogged self-assertion which had nothing aggressive in it...He was spotlessly neat, apparelled in immaculate white from shoes to hat, and in the various Eastern ports where he got his living as a ship-chandler's water-clerk he was very popular (p. 1).

The description of Jim in the manuscript increases his height and makes him 'overbearing' and this particularly suggests that Conrad had Williams in mind. 'He was over six feet and stared downwards at one with an *overbearing* air of overbearing watchfulness. You felt that if you happened to say something, some one special thing which he did not want to hear, he would [indecipherable] knock you down and without more ado.'[28] Later Marlow stresses his fair, sunburnt complexion and blue eyes—'the clear blue of his eyes...'[29] and 'these blue, boyish eyes looking straight into mine, this young face ...the open, bronzed forehead...'.[30]

Williams's height, powerful build, and neat dress were confirmed by Mrs Thornett. I asked her to compare the description in *Lord Jim* with her memories of her father and she wrote to me on 13 July 1962: 'I have read *Lord Jim* and it certainly does seem that reference is made to my Father & the description in Chapter 1 seems typical. From my recollection of him as a child, he was powerfully built, very tall and had a deep voice, though gentle at heart.' Later, on 30 September 1962, she added: '...my father did dress carefully, very neat, all in white, I believe they were called "tutop"... the jackets were buttoned up the front to the neck.' Miss Brooksbank, granddaughter of Captain Lingard, has told me that A. P. Williams was a big man, certainly not under six feet, over it, in fact, and broad, and another old Singaporean said he was 'bluff, handsome, head up in the air', and the photographs I have of Williams confirm this. Mrs P. Ward of Perth, Australia, another daughter, stated that her father 'had beautiful china-blue eyes' (letter of 21 August 1962).

Conrad also emphasizes Jim's essential youthfulness and honesty of feature. He stresses that Jim's manner, though displaying a kind of 'dogged self-assertion', has nothing aggressive in it. He is popular as a water-clerk, and Schomberg says of him, 'And, mind you, the nicest fellow you could meet... quite superior.'[31] Jim's looks separate him from the other deserters as they arrive at the Harbour Office to report to the Master-Attendant. He is 'upstanding, broad-shouldered... turning his back on the other two... He looked as unconcerned and unapproachable as only the young can look... as promising a boy as the sun ever shone on.'[32]

If Conrad met Williams in Singapore, he would have been aged about thirty-one at that time, for he was twenty-eight at the time of the *Jeddah* incident. Conrad made Jim twenty-four when he sailed on the *Patna*. The four photographs I have obtained of Williams show him at various stages of his life, and certainly in the first two photographs it is possible to trace those less easily definable aspects of manner and stance which were typical of Jim.

The first is dated 1868, when Williams was sixteen (Plate 2). He is leaning against a chair, legs crossed, hands in pockets and looking firmly and a little suspiciously into the camera. He is certainly 'upstanding, broad-shouldered, with his hands in his pockets', he is 'clean-limbed, clean-faced, firm on his feet', and given a few years more in age, he might well be the Lord Jim who turned away from the other deserters, looking 'unconcerned and unapproachable as only the young can look'.

In the second photograph (Plate 3), he is probably in his thirties or early forties and is photographed sitting, with his wife standing beside him. The features most noticeable about him here are his size, powerful build, and direct stare which could certainly be described as a 'kind of dogged self-assertion'. He looks out of the photograph with a kind of determined, aggressive pride which is lacking in the younger Williams, but which recalls the attitude of Lord Jim when in his determination not to be called names by any man he 'bullies' Marlow. This is obviously the man who impressed Conrad so much.

*

Williams did not spend years attempting to run away from his past as Jim did, but apart from this, his later life has certain similarities with that of Jim. Mrs Thornett could tell me only that 'he was sea-faring to start with and then joined McAlister & Co., as a ship's chandler'. Williams on returning to Singapore had obviously tried to continue as a seaman. He was taken on as first officer in the S.S. *Cleator*, a much smaller ship than the *Jeddah*, in January 1881.[33] He left this ship after two months, and seems to have been unemployed until he joined an even smaller vessel, the S.S. *Vidar*, as first officer in May 1882. This is a most important fact, for Conrad himself was first officer in the *Vidar* at a later date, from August 1887 to January 1888. Williams served on this ship for almost the same period of time (May to October 1882) as Conrad and made the same journeys from Singapore to Berau, the settlement in Eastern Borneo on the Berau river which was to become Conrad's source for Patusan in *Lord Jim* and Sambir in *Almayer's Folly* and *An Outcast of the Islands.* Williams must have met at Berau, as Conrad was to do later, Olmeijer (the original of Almayer), Captain Lingard, and Jim Lingard, whose Malay title 'Tuan Jim' provided Conrad with the title of his novel. We can now question the statement attributed to Craig and reported by Jean-Aubry: 'It was on board the *Vidar* that he [Jim Lingard] was first dubbed Lord Jim, "thanks to the swaggering manner he assumed, when meeting our ship"...He made two or three voyages from Bulungan to Singapore on board the *Vidar* when Conrad was mate.'[34] Augustine Podmore Williams made exactly three voyages in the *Vidar* in 1882 and a comparison of the photographs of Williams and Jim Lingard (Plate 5) makes it only too apparent that Lingard would be unlikely to be known for an assumed 'swaggering manner'. Captain Craig was seventy-eight when he gave this information to Jean-Aubry and was speaking of people he knew and of events which took place about forty years earlier. It is possible, therefore, that he had confused Williams and Lingard. One of Jim Lingard's daughters, now living in Singapore, has told me that the Lingard children, who were educated in Singapore, played with the Williams children, and this suggests a friendship between the two men. James Allen and John Niven, who had been with the *Vidar* at least as early as 1883, were probably able to tell Conrad something of Williams. He may also have met him, and perhaps seen him at work as a water-clerk in the port of Singapore. Conrad could also have met him elsewhere. It will be remembered that the novelist describes Emmerson's Tiffin-Rooms in the MS of *The Rescue* where Shaw hears something of the exploits of Captain Lingard. Since McAlister's, the ship-chandlers, was housed in the same building situated across the road from the Harbour Office, it is very likely indeed that Conrad visited the Tiffin-Rooms and saw Williams there. (See Plate 14*a*.)

The first reference to Williams as a ship-chandler's water-clerk is in the *Singapore and Straits Directory* of 1884. He was then working for McAlister's, a firm in those days quite small but well known and certainly well known today in Singapore.

Conrad tells us that Jim's work as a water-clerk consisted in: '...racing under sail, steam, or oars against other water-clerks for any ship about to anchor, greeting her captain cheerily, forcing upon him a card—the business card of the ship-chandler—and on his first visit on shore piloting him firmly but without ostentation to a vast, cavern-like shop...'

(pp. 1–2). Jim's speed and the risks he took are particularly stressed, 'a regular devil for sailing a boat; ready to go out miles to sea to meet ships in any sort of weather...a reckless sort of a lunatic you've got for water-clerk...more like a demon than a man...'[35] And Egström says, 'I tell you, Captain Marlow, nobody had a chance against us with a strange ship when Jim was out.'[36]

Mrs Thornett says that her father 'was...the first man out as the ships came into harbour'. Perhaps Williams also, like Lord Jim, was trying to prove himself after the *Jeddah* incident by taking these risks.

Just as Jim lived with his 'Jewel' so A. P. Williams married in the East, an indication perhaps of his determination to settle there, and also of the fact that he had given up the idea of returning home. Mrs Neill, his niece, writes: 'He shocked and horrified his father—also mine, by marrying a Eurasian! Aunt Jane I believe was clever—cultured, of high caste and attractive, and it was apparently a very happy marriage. They had a large family—some black—some white.' The record of Williams's marriage is in the registry held at St Andrew's Cathedral, Singapore. It records that George Augustine Podmore Williams, aged 30, Master Mariner, married E. Jane Robinson, aged 16 years, on 22 January 1883.

Seven years after A. P. Williams began working for McAlister's, he was promoted to Canvasser (*Singapore and Straits Directory*, 1891). In 1908 he was wealthy enough to celebrate his silver wedding in the Hotel de l'Europe, the hotel that Conrad describes as Malabar House in *Lord Jim*. Mrs Thornett wrote in answer to my request for photographs: 'I have a photograph of father and mother on a menu of their Silver wedding anniversary, a dinner held at the Europe Hotel.' This shows Williams as an older man and it is noticeable that the look of determined pride has gone. Perhaps he felt that he had successfully outlived the *Jeddah* affair. A year later he was made departmental manager of the Dubash department of McAlister's. McAlister's could provide me with no information, for all their records had been destroyed by the Japanese during their occupation of Singapore, but they had one old photograph of their employees. They did not know its age—or the names of the staff photographed. On it I recognized Williams, much older, stouter and no longer upright in stature. Yet something of his characteristic pose remained, in the bend of his shoulders, and spread of his hands on his knees (Plate 4). I have dated this photograph about 1911 because in that year A. P. Williams left McAlister's after twenty-seven years' service and began his own business.

In the year of his silver wedding, he drew up his will, 10 March 1909. It makes interesting reading. 'Deliver to my son Alfred Lockyer Williams my watch, large diamond ring and the family crest seal and seal with coat of arms.' To each child (and he had 16) he asked that a diamond ring should be given and to his brother Robert Bernard Williams of Dunedin, New Zealand, among other things, his 'silver cigar case with crest engraved on same'. To his wife he left: 'All my lands and houses and my ready money, furniture, jewellery, silver plate, pictures, horses, carriages, insurance policy of £1,000, tramway shares.' Two years later he began his own firm of ship-chandlers in Battery Road, Singapore, in the same street as McAlister's, which is close to the water-front. But on 22 October 1914 the *Straits Budget* reports:

In the Bankruptcy Court on Monday afternoon, before the Chief Justice, Mr J. A. S. Bucknill, K.C., A. P. Williams came up for his public examination. The debtor, who stated that his age was 62, said that he had been in Singapore for 35 years. For 28 years he was with Messrs McAlister and Company, leaving them at the end of 1910. He made a little money during the land boom. He bought three houses and, with his wife, a fourth. He started on his own as a shipchandler and then came the rubber boom, during which time he lost about $16,000...He was still endeavouring to earn a living as a shipchandler.

He was still in business in 1915, according to the Directory, but in 1916 Conrad's source for Lord Jim died. His death was recorded in the St Andrew's Cathedral register: 'Died 1916, April 17 Augustine Podmore Williams. Aged 64. Master Mariner. Buried 17 April 1916. Cause of death Bulbar Paralysis.' Two obituaries were published in the local newspapers. The *Singapore Free Press*, 20 April 1916, wrote:

> There passed away yesterday morning, at his residence, Shamrock, Barker Road, Mr Austin Podmore Williams, who for 27 years was employed at Messrs McAlister & Co., as their chief outside superintendent in the Dubash and Shipchandlery Department. He severed his connection with this firm some three to four years ago and set up on his own account in a ship-chandlery business in the Arcade, but this not proving as flourishing as expected, Mr Williams joined the firm of Dawood & Co., and it was while employed in his duties there that on the 15th of March, he slipped and fell, which resulted in a fractured hip bone. The deceased...never really rallied from this accident and died at 3.45 yesterday morning of paralysis of the brain. The late Mr Williams was chief officer of the Singapore Steamship Co's *Jeddah*, a pilgrim ship which met with an accident in the Red Sea and was abandoned with about a 1,000 coolies aboard. He held a chief officer's certificate and was for some time the Singapore representative of the Imperial Merchant Service Guild. Many wreaths were sent to the funeral having reference to his nautical career, besides many others from private friends...

So even at the end of his life, the incident of the *Jeddah* remained with him. He faced it but never lived it down. Yet he had made friends and was respected, as the second obituary shows: 'There passed away on Monday Mr A. P. Williams, known to his many friends and acquaintances as "Daddy", a very familiar figure in local shipping circles' (*Straits Budget*, 20 April 1916).

Jim died at the hand of his friend's father:

> The crowd, which had fallen apart behind Jim as soon as Doramin had raised his hand, rushed tumultuously forward after the shot. They say that the white man sent right and left at all those faces a proud unflinching glance. Then with his hand over his lips he fell forward, dead (p. 516).

A. P. Williams died much less melodramatically and he had a quiet funeral. In his will are the following words: 'I desire that my funeral should be quiet, cheap and simple and no fuss made about it.' His grave is in the Bidadari Cemetery, Upper Serangoon Road, Singapore. Williams, clearly, regarded himself to the last as a master mariner, in spite of his long years on land, for his headstone was engraved with an anchor.

In view of the strong parallels between Williams and Lord Jim, it is apparent that Conrad's inspiration depended upon a much closer contact with his source than he indicates in the Author's Note to *Lord Jim*—'One sunny morning in the commonplace surroundings of an Eastern roadstead, I saw his form pass by—appealing—significant—under a cloud—perfectly silent.'[37] Admittedly, there is no absolute evidence that Conrad had met Williams, but there is a great deal of circumstantial evidence. Conrad very likely heard of Williams's history, reputation, and character from Allen and Niven while he was on the *Vidar*. He very probably saw, and possibly met, Williams when the latter was working as a ship-chandler's water-clerk in Singapore during Conrad's periodic visits there.* And finally, the close parallels between Williams and

* While I was revising this book for publication, an article of mine on Conrad in Singapore appeared in *The Guardian*. In it, I stated (perhaps precipitately, but following my personal conviction) that Conrad 'met' Williams in Singapore. As a result, I received a letter from a Mrs Viola Allen of Surrey who, while taking me up on the question of Conrad meeting Williams, certainly confirmed that my research was accurate, and that Williams was the source for Jim. She wrote:

'...I think you are wrong when you say Conrad *met* Lord Jim in Singapore. We had many talks about people in Jim—a book I first met in 1902!! and Conrad told me he *saw* Williams in Singapore and wondered why a man of that—well—*class—should be a ship chandler's clerk* [my italics], and he was *told* Jim's story.'

'...Then I asked about Jim. "I used to see him in Singapore—a ship's runner he was—nearly six feet tall."

'"Yes, an inch, perhaps two, under six feet," I interrupted. For a moment—he gazed at me—not recognizing the opening words of Jim!!

'"Yes," he said, "and he had an expression like this"—and he gave a rather lowering frown. "He was a fine looking man of about forty—his name was Williams—but I used that name somewhere else, and so I called him Jim—I always wondered why a man like that was doing that sort of job. One day, I asked why. 'Oh, don't you know his

Lord Jim suggest that Conrad had spoken to Williams and perhaps heard his history from the man himself. I feel certain that it was his intimate knowledge of Williams's life and character, in fact, which led Conrad 'to seek fit words for his meaning' with all the sympathy of which he was capable.

story?' Apparently, everyone knew it in Singapore. I don't know the name of the ship—not *Patna*, but some name of that kind. Always, there was the shadow of that damn thing over him."' (letter of 20 February 1965).

'LORD JIM'

THE SECOND PART

'ALMAYER'S FOLLY'

'AN OUTCAST OF THE ISLANDS'

5
THE RAJAH LAUT

Captain Tom Lingard, 'the acknowledged king of them all... he whom the Malays...recognised as the "Rajah-Laut"—the King of the Sea',[1] plays a progressively important role in *Almayer's Folly*, *An Outcast of the Islands*, and *The Rescue*, yet little is known of the Lingard who was Conrad's inspiration for Captain Tom Lingard, and the nature of Conrad's contact with him has never been established. Jean-Aubry has this to say of Lingard:

> It was during these Singapore and Borneo voyages [in the *Vidar*] that Conrad also came across that Tom Lingard whom he afterward made the hero of two of his books; creating him out of the traits taken from the real man and others borrowed from Dominic Cervoni...The real Tom Lingard was the captain of a schooner which traded between Singapore, Benjarmassim, Cottu, Bulungan, and other Dutch places to the North.[2]

J. D. Gordan added to our knowledge of Lingard by visiting Bulungan in Dutch East Borneo in the summer of 1939.[3] There he was told that Lingard was a Scot (Lingard's granddaughter, Miss Brooksbank of Singapore, denies this); that he paid the Sultan of Sambaliung, who ruled Berau, a relatively large yearly tax of 700 florins; that he had business connections with the Getle Company of Singapore—I have found no reference whatsoever to such a firm existing then or now in Singapore; that he was closely connected with Olmeijer, who shipped his goods by Lingard's schooner; that Lingard represented Olmeijer in Bulungan for a time; that his voyages had brought him renown and his title of 'Rajah Laut'; and that he had discovered a channel for ships in the Berau river still called on the official chart 'Baak van Lingard'.

He concluded that Tom Lingard of *Almayer's Folly* and *An Outcast of the Islands* was apparently founded upon this Captain Tom Lingard whom Conrad met at Berau.

But this man was actually called Captain William Lingard and *it is unlikely that Conrad ever met him*. Conrad must, therefore, have been depending upon marine shore-talk for his information, and my aim was to rediscover the life of the 'Rajah Laut', looking always for those aspects of it likely to be part of a contemporary oral tradition. I knew that the Lingard children and the Williams children had played together, and it seemed to me that descendants of both families in Singapore might have stories to recall about the famous 'Rajah Laut'. I was to find that, oddly enough, they knew very little of Captain Lingard. But since Lingard had traded between Borneo and Singapore, the movements of his ship or ships might be traced through the 'Shipping in Harbour' columns of the Singapore newspapers.[4] A study of the newspapers for the period 1844 to 1890 provides sufficient new material for a reconstruction of at least part of the career and character of the original of Conrad's Rajah Laut. Some of the newspapers are in bad condition but, apart from those of 1868 and parts of 1880 which were not available, they provide a continuous record. Information from this source is supported by material obtained from public records, interviews, and contemporary accounts of the East during and after Lingard's time.

The earliest reference to Lingard was as master of a ship called the *Nina*,* which arrived in Singapore from Liverpool

* Conrad's heroine in *Almayer's Folly* is called Nina and it may be that Conrad gave her this name because he had heard of it in connection with Lingard. Gordan states (p. 43) that Mrs Gray, Olmeijer's daughter, had never heard of a Nina in her family, though Jim Lingard's daughter recalled, when I interviewed her in May 1962, a 'tanta Nina', Aunt Nina, who was an Olmeijer and, she said, though middle-aged when she knew her as a girl, very beautiful, with long black hair. She was the wife of William Olmeijer, who may have been a brother of Charles Olmeijer. I believe this woman to have been the natural daughter of Francis James Secretan, born on 13 November 1860 and mentioned in a codicil to his will (see p. 92, below). Lingard was appointed

on 28 February 1861. I was able to obtain a copy of the *Nina*'s registration from the Singapore Register of Shipping, and this provided some information about Captain Lingard.

The *Nina* was owned by Francis James Secretan, a merchant, who died on 16 May 1864. The registration stated that in his will, dated 20 September 1859, he appointed James Weir and William Lingard* as executors. The will showed that Secretan was 'a merchant of Lombock residing in Singapore for a temporary purpose' when he made his will, and William Lingard is also said to be 'a merchant of Lombock'. Lingard's arrival in the *Nina* in 1861 was not, therefore, his first arrival in the East, for he was established at Lombock prior to his becoming known in Singapore. It may even be that he was in the East as early as the 1840's, as the fictional Lingard's statement in *An Outcast of the Islands* suggests:

> Well, I said I would see her through it all right; help Willems to a fresh start and so on. I spoke to Craig in Palembang. He is getting on in years, and wanted a manager or partner. I promised to guarantee Willems' good behaviour. We settled all that. Craig is an old crony of mine. Been shipmates in the forties.[5]

But I found no reference to Lingard in the first sixteen years of Singapore newspapers (1844–60) that I checked. The Craig referred to in this quotation is not, of course, Captain James Craig, master of the *Vidar* during Conrad's service on that ship, but Thomas Morgan Craig who was indeed 'an old crony' of Lingard's and at one time captain of the *Nina*.

The years 1861–4 are significant when we are considering William Lingard as the source of Conrad's Tom Lingard.

guardian to both of Secretan's natural children, Phillippo and Ninette, and he may well have persuaded William Olmeijer to marry Ninette. Perhaps when Lingard in *Almayer's Folly* says, 'Nobody will see the colour of your wife's skin. The dollars are too thick for that', there is a connection with the money Ninette inherited under the terms of Secretan's will. With this marriage, both in fact and fiction, Lingard's long responsibility for her came to an end and it could be said that 'the old seaman was perfectly happy. Now he had done his duty by the girl.'

* James Weir was already a member of the firm of William Spottiswoode & Company (Singapore), and they were for many years consignees or agents for Lingard.

Lingard made his first appearance in Singapore as master of one of Secretan's ships, the *Nina*, and remained master of the *Nina* until 1864, making trading voyages to 'Ampanam, Sourabaya, and Macassar'. The *Nina*, according to her registration, was sold in September 1864. Lingard's connections with Craig seem to date from this period, for Craig had earlier arrived in Singapore as master of the *Swan*, another of Secretan's ships, which was also sold in 1864.

While Lingard was in Singapore in 1861 he was awarded a Certificate of Service. Two years previously an Act had been introduced in Singapore (Act 1 of 1859) which made it necessary for masters of ships to have a Certificate either of Competency or of Service. The first person to receive a Certificate of Service was Thomas Morgan Craig. William Lingard received his Certificate of Service on 15 March 1861 (*Straits Calendar and Directory*, 1866). The *Royal Almanac and Directory*, 1862, gives as Lingard's qualification for the Certificate of Service, that he had been a 'master for several years'.*

Secretan died on 16 May 1864. Five days later Lingard arrived in Singapore and on 23rd of the month he and Craig bought the *Coeran*.

Secretan's will and the documents preserved with it throw some light on the connections between these three men, and upon Lingard's history up to this point. A codicil to Secretan's will appoints William Lingard as guardian of Secretan's two children Phillippo and Ninette. 'The mother of the aforesaid Phillippo having on the 13th of November A.D. 1860, given birth to a female child, which I acknowledge to be mine and named "Ninette"...Ninette to be equal sharer with Phillippo in the property and advantages above specified.' The mother of these children—a Bali woman, Sumanty— is to be provided

* Other masters who received certificates stated the exact number of years they had commanded vessels, and the shortest term of service was three years.

for at 'the discretion of my Executors—I wish such provision to be extended only in case of actual want, she being now otherwise provided for'. Documents relating to the execution of the will by Lingard and Weir show that large sums of money were involved and suggest that Secretan was a wealthy man.*

Much of this is relevant to Conrad's portrait of Lingard, and perhaps of Stein in *Lord Jim*. It would appear that Lingard and Craig took over the trading interests of Secretan after his death and that Lingard later extended them at Berau and Bulungan. Moreover, the fictional Lingard's reputation for adopting protégés was obviously based on fact. As early as 1864 William Lingard is guardian of the two Secretan children. The connection between Lingard and Stein is less certainly proved, but remains, I think, a strong probability. In *Lord Jim* Conrad writes:

> ...Stein...remained with an old trader he had come across in his journeys in the interior of Celebes—if Celebes may be said to have an interior. This old Scotsman, the only white man allowed to reside in the country at the time, was a privileged friend of the chief ruler of Wajo States...I often heard Stein relate how that chap, who was slightly paralysed on one side, had introduced him to the native court a short time before another stroke carried him off...He dragged his leg, thumping with his stick, and grasped Stein's arm...'Look, queen, and you rajahs, this is my son...I have traded with your fathers, and when I die he shall trade with you and your sons'...By means of this simple formality Stein inherited the Scotsman's privileged position and all his stock-in-trade... (p. 251).

Conrad may be reflecting here Lingard's inheritance of Secretan's trading interests.

The registration of the *Coeran* shows that on 23 May 1864,

* The *Nina* in July 1863 carried a large cargo of gutta percha. There is a record of wages paid to Lingard after an Australian Expedition in 1864. In a schedule dated 18 March 1869, Thomas Morgan Craig, then residing in Fife, Scotland, deponed that he witnessed Secretan's will, and that he, Craig, was 'Master of the *Swan*...of which the said F. J. Secretan was owner, which was then trading between Singapore and Lombock and Borneo'.

Thomas Morgan Craig of Singapore, master mariner, and William Lingard, also of Singapore, master mariner, bought 32 shares each in the ship, a locally built sailing vessel of 134 tons. Lingard became sole owner on 18 June 1866 and remained her owner for eight years when the ship was sold.*

From June 1864 to July 1865 the *Coeran* came into Singapore harbour four times with Craig and Lingard alternating as master. Whenever Craig took the vessel out of port, Lingard was reported as bringing her in, and when Lingard took her out of port Craig brought her in. At this time the schooner travelled between Singapore and Borneo, which probably means the east coast of Borneo and may mean in particular Berau and Bulungan.

In 1864 we find Lingard connected for the first time with the Olmeijer (Almayer) family. On 18 November he brought the *Coeran* in from Macassar in Celebes and eight days later was married at the Presbyterian Church, Orchard Road, Singapore to Miss Johanna Carolina Olmeijer (spelt 'Olmeyor' in the marriage certificate). Lingard obviously brought his wife-to-be with him on board the *Coeran*, for the certificate records their place of residence as 'on board the *Coeran*'. It would appear, therefore, that Lingard had no settled residence in Singapore at this time in spite of the reference to 'William Lingard of Singapore' in the *Coeran*'s registration. According to the marriage certificate, his father's name was also William and he was an innkeeper by occupation. Johanna Carolina's father was Mathys Olmeyor, a clerk. The two witnesses were William Tod (he was then master of the British barque *Bencleuch*) and William Burrows, one time master of the ship *Crimea*. Burrows later became well known as a pilot in Singapore, and Lingard and he were clearly good friends.

* Craig, after selling his shares to Lingard, must have gone to live in Scotland (see p. 93 n., above), but it is possible that he later returned to the East and traded in 'Palembang' as the quotation from *An Outcast of the Islands*, pp. 189–90, suggests.

Lingard spent a short honeymoon in Singapore before putting out to sea, the *Coeran* leaving port with Lingard as captain and bound for Borneo, on 4 December 1864. No doubt he took his young wife with him.

During the next two years the *Coeran* returned to the port of Singapore only twice, in November 1865 and June 1866. It is on the latter occasion that Berau is first mentioned in the Shipping Column and, therefore, Lingard's trading at Berau cannot be placed later than 1866. The spelling given in the newspaper is 'Brow' and this agrees with Conrad's when by accident he failed to take the name out of the published text of *Almayer's Folly* and replace it with the fictional 'Sambir'. The passage reads: 'She [Nina] seemed to have forgotten in civilised surroundings her life before the time when Lingard had, so to speak, kidnapped her from Brow' (p. 49). Three days after arriving in port Lingard bought the *Coeran* outright on 18 June 1866.

The *Coeran* continued her trading voyages—often to Berau or Bulungan, and sometimes with Lingard as master. And on 4 April 1871, Lingard bought a second ship, the *West Indian*. Though Lingard continued to own the *Coeran* he did not appear as her master again but remained with the *West Indian*. The ownership of these two vessels at the same time, and for a period of three years, seems to indicate that there was a basis in fact for Conrad's constant references to Lingard's wealth. '"And Captain Lingard has lots of money", would say Mr Vinck solemnly, with his head on one side—"lots of money; more than Hudig".'[6]

Lingard was to sail in Eastern waters in the *West Indian* for the next nine years, though the *West Indian*'s registration shows that there was a slight break in ownership from 1 June 1875 to 3 August 1875. She was the largest vessel he ever owned, weighing 324 tons, and was already some thirteen years old when he bought her. She was a sailing vessel—

Lingard would have nothing to do with steamers—with one deck and three masts. Her figure-head was a 'woman half figure'.

*

All these details suggest certain possibilities with regard to William Lingard's life as a captain and trader in the East which would confirm that he was Conrad's model for Captain Tom Lingard, the 'Rajah Laut'. I will attempt to reconstruct William Lingard's life with these possibilities in view.

The death of Secretan in 1864 must have been something of a turning-point in Lingard's career. By that time Lingard was established as a merchant and captain in Lombock, was known in Singapore, and had met Craig and discussed with him the possibilities of trading in Borneo. The next stage was the partnership with Craig, which allows us to draw some conclusions about this trading. The method of sharing the command of the *Coeran* invariably brought only one of them into Singapore at any one time.* Moreover the journeys made are of approximately four months' duration, which might be taken to mean that they were already trading with Berau and Bulungan. It seems probable that one partner remained in Borneo to collect cargo or to explore, while the other brought the cargo into Singapore. The trading post at Berau might not yet have been established since it is not mentioned by name in the Shipping Columns until May 1866. But it is significant that, as soon as Craig dropped out of the partnership, Lingard found it necessary to employ other captains on the run between Berau and Singapore when, so far as I know, he owned only one vessel.*

Other sources might help us here in determining what Lingard was doing, and what the situation was at Berau. The trading situation described in *An Outcast of the Islands* is one

* See list of Lingard's journeys on the *Coeran* and *West Indian* in Appendix D, pp. 312–14, below.

which requires two men to carry it out. One remains at the trading post at Sambir to collect rattans from the natives, the other carries this cargo to Singapore. It is possible that after the break with Craig, Lingard remained at Berau to establish firm trading relations with the natives and therefore had to employ a captain for the *Coeran*. Mrs Oehlers told me during an interview in May 1962 that her father, Jim Lingard, made long journeys up river from Berau into the interior to collect rattans. It may well be that he was carrying on the custom established by his uncle, Captain Lingard, and made necessary by trading conditions at Berau—traders were discouraged by piracy, the unsettled state of the area and the 'scantiness of tonnage'. Lingard would seem to have been the first trader to form *permanent* trading relations with the local people by remaining at Berau to establish a post, and also by journeying into the interior. This would mean that he must have employed a captain for the *Coeran* after Craig left him.

I do not think that Olmeijer (Almayer) was at Berau at this time. Gordan stated that Olmeijer arrived in Berau in 1870.[7] This date is clearly a more sensible one than that quoted in the K.P.M. (Koninklijke Paketvaart-Maatschappij) report of 1893 by M. G. Van Der Burg which reports Olmeijer as having lived at Berau since 1880.[8] Miss Jerry Allen[9] refers to Mr Haverschmidt's discovery at Gunung Tabur (Berau) of the graves of Olmeijer's first and third sons, both of whom died young, one in 1876, the other in 1878. The journeys of the *Coeran* suggest that Olmeijer was established at Berau between 1869 and 1870. I feel inclined to suggest a date early in 1869 because Lingard came to Singapore in June of that year and afterwards dispensed with other captains, taking charge of the *Coeran* himself until he bought the *West Indian* in April 1871. He was travelling to Berau during this time and would appear to have had someone there permanently to carry on the trading.

In *Almayer's Folly*, Conrad describes the young Almayer sailing with the famous Lingard: 'Almayer...started in the *Flash* [this was never the name of a ship that William Lingard owned] on one of those long cruises when the old seaman was wont to visit almost every island in the archipelago' (pp. 8–9). These 'long cruises' seem to be based on the voyages of Captain William Lingard, for he was absent from the port of Singapore so long at times that some kind of exploratory journeys seem likely. For example, on one occasion he was away in the *Nina* over two years (March 1861 to May 1863).

On 24 August 1872 the *Coeran* left for Berau, the master being a Captain Merry, and Lingard followed in the *West Indian* on 4 September. This was the *Coeran*'s last journey for Lingard. She returned on 6 October 1873 and remained in port until she was sold in February 1874.

*

Two days after Lingard returned to Singapore on 1 February 1873, the *Singapore Daily Times* printed the following report:

> The British Barque *West Indian* arrived on Saturday afternoon, from North-east coast of Borneo; she has been away from Singapore for about five months, and those on board appear to have had a rather hard time of it, the Captain, Mr Bruce the consignee, and nearly the whole of the native crew being down with fever and ague. For the past week, the mate (himself very sick with the fever) and three Malays were the only ones on board at all well enough to work the ship, and during this time some very dirty weather was experienced.

The fever of captain and crew did not delay the *West Indian* to any appreciable extent, for she left for Berau within a month, on 28 February 1873.

Lingard returned to port on 15 August 1873, and the Register of Shipping records the sale to him on 1 September 1873 of a wooden steamer, schooner rigged, with a net tonnage of six tons. Lingard named her *Johanna Carolina* after his wife. Such a small vessel (it had one eight-horsepower engine and was 49 feet in length) would not, I think, be used for trade, though it might conceivably have been bought by Lingard for exploring the lower and upper reaches of the Berau river, a river notoriously reef-scarred, in places dangerously shallow, and with unexpected currents. In the *Johanna Carolina*, Lingard would no longer need to rely on the wind for movement. Whatever happened to her, she is not reported in the Singapore newspapers as appearing in the port of Singapore.

The *West Indian* continued her journeys to Berau and Singapore under the command of different captains until 28 April 1875, when she again arrived from Berau. The events which follow seem to suggest that Lingard went through some kind of financial crisis. The registration of the *West Indian* shows that the ship was sold on 1 June 1875 to 'Peri Aya'. On the same day 'Peri Aya' took out a mortgage for $7,000 and then by a bill of sale dated 3 August 1875 William Lingard bought back his ship. After Lingard regained possession of the *West Indian*, he changed his consignees, William Spottiswoode and Co., with whom he had had dealings since 1861. His new agents were Guthrie and Co., an important firm then as now. I suspect that Spottiswoode went out of business at this time (though I have found no newspaper reference to this) and that Lingard found himself short of money and had, until Guthrie's came to his aid, to sell his barque. The *West Indian* did one more journey in 1875 to Berau and Bulungan, leaving Singapore in August and returning on 19 December.

Up to this point, William Lingard's nephew, Jim Lingard, would not have come out from England. According to Jim's son, Mr Edward Lingard of Perth, Australia, his father was born on 25 August 1862, and Jim's daughter, Mrs Oehlers of Singapore, told me her father was brought out East by her grand-uncle, William Lingard, in a sailing ship, when he (Jim) was about fourteen years old. With him also came his brother Joshua who was, Mrs Oehlers thinks, two years older,* and Jim's sister Anne who was eighteen.† Mrs Oehlers's memory may well be at fault about the age at which her father left England, but if she is correct as to dates, it would mean that Jim came out about 1876 and that Lingard's ship went to England for him. But I found no reference to any of Lingard's ships going to England at this time. Mrs Oehlers recalls her father mentioning that her uncle was 'very strict with the brothers, Joshua and Jim, making them start at the bottom as cabin boys'.

There is a notable change in the entries in the Shipping Columns referring to the *West Indian* from August 1875 to the date on which Lingard sold this ship. The barque did her regular journeys of from three to six months in length to Berau and Borneo, but Lingard was her master throughout this period. For some reason he had dispensed with other captains. The ship was put up for sale in August 1878 but does not appear to have been sold, for she left for Borneo again.‡ Finally she was up for sale on 22 July 1879 and Lingard's name dropped out of the newspaper columns. The ship was in harbour until she was sold on 16 February 1880. But while the *West Indian* was up for sale, the irrepressible Lingard came into Singapore as master of another ship—the *Rajah Laut*.

Conrad makes much of Captain Tom Lingard and the title of 'Rajah Laut' given him by the Malays. In *An Outcast of the Islands*, he describes Lingard's attachment to his title:

* In fact he was five years older. His death certificate shows that he died on 29 November 1920. Jim's son, Mr Edward Lingard, says that his father was born on 25 August 1862.

† Anne returned to Manchester. She married a man called Burrows, probably related to William Lingard's best man, and a son of that marriage was called Lawrence Lingard Burrows. Another sister, Julie Lingard, stayed on in Manchester.

‡ Lingard returns to Singapore on 3 July 1878 in the *West Indian*, and the ship is up for sale on 17 August. No sale was effected, the ship being cleared on 3 September for the east coast of Borneo with Lingard as master.

'Those white men with whom he had business...could easily see that it was enough to give him his Malay title to flatter him greatly...they would drop the ceremonious "Captain Lingard" and address him half seriously as Rajah Laut—the King of the Sea' (p. 14). F. W. Burbidge the naturalist, in his book *The Gardens of the Sun*, describing a morning in Raffles Place, Singapore, where the 'enterprise and trade of Singapore' is discussed, proves that William Lingard *was* known as the 'Rajah Laut':

> You are sure to meet two or three captains of trading steamers. Captain Linguard [*sic*], perhaps, after one of his trips to the Coti river away on the south-east of Borneo, and then you will hear something of the rubber-market, or of the pirates, of whom, perhaps, few men know more than this energetic 'Rajah Laut', or 'Sea King', as he is called by the natives.[10]

Lingard's pride in his title is suggested by the fact that he gave his last ship the same name.

I failed to trace the registration of the *Rajah Laut*, but according to the *Singapore Daily Times* she was a Dutch barque of 320 tons and Lingard was her master until 1883 (Plate 6*b*).* During this period he continued trading with Berau and Bulungan, making two journeys in 1880, three in 1881, and four in 1882. He returned to Singapore in May 1883 and the ship was in port for three months. She eventually left on 13 August but Lingard was no longer listed as her master, though he was probably still connected with her. With Captain Archer as her master she returned to port on 1 December 1883, and left again on 20 March 1884. This was to be her last voyage and Lingard did not travel on her, for on 23 May 1884, his daughter, Caroline Lingard, was married in Singapore and he was present at the ceremony. The *Straits Times*, 28 May 1884, reports: 'At the Presbyterian church on Friday, the 23rd May, by the Rev. A. S. MacPhee, Frederick

* This picture of the *Rajah Laut* was sent to me by William Lingard's granddaughter. The ship was called the *Chineserin* before Lingard bought her and changed her name.

Havelock Brooksbank to Caroline Lingard both of Singapore.' Unfortunately all records of the Presbyterian Church, Singapore, were destroyed during the Japanese occupation, but the register of marriages still exists. The entry is as follows:

> Frederick Havelock Brooksbank 26 years (Mariner)
> residence Victoria Street, Singapore.*
> Father John Brooksbank.
>
> to
>
> Caroline Lingard 20 years
> residence Victoria Street, Singapore.
> Father William Lingard.
>
> at the Presbyterian Church in the presence of Fred. S. Pooles
> and Wm. Lingard.
> 23 May 1884.

Exactly three months after this marriage, the *Rajah Laut* returned on 23 August 1884 and the following month she is reported in the *Straits Times* as being up for sale. She remained unsold for over a year. No record of her sale was found but her name disappeared from the Shipping Columns on 21 September 1885. At this point Captain William Lingard seems to have disappeared, just as Captain Tom Lingard disappeared in *An Outcast of the Islands* and *Almayer's Folly*. But there is more to be said of William Lingard and some conclusions to be drawn which link him more closely to his fictional counterpart.

*

The character and reputation of Tom Lingard are fully presented in Conrad's Malayan novels, and correspond closely to the character and reputation of William Lingard. Part of Tom Lingard's reputation rests upon his success as a sea-adventurer. Conrad refers in *Almayer's Folly* to Lingard's 'desperate fights with the Sulu pirates', and in *An Outcast of the Islands* he gives the source of Lingard's fame: '...he soon became

* The number of the house in Victoria Street was not given in the marriage register but the register of births records that it was number 368.

known to the Malays, and by his successful recklessness in several encounters with pirates, established the terror of his name' (p. 14). I have discovered only two reports of William Lingard's encounters with pirates in the Singapore newspapers, but since the newspapers were very parochial at this time, he may have had others which were not mentioned in print. Events in Dutch East Borneo were not of great interest to readers in Singapore, but the nature of the two references suggests that Lingard had some reputation as a fighter against the pirates.

In the *Straits Times Overland Journal*, 7 October 1879, there is a letter from a master mariner called John Kelly. I give it in full.

Sir,—I notice in a paragraph in your issue of Wednesday last in commenting upon the action of H.M.'s *Kestrel* in burning a native piratical village on the North East coast of Borneo, you state that it is strange that you have not heard from Europeans who trade on the coast in question of any piracies having been committed, nor have you read of such in the Dutch or Manila papers. Well, Sir, I was attacked in the *Subahani* six months ago by pirates at the mouth of the Beelungan River [this is Bulungan]. I was apprehensive of an attack, knowing the coast, and put on deck rattans 8 ft. high and my guns were double shotted, when about 200 piratical sampans attacked me and I fired upon them. *Captain Lingard of the West Indian was attacked by pirates on the same coast* some time previous [my italics]. From Gunong Tabur to Sabuta, a horde of pirates infests the coast, and I, for one, am delighted that H.M.'s Gunboat *Kestrel* has taught them a lesson. As you wished for information on the subject from a European trader, I write this to give you my own experience, and remain, Sir,

Yours truly,

John Kelly,

late master of the Schooner *Subahani*.

Singapore, 3rd October 1879.

The Singapore newspapers sometimes carried accounts from other newspapers in the area and on 29 January 1876 the *Straits Times* reprinted the following account from the *Samarang Courant*:

Mr Lingard, commander of the *West Indian*, which vessel as we stated at length last week had been attacked by pirates off the East Coast of Borneo has again treated of the event in the *Macassar Handelsblad*. He is of the opinion that the honour of the Dutch flag is very badly maintained on the East coast of Borneo and that it is high time to guard that coast more effectively.

These reports suggest that Captain Lingard, at least by 1879, four years before Conrad's first arrival out East, was known well enough to be referred to quite casually.

Apart from these two references, John Dill Ross in his book *Sixty Years' Life and Adventure in the Far East*, relates an incident about William Lingard which seems characteristic of Conrad's Tom Lingard. Ross recalls Lingard holding the attention of the assembled company by telling 'the oft-told story of how he and his sailors stormed the Sultan of Bolongan's [*sic*] palace'.[11] Roland St J. Braddell in 'The Merry Past' gives us the reason for Lingard's attack on the palace: 'Captain Lingard, known as the "Rajah Laut", was also a great character. It is related of him that finding it impossible to obtain payment of a very large sum of money from a certain Bornean Sultan, he landed his crew, stormed the Sultan's palace, and captured His Highness, who promptly paid up!'[12]

The speed of Lingard's brig *Flash* is made much of in *Almayer's Folly*: 'Many tried to follow him and find that land of plenty for gutta-percha and rattans, pearl shells and birds' nests, wax and gum-dammar, but the little *Flash* could outsail every craft in those seas' (p. 7), and is returned to again in *An Outcast of the Islands*. Lingard says on being greeted by the Arab trader: ' "I know that this fellow will be under way and after me like a shot. I don't care! I have the heels of anything that floats in these seas," he added, while his proud and loving glance ran over and rested fondly amongst the brig's lofty and graceful spars' (p. 45). The part played by some of William Lingard's crew on two occasions in the Singapore annual regatta suggests that he may have had a similar reputation for speed:

> At 4.30 p.m. a challenge pulling race came off between four men of the *Glenlyon* against six Malays of the barque *West Indian*. Little or no excitement was caused by this race, as the difference of the build of the two boats was so great that there was not the slightest doubt from the first that the *Glen*'s would win. They had a smart Danish built boat, something between a skiff and a gig, while the *West Indian* had a common ship's gig intended for ordinary work in all kinds of weather, and it is quite astonishing how the natives held so well against the *Glen*'s; the coxswain of the *Glen*, all the more making frantic exertions to jerk off his head, and, as his boat neared the goal, he vainly tried to fling away his arms as well. Had there been a bit of a sea on, it is doubtful how this race would have ended (*Singapore Daily Times*, 8 January 1878).

In the following year, one of Lingard's boats took part in a race for six-oared gigs, against three other boats. Lingard's gig is rather oddly named 'No Name' but her flag is of interest, for it is the flag of 'Brow and Bulungan'. This would appear to indicate Lingard's pride in his influence in this area of Borneo. The newspaper printed a short report: 'This was a splendid race, and the contest between the P. & O. boat and the *West Indian*'s boat was exciting, the *Erewhon*, however, won, the *West Indian* boat, *No Name*, not withstanding that one of the rowers broke an oar, coming in second.' The regatta of 1879 was the most extensive to be held for many years, and in the account of it in the *Straits Times Overland Journal*, 4 January 1879, there is a further reference to Lingard: '...Captain Lingard of the *West Indian* notably—provided Lord Mayor's banquets on their own account, and their only grievance seemed to be that the whole of Singapore could not take seats at their tables.' Conrad's emphasis on Tom Lingard's generosity would again seem to be based on William Lingard's reputation. Conrad presents his hero as having a 'stupidly guileless heart', what Almayer calls his 'infernal charity', and what is earlier described as 'accesses of unreasoning benevolence'. Entertaining on the scale described must have cost a great deal and the passage can also be seen as a tribute to Lingard's wealth. A further reference to Lingard's generosity and wealth appears in John Dill Ross's book. His father was probably a friend and certainly an acquaintance of Lingard's.* He describes a party held in England at which Lingard was a guest. Lingard left the drawing room to go into the garden and Northwood (i.e. Captain Ross—Lingard is called 'Lugard') says:

> 'Lugard is an awfully decent fellow, and very generous with his dollars if anybody happens to want some of them, but off the quarter-deck of his old barque he is a bit of a nuisance. He'll be half-seas over before he thinks of going home to-night.' Everybody concurred, and everybody thought of the piles of money that Lugard made out of his gutta-percha trade.[13]

That William Lingard should be 'half-seas over' does not correspond with Conrad's view of Tom Lingard, since Conrad describes his ability to hold his liquor. In the early pages of *Almayer's Folly* it is reported that, after a night's carousal at the Sunda Hotel, Lingard would '...disappear quietly during the night from the roadstead while his companions were sleeping off the effects...Lingard seeing them drunk under the table before going on board, himself unaffected by any amount of liquor' (p. 7). He would, of course, have been an odd sea-captain at this time if he had not been a considerable drinker. Medical reports of the 1870's and 1880's show that a surprisingly large percentage of Europeans in the East died from the effects of over-drinking.

According to Miss Lena Brooksbank her grandfather was a bluff, outspoken man, and her father told her that Captain Lingard had said to him before he married Caroline: 'If

* It was Ross, Lingard, and Cowie who, in their different ways, first opened up the Bornean trade.

you play around with my daughter, I'll shoot you.' This could stand as a characteristic statement of the Tom Lingard Conrad reveals in his first two novels: 'Very soon, however, they found him out, and the word went round that Captain Tom's fury was less dangerous than many a man's smile' (*An Outcast of the Islands*, p. 14). And his remark to Willems could be an echo of the real Lingard: '... I am not going to mince matters. Never could! You keep quiet while I talk. Can't you?' (*ibid.* p. 32).*

*

I shall show in the next chapter that Conrad keeps close to the facts of the trading post at Berau. But it is difficult to discover whether or not the Arabs eventually took over Lingard's monopoly there and whether any treachery was involved, as is the case in *Almayer's Folly* and *An Outcast of the Islands.*

The Arabs who traded at Berau were the Al Jooffrees, owners of the *Vidar*. According to the *Singapore and Straits Directory*, Syed Mohsin Bin Salleh Al Jooffree was already owner of several steamers in 1883 and had branch houses at Berau and Bulungan. He had four sons and it was the eldest, Syed Abdulla, who traded at Berau. The wife of Syed Mohsin's youngest son is still living in Singapore. She is reputed to be over a hundred and, though unable to walk very much, is in possession of her faculties. She was unable to give very much information about the houses of Agency established at Berau and Bulungan, but she remembered that Syed Abdulla used to do a straight trade with the natives in red

* Miss Brooksbank mentioned to me a story she heard from her mother of her grandfather rescuing a sailor. She said, 'He was a strong swimmer and jumped overboard and saved a drowning man somewhere among the islands off the Borneo coast.' Conrad, in *An Outcast of the Islands*, p. 14, has Tom Lingard rescue 'the yacht of some big wig from home, somewhere down Carimata way'. (Cf. also *The Rescue.*) The only rescue I have found reported in the newspapers is quite different in character, and tells how Captain Lingard of the *Rajah Laut* picked up 'at sea a cargo boat with four men in which had drifted or been blown off the Java coast. The four men appear to have been in a very exhausted state when rescued.' The report gives Lingard's own account of the rescue (*Straits Times Overland Journal*, 10 March 1880).

and black cloth, beads and semi-precious stones, in exchange for rubber and rattans. According to Jim Lingard's daughter, Mrs Oehlers, her father used to trade with the Malays and Dyaks in Berau, doing a straight barter with salt and trinkets for rubber and rattans. No doubt he was carrying on his uncle's traditional method of barter.

The first ship of Syed Mohsin's I discovered going to Berau was the steamship *Vidar*, the ship that Conrad sailed in at a later date. It is interesting that the *Coeran* and the *West Indian* were both in Singapore harbour in August 1872 at the same time as the *Vidar*. This is the first mention in the newspapers of the *Vidar*, which arrived on 24 June. The consignee was 'Syed Massim' [*sic*] who bought the *Vidar* on 9 December 1872. Before 1879 a Captain Barrow had taken her at least in the direction of Berau on many occasions, that is to Sourabaya, Samarang, Pulo Laut, Coti and Macassar, though the first reference to her having gone to Berau occurs on 23 June 1879, with Captain Vincent as master. It is possible, therefore, that the Arabs were trading at Berau earlier than 1879. On the other hand, a more gradual approach would confirm Conrad's statement in *An Outcast of the Islands*:

> He [Abdulla] had found the river a couple of years ago, and had been anchored more than once off that estuary...He had never attempted the entrance, however, because men of his race, although brave and adventurous travellers, lack the true seamanlike instincts, and he was afraid of getting wrecked. He could not bear the idea of the Rajah Laut being able to boast that Abdulla bin Selim, like other and lesser men, had also come to grief when trying to wrest his secret from him (pp. 111–12).

And the movements of Lingard's ships and that of the Arab seem to confirm that Lingard's loss of his monopoly was a gradual process. During 1882, Lingard made only four journeys to Berau and Bulungan in the *Rajah Laut* while during the same period the *Vidar* appeared in Singapore harbour regularly every month, and every alternate journey of the *Vidar* was between Singapore and Berau and Bulungan. This is reflected in *Almayer's Folly*: 'He heard from her [Nina] oftener since Abdulla bought a steamer, which ran now between Singapore and the Pantai settlement.'[14] I have referred to the earlier attempt to sell the *West Indian* and this together with her sale a year later may indicate a growing realization on Lingard's part that the hey-day of Borneo trading was coming to an end for him as a result of competition from the Arabs. The *Vidar* departed for Berau only a month before the *West Indian* was put up for sale. Lingard's loss of the *Flash*, described by Conrad in *An Outcast of the Islands*, perhaps reflects the selling of the *West Indian*. It is because of this loss that Lingard, without a ship of his own, and without his own crew, is unable to take punitive action against Syed Abdulla and thus gives up without a fight.

> 'If it hadn't been for the loss of the *Flash* I would have been here three months ago, and all would have been well...'
>
> 'What? You don't mean to expel Abdulla out of here by force! I tell you, you can't.'
>
> 'Not I,' exclaimed Lingard. 'That's all over, I am afraid. Great pity. They will suffer for it. He will squeeze them. Great pity. Damn it! I feel so sorry for them if I had the *Flash* here I would try force. Eh! Why not? However, the poor *Flash* is gone, and there is an end of it. Poor old hooker. Hey, Almayer? You made a voyage or two with me. Wasn't she a sweet craft? Could make her do anything but talk. She was better than a wife to me. Never scolded. Hey?...And to think that it should come to this. That I should leave her poor old bones sticking on a reef as though I had been a damned fool of a southern-going man who must have half a mile of water under his keel to be safe!' (p. 173).

The fate of William Lingard's *West Indian* is more pedestrian than that of Tom Lingard's *Flash*, but the situation between William Lingard and the Arabs may have depended upon a historical situation with regard to ships; that is, the competition between sail and steam. The disadvantages of the sailing vessel in comparison with the steamer are apparent, and, though Conrad himself became master of a sailing barque, the *Otago*, as late as 1888, during Lingard's last year as a trader in the East, steamers were relentlessly chasing the sailing ships out of the South-east Asian archipelago trade, as the lists of shipping in Singapore harbour prove. So far as I know, Captain William Lingard never sailed in steamers, and when his career closed in 1884, the end of the sailing era was also near.

In *Sixty Years' Life and Adventure in the Far East*, John Dill Ross records Lingard saying to him: 'You are cut out for working on the Borneo coast; though after all, now that your dad has gone in for a damn steamer instead of the good old sailing-ships which made his money, it perhaps doesn't matter so much.'[15] Lingard is probably referring to the S.S. *Cleator* which John Dill Ross Snr. bought and which was registered on 14 February 1873. Ross had been in Eastern waters since the 1850's in his own sailing vessels and the *Cleator* marked his change to steam. He was a wiser person. It was literally a matter of changing to steamers or leaving the area and I suspect that finally Lingard left the area. On 13 January 1884, by which time Lingard was without a vessel of his own, the *Straits Times* had this to say: 'The day of sailing ships is almost done, and ere long they will have been crowded out of one more of their last strongholds, thus precluding them from obtaining freight to the East...' Whatever the reason, William Lingard's fortunes seemed to decline after the *West Indian*'s sale, and the beginning of Arab trade at Berau. In May 1883 the *Rajah Laut* returned to Singapore and eight days later the *Vidar* arrived from Sourabaya. Lingard's ship was unable to leave port at this time but the *Vidar* was busily in and out of harbour, and the *Rajah Laut* came up for sale in 1884 and after a year disappeared.

Returning to the fictional Lingard, we have references to his expeditions into the interior, after the Arab interference, in order to search for gold, all of which were unsuccessful.

Lingard returned unsuccessful from his first expedition, and departed again spending all the profits of the legitimate trade on his mysterious journeys (*Almayer's Folly*, p. 27).

The profits of past years had been swallowed up in Lingard's exploring craze. Lingard was in the interior—perhaps dead—at all events giving no sign of life (*Almayer's Folly*, pp. 28–9).

The next step in Lingard's decline was the failure of his bankers. 'The old man's banker, Hudig of Macassar, failed, and with this went the whole available capital' (*Almayer's Folly*, p. 28). Captain Whalley in 'The End of the Tether' also suffers through the failure of a Banking Corporation, 'the notorious Travancore and Deccan Banking Corporation'.

There was not to my knowledge a Hudig of Macassar, or a Travancore and Deccan Banking Corporation, but in 1884 an important and well-established bank in Singapore did fail. The Oriental Bank, called by the Malays 'the Bank Besar—the great or large bank', which was next door to Syed Mohsin's business premises, stopped payments. Roland St J. Braddell writes that 'when it stopped payment in 1884 there was a very big sensation in Singapore'.[16] A report of the winding up of the Oriental Bank is given in the *Straits Times*, 11 June 1884. The Occidental Bank (an obvious switch of name) is mentioned in *The Rescue* as Lingard's bank: 'Florid and burly he [Lingard] could be seen, for a day or two, getting out of dusty gharries, striding in sunshine from the Occidental Bank to the Harbour Office...' (p. 121). If there is any basis in fact for Conrad's suggestion that the fictional Lingard lost money through the failure of a bank, it must have been the Oriental Bank he had in mind. I think it likely that it was the failure of this Bank, which occurred just after his daughter's marriage, that resulted in Lingard ceasing to act as a trader.

The equally strange end of the *Johanna Carolina* may well be significant here. The *Singapore and Straits Directory*, 1885,[17] shows William Lingard as owner of the *Johanna*

Carolina, but the Directory is a year behind in its facts. The registration of the *Johanna Carolina* was closed on 5 December 1884, the certificate of registry having been lost and the ship having been already broken up at Sandy Point, Singapore.

*

Lingard's disappearance, at least in Conrad's novels, is made all the more startling by contrast with his previous position as benevolent despot and father figure. Lingard's generosity is constantly linked by Almayer with misfortune, and it does seem to bring disaster to his various protégés and to himself. Perhaps this is because it has such a strong aspect of possessiveness.

We see this possessiveness in relation to his 'river' and the people of the villages lying on the river. Beginning only with the thought of 'personal gain' he soon comes to dream 'of Arcadian happiness for that little corner of the world which he loved to think all his own'. He becomes convinced that only he 'knew what was good for them'. 'He looked proudly upon his work...He knew every settler on the banks between the sea and Sambir; he knew their wives, their children; he knew every individual of the multi-coloured groups...' (*An Outcast of the Islands*, p. 200). He tells Willems: 'I composed their quarrels, and saw them grow under my eyes. There's peace and happiness there. I am more master there than his Dutch Excellency down in Batavia ever will be when some day a lazy man-of-war blunders at last against the river' (*ibid.* p. 45). This benevolent despotism extends to his protégés Almayer and Willems, and they in turn give him love and admiration not unmixed with antagonism. Almayer thinks 'with dread of the separation from the only human being he loved'.[18] The situation is made more specific in *An Outcast of the Islands*:

All his life he [Willems] had felt that man behind his back, a reassuring presence ready with help, with commendation, with advice;...a man inspiring confidence by his strength, by his fearlessness, by the very weakness of his simple heart. Seeing him go away beyond his reach, Willems realised how much of himself belonged to that man; what an immense place that man had in his life, in his thoughts, in his belief in his own future...In his struggles with himself, with temptation; in his revolt and in his defeat, in his recklessness and in his remorse, he had always looked unconsciously towards the image of that man. And now that man was going away (p. 210).[19]

So far as the actual William Lingard is concerned, this desire to collect protégés seems to have been typical. I have already mentioned his guardianship of the Secretan children. Olmeijer was his first protégé at Berau, and we know that his nephews, Joshua and Jim Lingard, came East under his protection and that Jim was established, like Olmeijer, at Berau. It is likely that Frederick Havelock Brooksbank was also his protégé and served with Lingard in his ships. According to Miss Lena Brooksbank, her grandfather bought her mother, Caroline Lingard, the house in Victoria Street, Singapore, in which she and her husband were to live. There is some probability that F. H. Brooksbank contributed to the portrait of Almayer in that he married Lingard's adopted daughter.* It is significant that Almayer refers to Lingard as 'father', a term which would come naturally from Brooksbank whom Conrad might have heard using it. We do know that Olmeijer, at least in later years, was by no means the helpless figure that Conrad makes him. Van Der Burg, in the K.P.M. report of 1893, writes that Olmeijer was 'in fact the head of the area' and that 'the sultans seek his counsel in all circumstances'.[20]

That Joshua Lingard was also a protégé is suggested by the

* Gordan, p. 45, states that Lingard and his wife were childless. If this is true, who is Caroline Lingard? Mrs Oehlers told me that she had herself, many years ago, been told that Caroline Lingard was actually an Olmeijer. I later asked Miss Brooksbank whether her mother was adopted. She replied that her mother called Johanna Carolina mother and William Lingard father. But this doesn't answer the question. I also asked if her grandfather had married again. She replied that he did not need to. He was 'one for the women'.

fact that in the *Singapore and Straits Directory* for 1879 Joshua Lingard is listed as mate of the *West Indian*.* Both Mrs Oehlers and Miss Brooksbank agree that Joshua stayed at sea and became a master mariner sailing in the same waters as his uncle. Further, Miss Brooksbank recalls him as a regular and welcome visitor at her father's home and originally master of a Siamese ship. She recalled that Joshua and her mother became friends through sailing together in Captain Lingard's ships. This friendship continued long after the old sea captain had disappeared from Singapore.

*

In the novels, Lingard leaves Sambir for Singapore and considers going to Europe in order to get together enough money for his expedition.

> He wrote once from Singapore saying...that he...was going to Europe to raise money for the great enterprise. He was coming back soon. There would be no difficulties, he wrote. People would rush in with their money. Evidently they did not, for there was only one letter more from him saying he was ill, had found no relation living, but little else besides. Then came a complete silence. Europe had swallowed up the Rajah-Laut... (*Almayer's Folly*, p. 31).

By page 37 Almayer is asking Captain Ford 'to write to his friends in England making inquiries after Lingard. Was he alive or dead?' In *An Outcast of the Islands*, the same story is repeated. Talking of Willems, Almayer says,

> He knocked everything here into a cocked hat; drove father to gold-hunting—then to Europe, where he disappeared. Fancy a man like Captain Lingard disappearing as though he had been a common coolie. Friends of mine wrote to London asking about him. Nobody ever heard of him there! Fancy! Never heard of Captain Lingard! (p. 364).

It is a strange coincidence, but I have not been able to discover what finally became of William Lingard.

* The reference in the Directory is to 'J. Lingard mate *West-Indian*'. Jim Lingard's daughter was adamant that her father never stayed at sea.

The last reference to him shows that he was in the East early in 1887. W. G. St Clair, in his article in the *Malay Mail*, relates how he met William Lingard at that time, and also gives us the only description I have discovered of him:

Another personage I referred to in my letter...was one whose name is familiar to readers of Conrad. That is Captain Lingard, the type of the adventurer—skipper of those seas in the old days, now quite extinct. Curiously I met Capt. Lingard before Conrad had ever heard of him. It was on my way out to Singapore at the beginning of 1887, in the then brand new China Mutual steamer—*Tsinan*, on her maiden voyage from Glasgow to Hongkong.... At Penang, two extra passengers came on board, Captain Lingard and his niece. He and I soon made acquaintance, and I was told a good deal about himself and his wanderings through the Dutch Archipelago. He mentioned that he was popularly known among the Malay, Bugis, and Javanese sea-going people, mostly pirates, when a chance offered, as 'Raja Laut', the 'Sultan of the Seas'. When I told him that on the voyage out I had picked up about 800 Malay words from Swettenham's *Vocabulary*, he at once held an examination of a searching character, and when I promptly solved his nautical queries as to the Malay equivalents for scores of sea terms, I was passed with much credit.

Lingard, who was a personage of almost mythical renown, a sort of ubiquitous sea-hero, perhaps at times a sort of terror to evildoers, all over Eastern waters from Singapore to Torres Straits, and from Timor to Mindanao, was a well-set-up man of perhaps fifty-two when I saw him. Alert, decisive in his movements, just above middle height, with grizzled hair, moustache and beard, cut short after the naval style, he had two kenspeckle peculiarities. One of these was the texture of skin of his face, well tanned and wrinkled but with many small areas of smooth almost glossy cuticle, giving his features a hardbitten weather-beaten impression of a remarkable character. Another was the exceptional definiteness of the 'arcus senilis' that surrounded and encroached upon the corner of his eye. In that Lingard presented to me the most strongly marked case of this recognised token of advancing age, in his case evidently rather premature.*

I have found no trace of William Lingard after this date.

Neither Miss Brooksbank, Lingard's granddaughter, nor Mrs Oehlers, Jim Lingard's daughter, knows what happened to him. Mrs Oehlers says that she was told many years ago

* See Appendix E, pp. 315–16, below.

by an old Singaporean that William Lingard died in Singapore and was buried in the old cemetery on Bukit Timah, Singapore. She also said that she had looked for the grave. Since my interview with her, I have also searched for it. Neither of us has had any success. Miss Brooksbank thinks her grandfather died in England, probably somewhere in Lancashire, his home county. But I have checked the registers of deaths in Singapore, Penang, and the British Isles from 1884 to 1933 and found no record of his death. It would seem that Europe had swallowed up the Rajah Laut.

*

The disappearance of the actual Lingard seems to have impressed itself upon Conrad, so much so that the mysteriousness of Lingard's end is touched on in his first two novels. That Conrad was so impressed can, I think, be accounted for by considering the circumstances under which he was likely to have learnt the story of the real William Lingard.

Conrad came into Singapore for the first time in the year 1883 which was Lingard's last year at sea as master of a ship. Lingard left Singapore in the *Rajah Laut* for Berau and Bulungan on 16 November 1882 and returned on 20 May 1883. Conrad Korzeniowski was brought to Singapore in the S.S. *Sissie* on 22 March 1883 by Captain Choppard after the *Palestine* in which he was mate had burnt at sea. Conrad left Singapore and took a passage for Liverpool in a passenger steamer at the beginning of May, and could not have met William Lingard on this occasion. He might, however, have heard of him from Choppard who nine years previously was listed as master of Lingard's *West Indian* during the short period Lingard lost control of her.

There is one other possible source at this time. Another Captain Lingard was already in port when Conrad arrived, for the newspapers show that the steamer *Paknam*, master

Captain Lingard, came into port on 18 January 1883. This was Joshua Lingard, for on 26 July 1883 the *Paknam* again came in with Lingard as master at a time when the *Rajah Laut* with William Lingard as master was still in harbour. Conrad could have met Joshua Lingard during March and April.

On 22 September 1885 Conrad arrived for the second time on board the *Tilkhurst*. The *Rajah Laut*, which had lain in port for a year, disappeared from the Shipping in Harbour columns on the day before he arrived. If my earlier suppositions about the gradual failure of William Lingard's trade are correct, Conrad would most likely hear of this and might have watched the *Rajah Laut* leaving harbour.

Whatever Conrad may have heard of Lingard before his third visit in 1887 was probably casual and a matter only of minor interest. But in joining the *Vidar* on 22 August 1887 he must have found himself in contact at many points and through many people with Lingard's story. He was in the position of seeing the result of Lingard's actions, and of meeting people actively concerned in Lingard's past. Conrad was now mate in that same steamer which had threatened Lingard's trading monopoly, and was employed by the powerful Arab trader who had been his rival. He was engaged in the same trade in which Lingard had engaged and made the same journeys. He visited the settlement at Berau at regular intervals, navigating the difficult estuary and meeting Olmeijer, Jim Lingard, and Syed Abdulla. On board the *Vidar*, Captain Craig, and James Allen and John C. Niven particularly, were able to give him information about these people.

I had never believed that Conrad met William Lingard, for it seemed to me that Conrad's Tom Lingard was created from hearsay. Conrad's letter to W. G. St Clair, which was published in the latter's article in the *Malay Mail*, confirms this:

The only man I chummed with was Brooksbanks, then chief officer of the S.S. *Celestial*...I've heard of course a lot about the men you mention.

Old Lingard was before my time but I knew slightly both his nephews, Jim and Jos [my italics], of whom the latter was then officer on board the King of Siam's yacht.*

I suspect that Conrad knew Jim and Jos Lingard much better than he admits here, and that he visited the Brooksbanks at their house in Victoria Street which William Lingard bought for them. Miss Lena Brooksbank stated that her mother told her that Conrad was a good friend of her father and knew Joshua Lingard and visited their home during his stays in Singapore.

Although Conrad never met William Lingard, he obtained a great stock of information about him in a vivid form even though at second hand, and the fascination he had for Conrad as the type of the adventurer and protective father-figure resulted in his frequent appearance in the Malayan novels. The close parallels between the actual and the fictional Lingard are supported by a book review of *An Outcast of the Islands* which I found in the *Straits Budget*, 19 May 1896. The review itself is of no significance but the remarks about Lingard are.

It is very much to be regretted that, in this novel, as in 'Almayer's Folly', Mr Conrad should have given to the most interesting figure the name of a man who has actually played a real part in the history of the Archipelago, and who is no longer alive to defend the credit of his name. In justice to the author we must add that the portrait of the deceased 'Raja Laut' whether true or not, is calculated to enlist the sympathies of the reader. His friends, however, are not satisfied with it, and consider it a libel on his memory. They knew him and can judge best...Our enquiries have only given us reason to believe that the portrait of the 'Raja Laut' is not the only one which has been drawn from real life.

Conrad kept very close to the 'real life' he knew in the East, as this review confirms, and obviously this was recognized in Singapore from the beginning. He was speaking truthfully of his own creative method when he claimed that 'one's literary life must turn frequently for sustenance to memories and seek discourse with the shades...'[21]

* See Appendix E, p. 317, below.

6

AN EASTERN RIVER

An Eastern river, with a native settlement and a European trading post on its banks, is the setting for *Almayer's Folly*, *An Outcast of the Islands*, and the second part of *Lord Jim*. Conrad calls the river the Pantai, and the settlement Sambir in the first two novels, and in *Lord Jim* the settlement is called Patusan. The fictional Eastern river in these three books (and perhaps also in *The Rescue*) is based on Conrad's knowledge of the river Berau* in Dutch East Borneo which he visited as mate of the *Vidar*.

Conrad called the area 'one of the lost, forgotten, unknown places of the earth'[1] and Berau was, and still is, this. Little is known, even now, about the area. It is known that Captain William Lingard had established his trading-post on that river, and that Olmeijer and Jim Lingard were traders there. (See Chapter 5.) The native settlement on the banks of the river[2] is called Tandjong Redeb (or Gunung Tabur on some occasions). However, there has been no inquiry into the degree of exactness with which Conrad reflects the Berau setting, or into the question of how much of the human situation there appears in the Malayan novels. It is these two aspects that this chapter is concerned with. Some information about the area can be found in newspapers, Pilot Books, and travellers' tales about Borneo and this enables us to reconstruct the setting Conrad knew.

* In his first two novels, the river on which the village stands is given the name Pantai. In 1887, the year Conrad visited the river Berau in the *Vidar*, it was actually called the Pantai as the *Singapore and Straits Directory*, 1887, shows. Conrad was not, therefore, changing the name of the river from Berau to Pantai for fictional purposes as Gordan suggests (p. 51).

Conrad relied primarily upon observation and hearsay for his knowledge of conditions on the Berau river and his information could not have been extensive; yet the surprising thing about his fictional accounts of the area is their accuracy so far as the settlement was concerned.

*

The coast of Patusan [Marlow says]...is straight and sombre, and faces a misty ocean...Swampy plains open out at the mouth of rivers, with a view of jagged blue peaks beyond the vast forests. In the offing a chain of islands, dark, crumbling shapes, stand out in the everlasting sunlit haze like the remnants of a wall breached by the sea (*Lord Jim*, p. 298).

In terms of geography, Conrad had the Berau river in mind here. The chart of the Berau (opposite) shows the 'wide estuary' and the 'chain of islands...broken and massive' facing it (pp. 410–11). But whereas such a coastline might be common to many Bornean estuaries, other details given by Conrad show that he was describing Berau. Patusan, we are told, is

a remote district of a native-ruled state, and the chief settlement bears the same name. At a point on the river *about forty miles from the sea* [my italics], where the first houses come into view, there can be seen rising above the level of the forest the summits of two steep hills... (p. 270).

And speaking of his departure from Patusan Marlow says that 'at the first bend of the river shutting off the houses of Patusan, all this [the settlement] dropped out of my sight bodily'.[3] Of the settlement of Sambir in *Almayer's Folly*, Conrad writes:

From the low point of land where he [Almayer] stood he could see both branches of the river. The main stream of the Pantai was lost in complete darkness...but up the Sambir reach his eye could follow the long line of Malay houses crowding the bank, with here and there a dim light twinkling through bamboo walls, or a smoky torch burning on the platforms built out over the river (pp. 15–16).

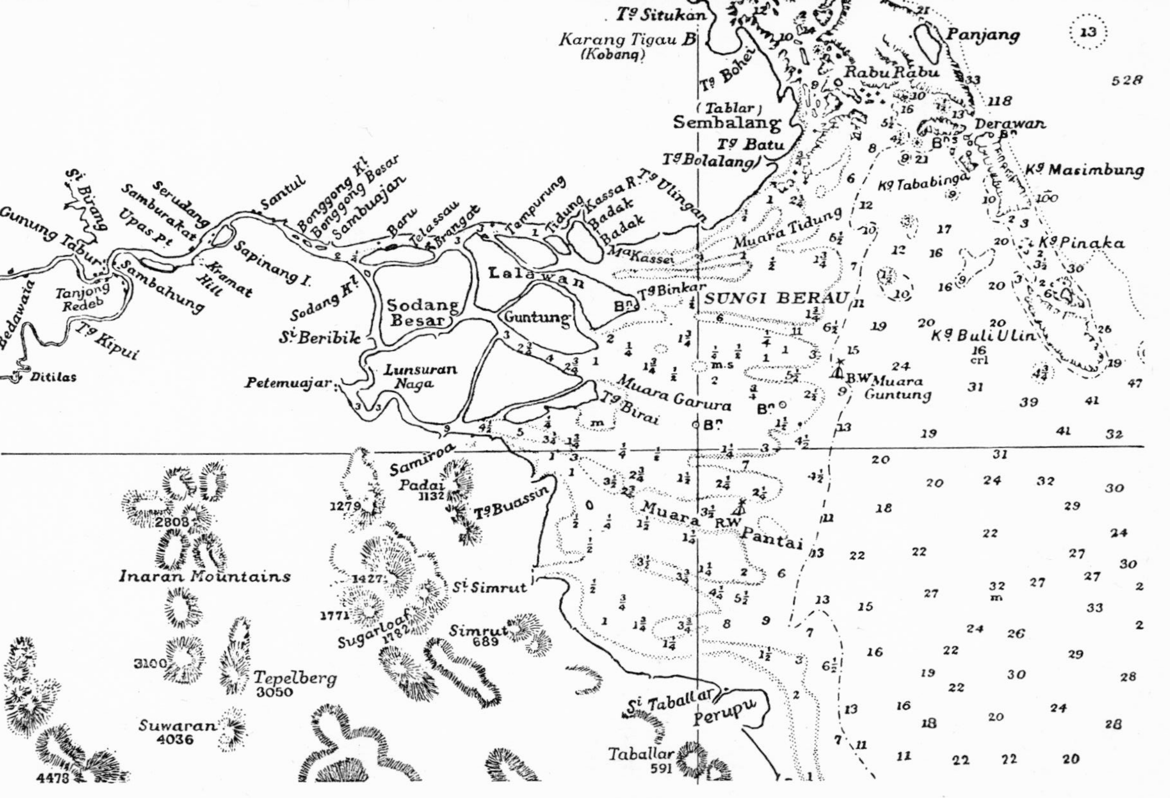

Chart of the river Berau.

Conrad's settlement has, therefore, certain distinctive features—the situation of the village forty miles from the sea, the junction of two rivers near the settlement, the bend in the river which shuts out the view of the settlement. It seemed to me that information about Berau must exist in the Pilot Books of the period, books with which Conrad would be familiar and which could be accounted one of his sources. In the *Eastern Archipelago Pilot*[4] I found confirmation of Conrad's statement that the settlement was 'about forty miles from the sea'. The Pilot Book gives this information: '...the rivers Segah and Kalai...unite opposite the towns of [Gunung] Tabur and Sambaliung, at a distance of 34 miles from the sea.' The chart of Berau (p. 121) confirms these details of topography. Just above Gunung Tabur and Sambaliung the river branches, as Almayer saw, and just below there is a sharp bend which would indeed shut off the houses of that settlement from view.

We are given a more elaborate description of the settlement in *An Outcast of the Islands*:

> The houses crowded the bank, and, as if to get away from the unhealthy shore, stepped boldly into the river, shooting over it in a close row of bamboo platforms elevated on high piles...There was only one path in the whole town and it ran at the back of the houses along the succession of blackened circular patches that marked the place of the household fires (p. 65).

I had the good fortune to obtain a photograph of the settlement of Tandjong Redeb from Australian Intelligence, and it shows the characteristics described by Conrad (Plate 6*a*). There is one row of houses, a single path, and the houses near the river are built out on stilts.

*

The Berau river has an added importance because Conrad's hero, Captain Lingard, is said to have discovered a river. His reputation to a large extent rests upon this discovery, and the entrance to the river is kept a well-guarded secret. The secret is revealed by Lingard's protégé, Willems, to Arab traders, whose competition eventually destroys Lingard's monopoly. In *Almayer's Folly*, Conrad writes:

He had discovered a river! That was the fact placing old Lingard so much above the common crowd of sea-going adventurers...Into that river, whose entrances himself only knew, Lingard used to take his assorted cargo...Many tried to follow him and find that land of plenty for gutta-percha and rattans, pearl shells and birds' nests, wax and gum-dammar... and for many years the green and peaceful-looking islands guarding the entrances to the promised land kept their secret with all the merciless serenity of tropical nature (p. 7).

In *An Outcast of the Islands*, Lingard's discovery is stated in rather different terms:

A good many years ago—prompted by his love of adventure—he, with infinite trouble, *had found out and surveyed*—for his own benefit only—*the entrance to that river* [my italics], where, he had heard through native report, a new settlement of Malays was forming (p. 200).

The stress here is upon one entrance to one river, but in *Almayer's Folly* Conrad seems to be admitting to two main entrances when Babalatchi whispers to his master Lakamba: 'There is one of our praus at the southern mouth of the river. The Dutch warship is to the northward watching the main entrance.'[5] The chart of the Berau river and the *Eastern Archipelago Pilot* show that there is not one or two but three main channels up to the settlement at Tandjong Redeb. There are also numerous entrances—Conrad mentions twenty outlets in *An Outcast of the Islands*[6]—and the *Eastern Archipelago Pilot* describes them:

In the approach to Beraoe (Berau) river is an extensive estuary, formed by many uninhabited islands, with various passages between them...the channels through the estuary are only suitable for small vessels with local knowledge...The principal channel of approach leads through...the upper reaches of Muara* Garoera (Garura)...There are also navigable approaches through Muara Pantai, on the southern side of the estuary, and Muara Tidoeng on the north side...Muara Pantai is now seldom used.[7]

The *Eastern Archipelago Pilot* also confirms that the actual Lingard had made a discovery relating to the navigation of the river, for in it there is a reference to a Lingard crossing:

Two beacons, equipped with reflectors one on each side of the river serve as crossing over marks for the bar in the channel westward of Sodang besar; this is known as the Lingard crossing. The western beacon was reported in 1946 to have disappeared.[8]

Lingard's Cross is on the Pantai branch of the river. The first edition of the *Eastern Archipelago Pilot* (1893) states:

Below Gunong Tabur, the Berau river has a breadth of from 660 to 1,310 yards, its mean depth at ordinary low water being 18 feet, with a minimum depth of 12½ feet at a spot on the west side of Sandang-besar island, known as 'Lingard's Cross'.†

We can conclude, therefore,[9] that Captain William Lingard did survey the river and made a contribution to the knowledge of its navigation, and that the statement in *An Outcast of the Islands* is very likely based on this. Lingard probably did find out and survey the entrance to that river. It is possible also that a legend had developed of his actually discovering a river and being the only one who knew the secret of its navigation. Moreover, Lingard's Cross is on the Pantai channel of the river, which was at one time the principal channel, though the later edition of the Pilot Book shows that it fell into disuse afterwards:

There is an extensive delta at the mouth, the principal channels through which are the Pantai, Garura, Manussur, and Tidung. The first named, which is in fact the mouth of the river of the same name, is one of the most frequented by ships, and its entrance is well defined by several isolated hill tops, which rise from the otherwise low and marshy shore.[10]

* 'Muara' is Malay for 'estuary'.

† See chart on p. 121.

If an Arab trader *had* been surreptitiously brought into Lingard's river, as Conrad records in *An Outcast of the Islands*, he would presumably have been taken up the Pantai channel and over the bar Lingard had surveyed.

Conrad's fictional account of the river is more dramatically in keeping with the character of the fictional Lingard, but the actual Lingard did not discover the river Berau in the sense that he was the first to travel up it. There had been other Europeans up the Berau river long before Lingard's time and some trading with the natives had already taken place. We can in fact go back to the eighteenth century, when the famous explorer Dalrymple travelled in that area. Dalrymple writes: 'The next river is a very large one, sometimes called *Barow* [Berau] and sometimes *Curan*, from different places near it, the first is an independent state, in alliance with Sooloo...'[11] There is no indication that Dalrymple travelled *up* the river Berau but he certainly knew it and had probably anchored at its mouth.

Dalrymple's voyage into unknown Eastern Seas took place during the years 1759–64. It was not until 1845 that Captain Sir Edward Belcher explored the river Berau: 'This river... is the Pantai, one of the branches, or properly the main stream, which takes the name of Brraou, and gives its name to people of the district, the city being Gunung Taboor...'[12] Belcher came to Gunung Tabur in search of some British seamen whose ship had been lost at the entrance to the river Pantai and who had been taken prisoner by the Malays to Gunung Tabur (Tandjong Redeb). In his book, *Narrative of the Voyage of H.M.S. Samarang*, he described his first view of the settlement of Gunung Tabur, forty years before Conrad visited the river:

> In the morning we again moved forward, still without any signs of human beings, although every mile that we advanced the cleared condition of the land...satisfied us that we could not be far distant from their dwellings. Shortly before eight, we discovered the first inhabited house, and immediately afterwards the outskirts of the town of Gunung Taboor...

we advanced towards the town; it was found to be closely stockaded... On the range of stockade, numbers of small Dutch flags were displayed.[13]

In *An Outcast of the Islands*, Conrad relates how the Dutch influence came late to Sambir and was the result of Willems's betrayal of Lingard's secret. As for Gunung Tabur, upon which Sambir is based, Edward Belcher found, when he first arrived there in 1845, that the Dutch had preceded him. Belcher, ever-conscious of British sovereignty and power, inquired why the Dutch colours predominated on the stockade and the reply of the Malayan ambassador was: '...the colours you see are Bugis, from Celebes, excepting that large Dutch flag, which was a present from the Governor of Macassar.'[14]

*

Conrad went to Berau in 1887 in a trading ship, and the people he met there were concerned with trade. It was inevitable, therefore, that trading concerns should enter into his stories about the area. Stein in *Lord Jim* is a successful trader, Almayer an unsuccessful one, and Captain Lingard is reputed to be very wealthy as a result of his trading: 'And so Lingard came and went on his secret or open expeditions, becoming a hero in Almayer's eyes by the boldness and enormous profits of his ventures.'[15]

In 1845, about twenty years before Captain Lingard set up a trading post at Berau, Captain Sir Edward Belcher concluded a treaty of 'Friendship and Commerce' with the Sultan of Gunung Tabur. He was not alone in wishing for trade—the Sultan himself offered very generous terms:

In proof of his anxiety to befriend the English, the Sultan offers to give them a separate place within his town to live in, to protect them, to give them a preference in trade, and as a further exhibition of his sincerity to open trading connexions, he gave me a letter under his official seal, containing the list of goods which he would engage as certain cargo, to any vessel which I would send in the May following...[16]

In a footnote Belcher adds: 'This letter was delivered to Mr Wyndham, and I have the satisfaction of learning from him that the vessel he sent was very handsomely received, and that great anxiety was expressed for his personal visit.'*

Wyndham, then, was the first English *trader* to send a trading vessel to Berau but, unlike Captain Lingard, he did not set up an agency there. At this early date trading on any substantial scale was not possible, though trading in so far as it could be carried out was very profitable. Belcher gives reasons for the possible limitations of future trading:

> ...I not only used every effort to open trade direct with Gunung Taboor ...but at my persuasion, two persons have made the attempt; others met me with the observation: 'All which you state is very true, and the prices are favourable in the highest degree, *but you cannot warrant half a cargo, even for a small schooner.*' At Gunung Taboor the Sultan bound himself to supply a cargo for one vessel filling up with rattans, Cassia bark, &c., but more he could not promise, as the collection of *one year*...Until the colony is firmly settled, and piracy annihilated on the range of coast by which trade must pass, this state of affairs will be slow of arriving...the same scantiness of tonnage must prevail.[17]

At Berau Lingard presumably met with a friendship from the local people which did not exist in other parts of Borneo. But he was fully aware of the other conditions which prevailed. He knew he would have to deal with pirates and his ship was armed for that purpose; he knew he would have to set up a trading post at Berau to organize the collection of rattans and gutta-percha, and so Olmeijer became the first trader to be settled permanently at Gunung Tabur (Tandjong Redeb).

In the first edition of the *Eastern Archipelago Pilot*, I found an official account of the trading situation at Berau. This edition was published in 1893, but I think we can assume that the information given in it relates to a situation at least ten

* Wyndham had once been a mate of Sir Thomas Cochrane's ship, *Nemesis*; had, like Lingard at a later date, fought pirates; and had settled down as a trader and as British representative on the island of Sulu. He was a friend of the Sultan of Sulu, and something of Lingard's influence and power as Conrad presents it is probably taken from the life of Wyndham. In a letter to William Blackwood of 6 September 1897, Conrad refers to him as a 'great nuisance' to the Dutch (*Joseph Conrad. Letters to William Blackwood and David S. Meldrum*, ed. William Blackburn (North Carolina, 1958), p. 10).

years earlier, since the account refers to 'the vessel of Messrs Lingard and Co.'. I have already shown that after 1883 Lingard was no longer a shipowner. But the account confirms the existence of Lingard and Co., and the nature of their trading as Conrad later wrote of it:

> The principal articles of export are *rattan, gutta-percha, and dammar* (gum copal), in quantities of about 250 tons, 120 tons, and 300 tons respectively, a year. The principal trade is with Singapore, chiefly in the vessels of Messrs *Lingard & Co.*, and only a small portion goes to Java or Dutch East India ports. The forests in the Berau lands could furnish an inexhaustible supply of good and fine timber[18] [my italics].

In *Almayer's Folly*, Conrad lists the produce Lingard traded in: '*gutta-percha* and *rattans*, pearl shells and birds' nests, wax and gum-dammar'[19] [my italics]. *An Outcast of the Islands* deals in part with Willems's betrayal of Lingard and, having been told of this betrayal by Almayer, Lingard says, 'Never you mind about Willems...Have you got any cargo for the schooner that brought me here?' And Almayer answers: 'The shed is full of rattans...and I have about eighty tons of guttah in the well. The last lot I ever will have, no doubt' (p. 174). Lingard's office, forty miles up the Bornean river, is described in *Almayer's Folly*: 'In one of the side walls there was a doorway. Half-obliterated words—"Office: Lingard & Co."—were still legible.'[20] There is a fuller description in *An Outcast of the Islands*:

> To the left of him, in the whitewashed wall of the house that formed the back of the verandah, there was a closed door. Black letters were painted on it proclaiming the fact that behind that door there was the office of Lingard & Co. (pp. 298–9).

Under the heading 'Communications' the Pilot Book is also revealing:

> A tolerably regular steam service between Singapore, Pasir, Berau river, and Bulungan, is maintained by a vessel belonging to an Arab at Singapore, but running under the British flag. There is also irregular steam communications with Makassar, and occasionally with Pontianak.[21]

The only vessel visiting the area during Conrad's time must have been that of the 'Arab at Singapore', Syed Mohsin Al Jooffree, owner of the *Vidar*.

I think we can conclude, therefore, that Conrad's picture of the trading situation in that part of Borneo of which he wrote was accurate. The goods he mentions in his fiction are the goods in which trade was carried on; Lingard's trading post, with Olmeijer in charge, certainly existed when Conrad was in the area, though Lingard was no longer actively involved in running it. The Arabs for whom Conrad worked were in charge of communications.

This may seem to disprove the story of Lingard, his secret river, and the Arab treachery, but I think that it confirms the story in part. The actual Lingard discovered the river in the sense that he was the first European to survey it for his own trading purposes; to establish a trading post in order to collect the produce of the area for shipment; and place a man (Olmeijer) there to run it. The Arabs certainly arrived eventually, and probably in time took over from Lingard the carrying of the produce, and they also established a trading post there. But the competition may have existed, not in the finding of the navigable channel up the Berau, but, as I have already suggested, in the growing competition between sail and steam as a means of trade and communication.

*

A report in the *Straits Times Overland Journal*, 26 March 1883, provides an account of conditions at Berau only a few years before Conrad visited the area in 1887, and this report agrees with several details that appear in Conrad's novels:

> ...Gunong Thabor and Sambaliung, formerly forming together the State of Berouw [Berau] are situated right and left on the Berouw river. *The villages therein are insignificant*; even the Sultan's house appears miserable. *In* 1879 *only one European resided there, he being a storekeeper from Macassar.*

There is very little trade, though the soil is very rich and fruitful. Rattans, gutta percha, and coals are the principal products. The inhabitants are lazy and unenterprising. Labour is for women and slaves only. Slaves are met with in almost every house. *On the lower river*, *there is even a large village wholly inhabited by slaves.* The authorities allow this, in spite of Art. 115 of the Government reg. whereby slavery in Netherlands India has been abolished. Most of the slaves are fairly well off excepting those who have to work in the mines. The number of these unfortunates yearly sold at Gunong Thabor is estimated at 300. These people are bought in or kidnapped from the islands of Sooloo and the other Philippines, and then bartered for gunpowder, muskets, revolvers, lillas, cloths, calico, opium, Dutch candles etc. [my italics].

The 'large village wholly inhabited by slaves' was introduced into *Lord Jim*, the first reference to it appearing on page 298: 'There is a village of fisher-folk at the mouth of the Batu Kring branch of the estuary.' The village is described thus:

This bunch of miserable hovels was a fishing village that boasted of the white lord's especial protection, and the two men crossing over were the old head-man and his son-in-law...The Rajah's people would not leave them alone; there had been some trouble about a lot of turtles' eggs his people had collected on the islets there (p. 411).

A day or two before Jim's arrival 'several heads of households in the...fishing village...had been driven over the cliffs by a party of the Rajah's spearmen, on suspicion of having been collecting edible birds' nests for a Celebes trader'.[22] Jim tells Marlow: 'The trouble is...that for generations these beggars of fishermen in that village there had been considered as the Rajah's personal slaves...'[23]

The 'one European' residing there, 'he being a storekeeper from Macassar', is almost certainly a reference to Olmeijer, and recalls *Almayer's Folly*:

Macassar! Almayer's quickened fancy distanced the tree on its imaginary voyage, but his memory lagging behind some twenty years or more in point of time saw a young and slim Almayer, clad all in white and modest-looking, landing from the Dutch mail-boat on the dusty jetty of Macassar, coming to woo fortune in the go-downs of old Hudig (p. 3).

The statement that 'the villages therein are insignificant; even the Sultan's house appears miserable.... There is very little trade...' suggests that the settlement Conrad visited was not thriving, and that the picture he presents in *Almayer's Folly* is probably accurate. The prosperous days of Lingard's trading appear to be over and Olmeijer was no doubt affected by this. Olmeijer may very well have talked nostalgically about the great days of Lingard.

There is no mention in the newspaper report of any equivalent of Willems as Conrad refers to him in the Author's Note to *An Outcast of the Islands*, or of Jim Lingard; but according to Mrs Oehlers, his daughter, Jim Lingard probably went to Berau in 1880 when he was about eighteen. He was certainly there when Conrad first visited the settlement.

*

I have shown in the previous chapter how closely Conrad kept to the basic facts of the life and reputation of Captain William Lingard; but the situation at Berau, involving the trading post, the secret navigable channel, and Lingard's two protégés Olmeijer and Jim Lingard was also one which Conrad remembered and which he made use of at least three times. The situation appears in *Almayer's Folly* and *An Outcast of the Islands*, and it is present to some extent in the second part of *Lord Jim*.

Captain Lingard in *Almayer's Folly* and *An Outcast of the Islands* and Stein in *Lord Jim* are both old traders who have established trading-posts on an Eastern river, which are run by their agents, Almayer and Cornelius, respectively. Each trader introduces a second person into his trading-post (Willems/Lord Jim) who arouses the antagonism of the older man already at the post. Cornelius plots to bring about Jim's downfall, and Almayer plots against Willems. Almayer's attitude towards Willems corresponds in part with Cornelius's attitude to Jim. In *An Outcast of the Islands*, Almayer is afraid of the influence Willems has on his 'father' the Rajah Laut:

> The appearance of that man, who seemed to have a claim of some sort upon Lingard, filled him with considerable uneasiness...Suspicious from the first, Almayer discouraged Willems' attempts to help him in his trading...From cold civility in their relations, the two men drifted into silent hostility, then into outspoken enmity, and both wished ardently for Lingard's return and the end of a situation that grew more intolerable from day to day (p. 64).

And later, Almayer meditates on the possible future: 'He had no mind to share Lingard's money with anybody...if Willems managed to become friendly with the old man it would be dangerous for him...He would oust him from his position' (pp. 295–6). Cornelius's hatred for Jim is immense and he is infuriated by his arrival: 'What did Mr Stein mean sending a boy like that to talk big to an old servant?'[24]

The relationship between these two versions of what is basically the same situation, and the facts of the trading post at Berau as Conrad knew them, or had heard of them, cannot be definitely established. But Conrad may well be reflecting the true situation to some extent. It is certain that when Conrad visited Berau there were two men there, Charles Olmeijer and Jim Lingard, and a cause for jealousy possibly existed. For one thing, Olmeijer had been ten years at his trading outpost when Captain Lingard settled his young nephew, Jim, at Berau. Olmeijer was related by marriage to Captain Lingard and he might very well have seen Jim Lingard as a dangerous rival. This may well be the origin in Conrad's fiction of the Willems/Almayer and Jim/Cornelius antagonism.*

* I have not discussed here Conrad's reference in his Author's Note to *An Outcast of the Islands* to the 'mistrusted, disliked, worn-out European' at the settlement. This man is said to have been an alcoholic Dutchman, Carel de Veer. If Conrad saw this man it is possible that he combined in Willems the two characters of Jim Lingard and de Veer.

The Lingard story in actual life seems to have involved Secretan, the old trader who was the employer and friend of Lingard; William Lingard, who appears to have taken over Secretan's trading concerns; Olmeijer, who managed the trading post at Berau; and then Jim Lingard. This pattern recurs in Conrad's fiction. In *An Outcast of the Islands*, Lingard is the old trader who adopts first Almayer, as his protégé, and then Willems. In *Lord Jim*, the pattern of benefactor and protégé is even closer to the pattern of William Lingard's experience—there is Alexander M'Neil, the old Scotsman, who takes Stein as his protégé and hands on to him his trading interests and local influence; Cornelius, the unpopular protégé of Stein; and Jim, the young man who is sent to the trading post as a second protégé. There is a minor duplication of this pattern in *An Outcast of the Islands*, where Hudig is for a time the benefactor of Willems before he is taken up by Captain Lingard.

It seems clear to me that the whole complex of Lingard's relatives and protégés, including the Brooksbank family in Singapore, fascinated Conrad, and he shuffled the relationships about a little each time he made use of them so as to obtain a slightly different perspective for each novel.

Marriages are central to the Tom Lingard story—the arranging of marriages for his protégés, usually joining a white man and a Eurasian or native woman. The marriage theme is present several times in these stories in similar forms. Cornelius, like Almayer, is managing the trading-post partly because he has married a female protégé of his benefactor Stein:

> ...she had been an educated and very good-looking Dutch-Malay girl, with a tragic or perhaps only a pitiful history, whose most painful part no doubt was her marriage with a Malacca Portuguese who had been clerk in some commercial house in the Dutch colonies...It was solely for his wife's sake that Stein had appointed him [Cornelius] manager of Stein & Co's trading post in Patusan...and now the woman had died.[25]

She has left one daughter. Jim is introduced into this situation: 'This man Jim would have to relieve'[26] and Jim falls in love with a native girl. Almayer is similar to Cornelius in that he 'had married a Malay girl whom the old seaman [Lingard] had adopted in one of his accesses of unreasoning benevolence'.[27] Almayer's marriage is also unhappy, and he has one child, a daughter. Willems, like Jim, after being introduced into this situation, becomes attracted to a native girl. But Willems already has a wife, whom he has deserted, and the same influence has been at work in his marriage. Without knowing it, he has married the daughter of his first benefactor—the Eurasian daughter of Hudig of Macassar.[28] Willems's marriage to Hudig's daughter may reflect something of Brooksbank's marriage to William Lingard's daughter. Willems is asked, after he has left his wife: 'But did you really think that Hudig was marrying you off and giving you a house and I don't know what, out of love for you?'[29] William Lingard, it will be remembered, bought his daughter a house in Victoria Street, Singapore, on the occasion of her marriage. It is interesting, also, that the fictional Almayer was supplied with a house at Sambir, by Captain Lingard, on marrying Lingard's adopted daughter.

Further connections between Conrad's fictional characters and the actual Lingard family appear in the names scattered throughout these stories. Not only do we have Captain Lingard, Jim, and Almayer, but Willems's wife is called 'Joanna' (Captain William Lingard's wife was Johanna Carolina), and Almayer's daughter is called Nina (Lingard's first protégé was Ninette Secretan).

It has not been possible for me, at this distance of time, to learn more of the relationships within the Lingard and Olmeijer families, but I feel sure Conrad had them in mind in writing these three novels. No doubt he moved from the facts, either for romantic or tragic purposes, but the basic situations recur.

One further point may be made. Conrad asserted that he had few social shore connections in the East. Perhaps his attachment to and recurrent use of a basic situation in the Lingard family goes far to prove his assertion.

*

There is a change in the character of the hero in *Lord Jim* once he goes to Patusan. This change is not simply the result of his more active role. It obviously involved a change in Conrad's conception of his hero, and it marks a weakness in the book as a whole. It is apparent that the change in character depended upon a shift from A. P. Williams to some other source.

J. D. Gordan suggested that 'countless details confirm the probability that the Patusan episode derived from Conrad's reading about the Rajah James Brooke of Sarawak' and[30] that 'the probability of this literary influence is nowhere more apparent than in *Lord Jim*'.[31] I think he is correct in saying:

> The romantic aspiration and energy of the English Rajah were of the sort to fire the novelist's imagination. The great work the Englishman had accomplished in the teeth of danger, far off the map of Western civilisation, was material after Conrad's heart.[32]

though I would wish to qualify these statements by adding that Conrad was mistakenly inspired. It was not in fact material suited to Conrad's genius. But, in any case, the influence of Brooke (in *Lord Jim* though not in *The Rescue*) seems to me less important than Gordan believes. It would appear to exist in the general idea of the benevolent white ruler, but this influence was probably grafted on to certain characteristics of Jim Lingard which helped to complete the portrait of Lord Jim. These characteristics could not be, as I have shown, those ascribed to Jim Lingard by Jean-Aubry on the testimony of Captain Craig. It was not a swaggering manner or a physique that Conrad found in Jim Lingard, but the devotion for him of a native woman and a native servant, possibly his name, his position and influence in the jungle and the general inexplicableness of his being at Berau at all.

So far as I can gather Jim Lingard lived with a Sea Dyak. Perhaps the romantic love Jim had for Jewel in *Lord Jim* and the love that Willems had for the native girl Aïssa had its origin in the love Jim Lingard had for his Sea Dyak.

Lord Jim has a trusted servant Tamb' Itam, whose function in the story is as body-guard—'He was inseparable from Jim like a morose shadow':[33]

> ...even Tamb' Itam allowed himself to put on the airs of uncompromising guardianship, like a surly, devoted jailer ready to lay down his life for his captive. On the evenings when we sat up late, his silent, indistinct form would pass and repass under the verandah, with noiseless footsteps, or lifting my head I would unexpectedly make him out standing rigidly erect in the shadow...Later on, tossing on my bed under the mosquito-net, I was sure to hear slight creakings, faint breathing, a throat cleared cautiously—and I would know that Tamb' Itam was still on the prowl. Though he had...a house in the compound, had 'taken wife', and had lately been blessed with a child, I believe that, during my stay at all events, he slept on the verandah every night (pp. 350–1).

Mrs Oehlers told me that her father had a remarkable servant called Lias. When her father went up river into the dangerous interior, Lias always went with him and she recalled that he always slept on the verandah of her father's home. Tamb' Itam may have had his origin in Lias.

Jim Lingard has previously been looked upon as a person of little importance—the strength of his influence in the area of Berau and Bulungan has not been known. I have discovered a letter written to the Foreign Office by Mr Alex Cook, at that time Treasurer General of British North Borneo, in which he describes a visit to Bulungan on 31 August 1887. Cook says of Jim Lingard: 'I arrived at Balangan [*sic*] per S.S. *Royalist* on 31st August: next morning I sent my letter of introduction accompanied by a small present to the Sultan...Wm. James Lingard who is on very friendly terms with the Sultan agreed to go with me...'[34] This gives us an authentic account of Lingard's standing in the area at the time of Conrad's first visit there, and it shows Lingard—a young man of twenty-five—as a person of some influence with the Sultan. In his early years he may have found Olmeijer unfriendly, but when Conrad arrived in the area Jim Lingard must have been an influential man, one who, in a minor way, corresponded to the more influential Rajah Brooke of Sarawak. I believe it was Jim Lingard's position in the area which led Conrad to conclude Lord Jim's early adventures in the pilgrim ship *Patna* with a final period in the jungle. And he may be referring to him as well as to his uncle, Captain Lingard, at the beginning of *The Rescue* when he writes:

> He [Brooke] belongs to history. But there were others—obscure adventurers who had not his advantages of birth, position, and intelligence; who had only his sympathy with the people of forest and sea he understood and loved so well. They can not be said to be forgotten, since they have not been known at all. They were lost in the common crowd of seamen-traders of the Archipelago... (p. 4).

It might be also that we can apply Conrad's remarks about Lord Jim's success to Jim Lingard's—certainly they are not applicable to his other source, Rajah Brooke:

> The conquest of love, honour, men's confidence—the pride of it, the power of it, are fit materials for an heroic tale; only our minds are struck by the externals of such a success, and to Jim's successes there were no externals. Thirty miles of forest shut it off from the sight of an indifferent world, and the noise of the white surf along the coast overpowered the voice of fame (p. 277).

In *Lord Jim*, Doramin expresses his doubt whether Jim will remain in Patusan:

> The land remains where God had put it; but white men—he said—they come to us and in a little while they go. They go away...They go to their own land, to their people, and so this white man, too, would...I don't know what induced me to commit myself at this point by a vigorous 'No, no' (pp. 338–9).

Conrad had provided his hero with a strong reason for staying in Patusan, but Jim Lingard presumably had no such strong reason for remaining at Berau. I think that Conrad was probably impressed that a man five years younger than himself should be prepared to spend the rest of his life—and he did—in such an isolated place. Almayer says of himself, 'I believe I am the only white man on the east coast that is a settled resident'[35] but this was not quite true of Olmeijer. Olmeijer was a Eurasian who was born and died in Sourabaya, Java. It was Jim Lingard who was the only white man living in the area and his daughter has frequently told me that her father used to say: 'I am the only Englishman on the east coast.' Conrad probably never understood Jim Lingard, but he was impressed by his situation and it inspired him to put Lord Jim into a similar situation in order to work out his salvation.

And so, in the second half of the novel, Conrad's source changed from A. P. Williams to Jim Lingard. But Conrad could know little about Jim Lingard or his way of life, and he was therefore forced to make the source a composite one. Thus he drew upon the inspiration of Brooke for the success of his hero, and upon travellers' tales for the incidents and details of his life.

This reconstruction of conditions at Berau, so far as it goes, shows that again, wherever it did not hinder the fictional working out of his theme, Conrad kept to the truth of his experience and observation. The trading conditions and the geography of the area, as well as the situation of the Europeans there, are reflected with a great deal of accuracy. But, perhaps more so than in his use of other sources, Conrad continually moves from the basic facts of his knowledge of Berau into fictional worlds which involve the romances, the inadequacies, and the deaths of Almayer, Willems, and Jim. Whatever the true story was of conditions at Berau, Conrad seemed to view the area as a setting for unavailing struggle, and death.

7
UNDOUBTED SOURCES: DULL, WISE BOOKS

Malayan settings and Malayan peoples are important in Conrad's Eastern novels and stories. What is most impressive about Malayan characters is the convincing way in which they are presented. This is even more remarkable in view of what has already been said about Conrad's brief contact with the East, and particularly with the settlement on the Berau river. Assuming that the *Vidar* stayed at Tandjong Redeb for about three days at a time (Conrad says of the *Sofala* 'There was a three days' rest for the old ship before he [Whalley] started her again in inverse order'),[1] and knowing that Conrad made only four journeys in all to Berau, we can conclude that he was in this area for some twelve days only. It could not have been possible for him to learn much about the indigenous population in that short time.

Indeed, Conrad has been criticized for the inaccuracy of his picture of the Malays and their way of life. In particular, he was criticized by Sir Hugh Clifford in an article in the *Singapore Free Press*.[2] Clifford objected that the Malay wife of Almayer in *Almayer's Folly* would not wish her English-educated daughter to return to the Malay way of life, and referred, more sweepingly, to Conrad's 'complete ignorance of Malays and their habits and customs':

> The prime minister, Babalatchi, yawns and stretches himself while conversing with his King. Had he done so in real life the poor dear man would have ceased to live...The youths in the King's presence are represented as lying about sprawling over the floor and kicking their heels in the air. Mr Conrad's Malays eat *sirih* in a manner for which Mr Conrad alone is responsible. It is, perhaps, merely a detail, but *sirih* could not be consumed in the manner described.

When Conrad read this article some two months later, he was troubled, for it seemed to him unfair. In a letter to W. Blackwood, he wrote:

> I had a treat in the shape of a N° of the *Singapore Free Press* 2½ columns about 'Mr Conrad at home and abroad'. Extremely lauditory [*sic*] but in fact telling me I don't know anything about it. Well I never did set up as an authority on Malaysia. I looked for a medium in which to express myself. I am inexact and ignorant no doubt (most of us are) but I don't think I sinned so recklessly. Curiously enough all the details about the little characteristic acts and customs which they hold up as proof I have taken out (to be safe) from undoubted sources—dull, wise books. It is rather staggering to find myself so far astray. In *Karain*, for instance, there's not a single action of my man (and a good many of his expressions) that cannot be backed by a traveller's tale—I mean a serious traveller's. And yet this story 'can only be called Malay in Mr Conrad's sense'. Sad.[3]

Conrad, then, by his own acknowledgement, felt the need to add to his limited knowledge of the Malays, and found a definite source for their 'little characteristic acts and customs' in travel books.

A further attack came from Clifford in a talk given to the English Association, Ceylon Branch, in February 1927, when he said: 'Hardly a proper name, or a Malayan word, from one end of the book to the other, was not mis-spelt'—the book under discussion was *Almayer's Folly*. Clifford is being rather hard on Conrad here. An example of the kind of mistake Conrad made with regard to names is found in the name of his Malay heroes, Dain Maroola in *Almayer's Folly* and Dain Waris in *Lord Jim*. In each case Dain is a Bugis title of distinction, but should be spelt 'Daeng'. Yet Conrad was only following the spelling of such writers as Mundy,[4] Keppel,[5] and St John.[6] Conrad was afraid of making mistakes, and was careful not to mis-spell. Even names that might be thought to have the slightly comic flavour of error, like 'Mohammed Bonzo' in *Lord Jim* and 'Wasub' in *The Rescue*, are taken from an early account of Malaya edited by Marsden.[7]

Undoubted Sources: Dull, Wise Books

In this chapter I hope to show the nature and extent of Conrad's borrowings from serious travellers' tales. Some research into the books Conrad might have read has already been undertaken.[8] But the extent of Conrad's reliance on travel books has not been fully explored. Where he makes use of travel books, he follows the experience and knowledge of the writers closely. Obviously, because of his lack of personal experience in these matters, he did not feel free to alter the details these books gave when he made use of them in his fiction.

But Conrad's borrowings from travel books were extremely varied and did not consist simply in taking over Malay names. They ranged from small incidents to complete characters, though his method of using these sources was so intricate that it is not always easy to relate the fictional result to the non-fictional source.

It is already known that Conrad used Wallace's *The Malay Archipelago*,[9] McNair's *Perak and the Malays*,[10] and the Brooke journals, but a close study of the books by Wallace and McNair has revealed Conrad source material which has not been noticed previously. Of the other travel books written about the South-east Asian archipelago which were, according to their dates of publication, available to Conrad, I have discovered four which can be shown to have influenced him, though there may be others that I have not been able to trace. These books were Captain Sir Edward Belcher's account of the voyage of H.M.S. *Samarang*, Sherard Osborn's *My Journal in Malayan Waters*,[11] *Life in the Forests of the Far East* by Spenser St John, and Frank S. Marryat's *Borneo and the Indian Archipelago*.[12]

*

Richard Curle—referring to one of these travel books—remarked, 'He [Conrad] loved old memoirs and travels—and

I think Wallace's *Malay Archipelago* was his favourite bedside book.' Conrad read this

> ...over and over again...It was his favorite bedside companion. He had an intense admiration for those pioneer explorers—'profoundly inspired men' as he called them—who have left us a record of their work; and of Wallace, above all, he never ceased to speak in terms of enthusiasm. Even in conversation he would amplify some remark by observing, 'Wallace says so-and-so', and *The Malay Archipelago* had been his intimate friend for many years.[13]

Following this comment by Curle, Florence Clemens made a study of Conrad's use of Wallace's book, and found that, both in a detailed and in a general way, the account of the naturalist's travels in the East influenced *Lord Jim.* It was Miss Clemens who pointed out that 'Conrad modeled the country life of Stein on that of Wallace's friend, Mr Mesman';[14] that the description by Wallace of the Rajah of Goa 'is the shadowy basis for Doramin's household in *Lord Jim*';[15] that the fear Wallace excited in the Malays because he was a white man, culminating in an incident when some buffaloes broke loose from their halters, is used by Conrad to enhance Willems's sense of exile in *An Outcast of the Islands*;[16] and that finally, Wallace himself, his nature, background, and activities as a naturalist, was used by Conrad in his creation of the character of Stein in *Lord Jim.* Miss Clemens's discussion of Conrad's use of Wallace's book, though interesting, is perhaps a little sketchy, for Wallace's influence in Conrad's work is at once stronger and more complicated than she allows. While she suggests that 'it may be that Stein's very appearance was based on Wallace's, for Stein has certain striking physical characteristics which belonged to Wallace',[17] and while she points out some physical similarities, she forgets that Stein was beardless while Wallace was not. She is, of course, correct in stating that 'it is as a naturalist, indeed, that Stein owes most to Wallace'.[18] Conrad made use of Wallace's emotions on catching a rare butterfly, providing Stein with similar emotions when he likewise catches a rare butterfly. But Wallace provides only one element in Stein's character. Stein is derived from a composite source and, in addition to Wallace, Conrad drew upon the character of a man called Dr Bernstein, another called Charles Allen, and upon Captain William Lingard.

Wallace makes one brief reference to Dr Bernstein: 'Since I left, the German naturalist, Dr Bernstein, stayed many months in the island with a large staff of hunters collecting for the Leyden Museum'.[19] In this way Conrad found for his character Stein a name (by taking the last syllable of 'Bernstein'), a nationality and a career.

Describing how Stein became both an amateur naturalist and a trader of note—which of course was not the case with A. R. Wallace—Conrad writes in *Lord Jim*:

> ...it was there he came upon a Dutch traveller—a rather famous man, I believe, but I don't remember his name. It was that naturalist who, engaging him as a sort of assistant, took him to the East. They travelled in the Archipelago together and separately, collecting insects and birds, for four years or more. Then the naturalist went home, and Stein, having no home to go to, remained [out East] (pp. 250–1).

Stein builds up a large and prosperous business as a 'merchant adventurer' in the East though he does not forget his training as a naturalist and 'his collection of *Buprestidae* and *Longicorns*...and his cabinet of butterflies...had spread his fame far over the earth'.[20]

This description does not fit Wallace, except for the reference to the collections. Wallace was not an assistant to a naturalist in the Eastern Archipelago, nor did he remain in the East after he had made his collections, but Wallace's assistant Charles Allen did. Wallace writes: 'Charles Allen, an

English lad of sixteen, accompanied me as an assistant',[21] and later he tells us:

Charles Allen made a voyage to New Guinea...On his return he went to the Sula Islands, and made a very interesting collection, which served to determine the limits of the zoological group of Celebes...His next journey was to Flores and Solor, where he obtained some valuable materials, which I have used in my chapter on the natural history of the Timor group. He afterwards went to Coti on the east coast of Borneo, from which place I was very anxious to obtain collections... On his return thence to Sourabaya in Java, he was to have gone to the entirely unknown Sumba or Sandal-wood Island. Most unfortunately, however, he was seized with a terrible fever on his arrival at Coti, and, after lying there some weeks, was taken to Singapore in a very bad condition, where he arrived after I had left for England. When he recovered he obtained employment in Singapore, and I lost his services as a collector (p. 419).

Allen was not born in Bavaria, as Stein was, but he was similar to Stein in three ways. He was an assistant to a famous naturalist, he remained out East while the famous naturalist returned home, and he did prosper. In the *Singapore and Straits Directory*, 1883, he is stated to be manager of the Perseverance Estate, which was owned by a Mr J. Fisher and extended over 1,000 acres. In 1888, Conrad's last year in the East, the Directory shows that Allen was then owner of this estate.*

In composing the character of Stein, Conrad must have had in mind Bernstein, Wallace and Allen. But the man known to Conrad as having established trading posts at Berau and Bulungan was Captain Lingard. Lingard was, like Stein, a merchant adventurer, and it is very likely that Lingard was in life 'the only one to have an agency by special permit from the Dutch authorities'.[22] At one time Lingard was the only trader in the Dutch-controlled area of Berau and Bulungan

* In *British Malaya: Twentieth Century Impressions*, ed. Arnold Wright (London, 1908), p. 664, there is a photograph of Perseverance Estate which is said to be situated three miles out of town. It will be remembered that Stein's house is 'three miles out of town'.

and he had married into a Dutch family. The reference to Lingard in the *Samarang Courant*[23] suggests that he was accepted by the Dutch, and, being well established at Berau, he must have formed friendly relations with the Sultan of the area. This could be the source of the relationship in *Lord Jim* between Stein and 'Mohammed Bonzo'.

Conrad, therefore, was not drawing solely upon Wallace for his character of Stein, for Bernstein and Lingard and Allen also contributed. Nevertheless, Miss Clemens did establish that Conrad used Wallace's book as a source.

Wallace's book, *The Malay Archipelago*, provided Conrad with a great range of source material which included incidents, attitudes, backgrounds, and characters. The details of Lord Jim's imprisonment by Rajah Allang, for example, were obviously owed to Wallace. Wallace describes, during his visit to Lombock and Bali, how he and his companion Ross were received at the village of Coupang:

> ... we reached our destination...and entered the outer court of a house belonging to one of the chiefs...Here we were requested to seat ourselves under an open shed with a raised floor of bamboo, a place used to receive visitors and hold audiences. Turning our horses to graze on the luxuriant grass of the courtyard, we waited...As we had not yet breakfasted, we begged he [the Malay interpreter] would get us something to eat, which he promised to do as soon as possible. It was however about two hours before anything appeared, when a small tray was brought containing two saucers of rice, four small fried fish, and a few vegetables....At length, about four o'clock the Pumbuckle (chief) [presumably 'Penghulu': a head-man] made his appearance...[and] he seemed somewhat disturbed, and asked if we had brought a letter from the Anak Agong (Son of Heaven), which is the title of the Rajah of Lombock. This we had not done, thinking it quite unnecessary; and he then abruptly told us that he must go and speak to his Rajah, to see if we could stay. Hours passed away, night came and he did not return. I began to think we were suspected of some evil designs...The sun set, and it soon became dark, and we got rather hungry as we sat wearily under the shed and no one came. Still hour after hour we waited, till about nine o'clock, the Pumbuckle, the Rajah, some priests, and a number of their followers arrived...Then the Rajah asked

what we wanted...questions were asked about my guns, and what powder I had, and whether I used shot or bullets; also what the birds were for, and how I preserved them, and what was done with them in England. Each of my answers and explanations was followed by a low and serious conversation which we could not understand, but the purport of which we could guess. They were evidently quite puzzled, and did not believe a word we had told them. They then inquired if we were really English, and not Dutch; and although we strongly asserted our nationality, they did not seem to believe us (pp. 127–8).

The conference was interrupted by a meal and then the questioning continued:

At length, about one in the morning, the whole party rose to depart... We now begged the interpreter...to show us a place to sleep in, at which he seemed very much surprised, saying he thought we were very well accommodated where we were...all we could get after another hour's talk was a native mat and pillow, and a few old curtains to hang round three sides of the open shed and protect us a little from the cold breeze (pp. 128–9).

On the following morning, they were again neglected and eventually Wallace decided to leave. The interpreter then appeared and begged them to stay until the Pumbuckle (Penghulu) returned from another conference about them with the Rajah, but Wallace refused and his party rode off. In *Lord Jim*, Jim gives Marlow an account of his imprisonment on his first arrival at Patusan:

'This is where I was prisoner for three days,'...we were making our way slowly through a kind of awestruck riot of dependants across Tunku Allang's courtyard. 'Filthy place, isn't it? And I couldn't get anything to eat either, unless I made a row about it, and then it was only a small plate of rice and fried fish' (p. 307).

The unexpectedness of his coming was the only thing

...that saved him from being at once dispatched with krisses...They had him, but it was like getting hold of an apparition...What did it mean? What to do with it? Was it too late to conciliate him? Hadn't he better be killed without more delay? But what would happen then?...Several times the council was broken up...But...the deliberations upon Jim's fate went on night and day...He took possession of a small tumble-down shed to sleep in; the effluvia of filth and rotten matter incommoded him greatly...Now and again 'some fussy ass' deputed from the council-room would come out running to him, and...administer amazing interrogatories: 'Were the Dutch coming to take the country? Would the white man like to go back down the river? What was the object of coming to such a miserable country?' (pp. 310–11).

The similarities between the two situations are obvious. Both Wallace and Jim are confined in a courtyard and forced to wait about for a long time while the Rajah holds conferences about them. In each case, these conferences suffer interruptions. Both men are asked questions about their purpose in coming there and reference is made in each instance to the Dutch. There is difficulty in getting food, the food provided is similar, and the accommodation is limited to a shed in the courtyard. The reference to 'the effluvia of filth and rotten matter' comes from a later passage in which Wallace describes an attap house: 'Close to my house was an inclosed mudhold where three buffaloes were shut up every night, and the effluvia from which freely entered through the open bamboo floor' (p. 170). Both Jim and Wallace put an end to the situation by suddenly deciding to leave.

*

In his preface to Richard Curle's book *Into the East*, written *twenty-four years* after the publication of *Lord Jim*, Conrad describes a specific incident which took place in Malaya:

...to think that only fifty years ago, after a certain amount of jungle and stockade fighting, the Sultan of Perak, or perhaps his brother ruler next door in Selangor, having listened attentively to a lecture from a British Admiral on the heinousness of a certain notable case of piracy, turned round quickly to his attending chiefs and to the silent throng of his Malay subjects, exclaiming, 'Hear now, my people! Don't let us have any more of this little game.' Those words ought to have been engraved in letters of gold on a marble monument at the mouth of the Jugra River...'[24]

J. D. Gordan, noticing the connection here with *Lord Jim*, concluded, 'The character of Rajah Allang seems to contain details taken from reading other than in the Brookiana'[25] but did not attempt to trace the incident Conrad is referring to. Jocelyn Baines[26] found the source of the incident in McNair's *Perak and the Malays* and stated that Conrad took the names of Doramin,* Tamb' Itam and Tunku Allang as well as the Rajah's 'You hear, my people! No more of these little games' from this book. He pointed out also that Conrad had found in the same book the Malay proverb which appears in *The Rescue*, 'Even a lizard will give a fly time to say its prayers'. But he investigated no further than this.

Baines is right in suggesting that Conrad took the names of Doramin and others from McNair's book. The names appear in McNair's account of a Malay boat which was attacked by pirates in 1873, on the Jugra river, Selangor, Malaya. The sole survivor of the attack stated

> ...there were three Chinese passengers...and six Malays belonging to the boat, named Hadjee Doraman, who was the nacodah (skipper), Ah Kim, Tamb' Itam, Meman, Mambi, and myself...We left Bandar Langat about six o'clock A.M.; we arrived here (the stockade at the mouth) about one o'clock, and showed our pass to Arsat, who was in charge of the stockade...We anchored about three o'clock...One of the [pirate] boats came alongside...The other [pirate] boat came alongside on the other side...They talked to Doraman. About six o'clock Doraman told us to bring the rice. When he was about to begin eating, shots were fired from both boats. Doraman fell to the shots...Three of our people jumped into the water and were stabbed, and all the others in my boat were also stabbed and killed. I jumped into the water, hung on to the rudder, and after dark floated away to the shore... (pp. 283–4).

The pirates who slaughtered Doraman and his crew were eventually captured and tried at the place where the piracy

* He does not point out that Conrad changed the spelling of the Bugis leader's name from 'Doraman' to 'Doramin'. The survivor of the Jugra piracy called the headman in charge of the stockade 'Arsat' at one point and later 'Marsat'. When Conrad came to write his short story 'Lagoon' he used the name Arsat for the young Malay who stole one of the Rajah's women.

had taken place. McNair was one of two British Commissioners who watched the proceedings of the court which 'was composed of the Viceroy of Salangore, with three Native Commissioners appointed by the Sultan...The sitting of the court took place at a stockade',[27] and seven of the eight pirates were executed by the Sultan's kris. Before the trial and execution, a British Admiral had an interview with the Sultan who

was surrounded by his chiefs and people...The Admiral, in referring to the barbarity of the Jugra piracy, advised and urged upon the Sultan to caution his people against being guilty of such acts in future, pointing out how it was impossible that they could be left unpunished...The Sultan listened very attentively, and then turning quickly round to his people, he exclaimed: *Dungar lah, jangan kitah main main lagi*!—'Hear now, my people! Don't let us have any more of this little game!' (p. 289).

In *Lord Jim*, Conrad uses this speech with less effective irony, for the 'little game' was simple robbery and not piracy and murder as in the original.

Some poor villagers had been waylaid and robbed while on their way to Doramin's house with a few pieces of gum or beeswax which they wished to exchange for rice. 'It was Doramin who was a thief,' burst out the Rajah. A shaking fury seemed to enter that old, frail body...There were staring eyes and drooping jaws all round us. Jim began to speak. Resolutely, coolly, and for some time he enlarged upon the text that no man should be prevented from getting his food and his children's food honestly. The other sat like a tailor at his board...and fixing Jim through the grey hair that fell over his very eyes. When Jim had done there was a great stillness. Nobody seemed to breathe even; no one made a sound till the old Rajah sighed faintly, and looking up, with a toss of his head, said quickly, 'You hear, my people! No more of these little games.' This decree was received in profound silence (p. 308).

But it is obvious that Conrad has taken each stage of the initial interview and adapted it to his own ends—the attentive Malay leader and his subjects being addressed forcefully on a moral issue, which they had transgressed, by a white man of some authority, and the final proclamation on the part of the Malay leader. Conrad gives a stronger character to the Rajah, a more dramatic stillness to the scene, but the incidents are the same.

Conrad also found McNair useful in creating a specifically romantic incident in the life of Captain Lingard in *Almayer's Folly*:

> ...before he [Almayer] had been three days in Macassar, [he] had heard the stories of his [Captain Lingard's] smart business transactions, his loves, and also his desperate fights with the Sulu pirates, together with the romantic tale of some child—a girl—found in a piratical prau by the victorious Lingard, when, after a long contest, he boarded the craft, driving the crew overboard (p. 6).

As I have shown in Chapter 5, Lingard was a successful trader and fought against pirates, but there is no evidence that he had found a girl in a piratical prau. Conrad appears to have taken this story from Major McNair's book:

> The late Captain Edye, of H.M.S. *Satellite*, also brought down a little captive girl, who had evidently been taken by these people [the pirates] from one of the vessels they had destroyed. She was a Eurasian, and only about ten years of age, having in all probability been taken when quite an infant, for the language she spoke was very mixed, and she had no recollection of her capture.
>
> When received on board the vessel, she immediately became the pet of the sailors, and was treated with all the kindness for which the British bluejacket has made himself a worthy name...On her arrival at Singapore, she was first placed in the girls' school attached to the late Mr Keasberry's mission... (p. 277).

*

Perhaps Conrad's most interesting use of McNair as a source occurs in *Lord Jim*. In the second part of the novel, Conrad uses *one* incident from McNair on two occasions, making use of different aspects of the incident on each occasion. But the interest does not end there, for in typical fashion he blends this incident with information from other sources.

The incident taken from McNair was his account of the murder, on 2 November 1875, of the Resident of Perak,

J. W. W. Birch, who had fallen out of favour with the Sultan of Perak. Birch was attacked and murdered by the Malays while he was in his bathing-house:

> ...the infuriated Malays, armed with spears and krises, made a rush in a body down to the river-bank, where Mr Birch was ashore at the bathing-house, his orderly being on guard with a revolver. He let his leader, however, be taken completely by surprise...he [Mr Birch] was savagely attacked, some of the Malays driving their keen limbings through the rattan mat that formed a screen, while others went to the end of the bath, and, as the wounded Resident struggled up out of the water, one man cut at him with a sword, when he sank... (pp. 369–70).

A slight reflection of this incident occurs in *Lord Jim* when Cornelius suggests to Jim that he is in danger of being assassinated, one of the possible methods being 'to be stabbed in the bath-house'.[28]

The British brought up considerable military strength after the assassination of Birch in order to put down what looked to them like a rebellion. They travelled up the Laroot river, where the original Rajah Allang had his stockade, though there is no suggestion that the Rajah was in any way involved in the murder of Birch.

Conrad could have found many examples of stockade fighting in his reading of Brooke, but McNair's description of the campaign against the Malay rebels which followed the murder of Birch seems to have given him suggestions first for Jim's flight from Rajah Allang and secondly for his attack on Sherif Ali's stockade. The parallels are not easy to prove since Conrad is not taking over McNair's accounts verbatim, but I think it very likely that he developed in his own way these incidents in McNair. For example, McNair describes how a certain Captain Channer led a surprise attack on a Malay stockade:

> ...This jungle fort was composed of logs surrounded by a palisade, and sharp spiked bamboos were everywhere about the ground.
>
> This was an important moment; for if the Malays had caught sight

of the attacking force the alarm would have been given at once; but by using precautions, and watching the enemy, Captain Channer was able to learn the easiest way into the stockade. Then, supported by two Ghoorkhas, he leaped over the palisade, where he could hear the Malays talking inside—no look-out being kept, as the enemy was cooking; and then dashing forward, followed by his two men, he boldly attacked the twenty or thirty who constituted the garrison, shot down one man with his revolver, while the two Ghoorkhas each shot down theirs...the enemy, believing themselves to be surrounded, took to flight... (pp. 400–1).

This seems to have influenced Conrad's account of the attack on Sherif Ali. Jim organizes the Bugis for his attack on Sherif Ali's stockade in order to drive him out, since he has been terrorizing the local population. Jim gets the Bugis to mount 'two rusty iron 7-pounders'[29] on one of the two twin hills overlooking the stockade which is built on the other twin hill. Then with Doramin's son, Dain Waris, and the other Bugis he

lay in the wet grass waiting for the appearance of the sun, which was the agreed signal...With the first slant of sunrays...the summit of one hill wreathed itself, with heavy reports, in white clouds of smoke, and the other burst into an amazing noise of yells, war-cries, shouts of anger, of surprise, of dismay. Jim and Dain Waris were the first to lay their hands on the stakes...[Jim] put his shoulder to it [the stockade]...and went in head over heels...The third man in, it seems, had been Tamb' Itam, Jim's own servant...The rout...had been complete... (pp. 329–34).

Conrad has not taken over the Channer incident complete. There, no guns were mounted on a summit, nor did the attackers wait until dawn as Jim's party do. But in the case of both Jim and Channer there is a surprise attack. Channer, followed by two Ghurkhas, is first through the stockade and this parallels Jim, who is followed into the stockade by Dain Waris and Tamb' Itam.

Parts of this incident make their way into Jim's escape from Rajah Allang's stockade on his first arrival at Patusan. Jim is taken prisoner, and confined in the courtyard, and I have shown how Wallace was followed at this point. But when Jim escapes, Conrad turned to McNair for the method. When he attacks Sherif Ali's stockade, Jim does not, like Channer, leap 'over the palisade', but he had earlier made his escape from Rajah Allang in the way in which Channer made his entrance into the rebel stockade: 'his eyes fell on the broken stakes of the palisade...He started off...went over "like a bird", and landed on the other side with a fall that jarred all his bones.'[30]

According to McNair's account, the British troops had to make their way through difficult country dragging two 7-pounders and they encountered obstacles placed in their way by the rebels:

> Consequent upon the difficulties of the task, and the weight of the guns which had to be dragged over and through a variety of serious obstacles, only four miles were advanced in two hours and a half, and at the end of this time the first symptom of the presence of the enemy was found in the shape of several trees felled across the track...Nothing further occurred for a couple of hours, when the advance was again checked by trees felled across the path... (pp. 392–3).

At one point, 'while leaving the jungle, the land forces advanced through the thick Indian corn till fire was opened upon them'.[31] It will be recalled that Jim also makes use of two 7-pounder guns and that they have to be dragged through difficult country: 'two rusty iron 7-pounders...The thing was to get them up there...The last hundred feet of the ascent had been the most difficult.'[32] But the felled trees and the journey through the Indian corn take us back to Jim's escape from Rajah Allang:

> He swerved between two houses up a slope, clambered in desperation over a barricade of felled trees (there wasn't a week without some fight in Patusan at that time), burst through a fence into a maize-patch... blundered upon a path, and ran all at once into the arms of several startled men (p. 314).

Conrad has substituted the more usual term 'maize' for Indian corn, and probably he has taken the comment in parenthesis from Wallace: 'They told me it was quite a common thing, and that they are rarely without fighting somewhere near.'[33]

One final aspect of the Birch affair, as recorded by McNair, is of interest in that it finds its way into *Lord Jim*.

McNair describes a stockade which had been taken by the British during this expedition: 'It was a strong place, with deep ditch, earth-work, wattled fence, and pointed bamboos, while it was armed with a large iron gun and a small pivot "lelah"' (p. 380). In *Lord Jim*, we are told that Jim built a fort for himself which he called 'Fort Patusan' and it is described in the following manner: 'a deep ditch, an earth wall topped by a palisade, and at the angles guns mounted on platforms...'[34]

But Conrad borrowed from two other sources to complete the Sherif Ali incident. These were two separate accounts of the same incident, Belcher's search up the Berau river for the missing European seamen. The second account of this search was written by Frank S. Marryat who was at that time midshipman of Captain Belcher's ship *Samarang*.

In *Lord Jim*, there are two native powers at Patusan, the Bugis led by Doramin who 'formed the party opposed to the Rajah',[35] and the Rajah Allang whose 'idea of trading was indistinguishable from the commonest forms of robbery'.[36] When Jim arrived,

> The situation was complicated by a wandering stranger, an Arab half-breed [Sherif Ali], who...had established himself in a fortified camp *on the summit of one of the twin hills* [my italics]. He hung over the town of Patusan like a hawk over a poultry-yard, but he devastated the open country. Whole villages, deserted, rotted on their blackened posts over the banks of clear streams...The two parties in Patusan were not sure which one this partisan most desired to plunder. The Rajah intrigued with him feebly (pp. 317–18).

Later Marlow is shown the ruins of Sherif Ali's stockade by Jim: 'On the other hill, two hundred yards across a sombre precipice, I saw a line of high blackened stakes, showing here and there ruinously—the remnants of Sherif Ali's impregnable camp' (p. 324). Both Marryat and Belcher refer to a ruined stockade on a hill on the left side of the river Berau just before Gunung Tabur (Tandjong Redeb). Belcher writes:

> About 9 A.M., on the 30th of December, we noticed what at first appeared to be a Malay battery, or stockade, constructed upon the summit of a hill which completely commanded the whole reach of the river below this place...we soon discovered that the place was not only without inhabitants, but that the town which had been near it, had been lately burned... and the plantain and other fruit trees lately cut down, exhibited indubitable symptoms of recent war (I, 212–13).

This would seem to have suggested Sherif Ali's stockade and its ultimate fate at Jim's hands, and Marryat's account of the same stockade adds a further detail which confirms this. In *Lord Jim*, the fortified camp is on one of the twin hills and that these existed at Berau is confirmed by Marryat's reference to 'two small hills': 'We soon hove in sight of what appeared to be a town, although there were no signs of life visible. It was built on the left side of the river on two small hills' (p. 131).

*

J. D. Gordan believed that Conrad 'may have picked up the facts he gave in the story of Gentleman Brown from anecdotes never recorded in print'[37] but I think it likely that he took some aspects of the incident from Belcher and Marryat. Gentleman Brown's arrival at Patusan is similar to Belcher's arrival at Gunung Tabur; and the name Gentleman Brown—and in part his nature—appears to derive from Captain Brownrigg, whom Belcher had come to Berau to rescue. In *Lord Jim*, Brown and his crew left their schooner at the mouth of the river and travelled up to Patusan in their long-boat.[38]

They discovered at first that all was silent and deserted: 'They sailed in with the last flood; the Rajah's stockade gave no sign; the first houses on both sides of the stream seemed deserted.'[39] Belcher and his crew also left their vessel at the mouth of the river and travelled up by boat; as they approached the village they too were struck by the fact that all was deserted:

> In the morning we again moved forward, still without any signs of human beings, although every mile that we advanced the cleared condition of the land, and other objects, satisfied us that we could not be far distant from their dwellings. Shortly before eight, we discovered the first inhabited house, and immediately afterwards the outskirts of the town of Gunung Taboor.[40]

Though Conrad's Gentleman Brown is a much more outrageous villain than Brownrigg, Belcher did learn from the Sultan of Gunung Tabur that Captain Brownrigg had brought about a state of war between Sambiliong and Gunung Tabur, that he and his men used gross language, stood convicted of drunkenness and falsehood, and gave up their own lascars as slaves. Just as Gentleman Brown and his crew are forced to establish themselves 'on a little knoll about 900 yards from the stockade, which, in fact, they commanded from that position',[41] so Brownrigg and his men established themselves at 'Sambiliong, the fortified position on the heights, on the opposite side of the river, distant three miles'.[42] Just as Brown and Kassim (Rajah Allang's minister) collaborate to outwit the Bugis Doramin and Lord Jim, so Brownrigg reaches agreement with the Rajah Muda of Sambiliong: 'they leagued with the Rajah Muda, [the Sultan's] cousin, who had rebelled, and...he [Rajah Muda] required their aid to work his guns.'[43] Kassim begs Brown 'to have this big ship with his many guns and men brought up the river without delay for the Rajah's service'.[44]

*

From his limited experience of Borneo, Conrad would hardly have been able to distinguish between Malayan races such as the Malays and the Bugis. The physical characteristics of the two races, from the foreigner's point of view, are very much the same, and other differences involving character and way of life must have been quite beyond Conrad's knowledge. Yet in his novels, he distinguishes between Malay, Bugis, and Arab. In *Lord Jim*, he says of the Bugis, with whom Jim identifies himself: 'The men of that race [Bugis] are *intelligent*, *enterprising*, *revengeful*, but with a more frank *courage* than the other Malays, and restless under oppression' (p. 316, my italics).

Conrad appears to have taken this assessment of the Bugis people from the following passage in McNair's book:

> The Bugis are evidently a distinct race from the Malays, and come originally from the southern part of the island of Celebes. They compare most favourably with the Malays proper, being *intelligent*, *courageous*, and *enterprising*...The Malays fear and respect them above all the other races of the Archipelago; and among them are to be found the principal native traders and merchants...The character given to the Bugis is not always of the best, for he has been termed a beggar, treacherous, given to stealing, *braver than a Malay*, but not possessing the other's good points, being one who will lay his plans to obtain *revenge* on the offending party (pp. 130–1, my italics).

Conrad's attitude towards the Bugis changes from one work of fiction to another. In *An Outcast of the Islands*, for example, the Bugis settlers are against the kindly old Sultan Patalolo and are persuaded to rebel by Lakamba, a rebellion which would have succeeded but for the intervention of Captain Lingard:

> Once settled, he [Lakamba] began to intrigue. The quarrel of Patalolo with the Sultan of Koti was of his fomenting...Disappointed in that scheme, he promptly organized an outbreak of the Bugis settlers, and besieged the old Rajah in his stockade with much noisy valour and a fair chance of success; but Lingard then appeared on the scene with the

armed brig, and the old seaman's hairy forefinger, shaken menacingly in his face, quelled his martial ardour. No man cared to encounter the Rajah Laut... (p. 51).

This change in Conrad's attitude, and indeed this whole incident of the Bugis rebellion, might have been suggested by an account of an actual conflict between Bugis and Malays which took place, not at Tandjong Redeb but further down the east coast of Borneo in the Sultan of Koti's domain, as Carl Bock in his book, *The Head-Hunters of Borneo*, shows:

Samarinda, the chief trading-port of Koetei, is situated at the mouth of the Mahakkam, and occupies a considerable area on both banks of the river...That portion of the town which lies on the right bank is inhabited by Boegis of whom a large settlement has existed here for many years; they are in great force here and have at their head a 'kapitan' or chief, whose rank is officially recognized by the Sultan of Koetei...With their greater liberty and their annually increasing numbers they are, however, assuming too much power in Koetei, and, as they are a treacherous race, they will probably one day turn round and bite the hand that has fed them. Indeed they have already made an attempt to gain the upper hand at Samarinda, and for a time established a semi-independence, refusing to admit the authority of the Sultan and his Government (p. 22).[45]

This recalls the situation described by Conrad in *An Outcast of the Islands* after the Bugis rebellion:

Still faithful to his [Lakamba's] character of a prince-pretender, he would not recognize the constituted authorities, answering sulkily the Rajah's messenger, who claimed the tribute for the cultivated fields, that the Rajah had better come and take it himself (p. 51).

As one would expect, Conrad relied upon his reading particularly when it came to creating native characters. Doramin, Dain Maroola, and Babalatchi all derive, at least in part, from travel books, and often by a devious process.

Doramin in *Lord Jim* is a Nakhoda, as was the Malay of the same name who died in the Jugra piracy, but he differs in other ways from his namesake. In this instance, Conrad seems to be using both McNair and Wallace to build up the character of Doramin and also of his wife. In *Lord Jim* we meet Doramin for the first time when Jim escapes from the Rajah Allang's stockade to the Bugis enclosure:

He remembers being half carried, half rushed to the top of the slope, and in a vast enclosure with palms and fruit trees being run up to a large man sitting massively in a chair...Doramin's people were barricading the gate and pouring water down his throat; Doramin's old wife, full of business and commiseration, was issuing shrill orders to her girls... 'They put me into an immense bed—her state bed——'...

He seemed to have a great liking for Doramin's old wife...She had a round, nut-brown, soft face, all fine wrinkles, large, bright red lips (she chewed betel assiduously), and screwed-up, winking, benevolent eyes. She was constantly in movement, scolding busily...a troop of young women with clear brown faces and big grave eyes, her daughters, her servants, her slave-girls...She was very spare, and even her ample outer garment...had somehow a skimpy effect...She uttered homely, shrewd sayings, was of noble birth...In the afternoon she would sit in a very roomy arm-chair, opposite her husband, gazing steadily through a wide opening in the wall which gave an extensive view of the settlement and the river.

She invariably tucked up her feet under her, but old Doramin sat squarely, sat imposingly as a mountain sits on a plain. He was only of the *nakhoda* or merchant class, but the respect shown to him and the dignity of his bearing were very striking (pp. 314–16).

Miss Clemens points out that

Wallace...left a sketchy description of a large audience room with a great window overlooking the settlement, and two chairs—one for the Rajah who sat there in European fashion, and one for the Ranee, who had her feet tucked under her Oriental-fashion while she chewed siri. About them were respectful attendants. This room, the window, the chairs, and the positions of their occupants were all borrowed entire for Doramin and his wife and servants (p. 310).

A consideration of the relevant passages in Wallace, which Miss Clemens does not quote, reveals the scope of Conrad's borrowings:

As soon as I was well, I again went to Goa, accompanied by Mr Mesman, to beg the Rajah's assistance in getting a small house built for me near the forest. We found him at a cock-fight in a shed near his palace, which however he immediately left to receive us, and walked with us up an inclined plane of boards which serves for stairs to his house. This was large, well built, and lofty, with bamboo floor and glass windows. The greater part of it seemed to be one large hall divided by the supporting posts. Near a window sat the Queen squatting on a rough wooden arm-chair, chewing the everlasting sirih and betel-nut, while a brass spittoon by her side and a sirih-box in front were ready to administer to her wants. The Rajah seated himself opposite to her in a similar chair, and a similar spittoon and sirih-box were held by a little boy squatting at his side... Several young women, some the Rajah's daughters, others slaves, were standing about; a few were working at frames making sarongs, but most of them were idle...Everything had a dingy and faded appearance... The only thing that excited some degree of admiration was the quiet and dignified manner of the Rajah, and the great respect always paid to him (pp. 167–8).

In Wallace's description, the queen sits opposite the Rajah as she does in *Lord Jim*: 'Near a window sat the Queen squatting on a rough wooden arm-chair, chewing the everlasting sirih and betel-nut.' This parallels Conrad's '(she chewed betel assiduously)' and 'in the afternoon she would sit in a very roomy arm-chair, opposite her husband, gazing steadily through a wide opening in the wall which gave an extensive view of the settlement and the river'. Conrad, remarking that the queen sat beside the window, goes into detail about what could be seen through it. He does not mention glass windows because these must have been rare even in a Rajah's home. Wallace's statement: 'Several young women, some the Rajah's daughters, others slaves, were standing about', is taken up by Conrad in 'a troop of young women...her daughters, her servants, her slave-girls'. Wallace stresses 'the quiet and dignified manner of the Rajah, and the great respect always paid to him' and Conrad notes that 'the respect shown to him [Doramin] and the dignity of his bearing were very striking'.

In certain details, the account of the Rajah of Goa does not fit Doramin. The Rajah was a Malay and not a Nakhoda, whereas Doramin was Bugis and a Nakhoda; and while Doramin married someone of 'noble birth', so improving his own social standing, the Rajah had no need to do this. For these aspects of Doramin we have to go back to McNair's *Perak and the Malays*. McNair, as I have shown, compares the Malays with the Bugis and gives this further information about the Bugis:

> The Bugis race has kept itself very distinct from the people amongst whom it dwells, but occasionally inter-marriages take place. One of the most important of late has been that of the well-known Bugis chief of Perak, Nakhoda Trong, who led to the hymeneal altar one of the Perak ladies of distinction, Inche Maida, or Princess Maida. Their portraits are given in the accompanying engraving, with the female attendants (p. 131).

I think there is no doubt that we have here a further addition to Conrad's Doramin, the Bugis Nakhoda who married a lady of noble birth. The engraving, which is the frontispiece of McNair's book, supports this theory (Plate 7). It shows Nakhoda Trong who is, like Doramin, bulky—'His bulk for a Malay was immense'[46]—though he is not as large as Doramin. Conrad describes Doramin in the following fashion:

> This motionless body, clad in rich stuffs, coloured silks, gold embroideries; this huge head, enfolded in a red-and-gold headkerchief; the flat, big, round face, wrinkled, furrowed, with two semicircular heavy folds starting on each side of wide, fierce nostrils, and enclosing a thick-lipped mouth (p. 319).

Apart from the introduction of coloured embroideries, Conrad is giving a reasonably precise description of Nakhoda Trong. And when he describes Doramin's wife—'she, light, delicate, spare, quick, a little witch-like, with a touch of motherly fussiness in her repose'[47]—he appears to have had Inche Maida, Princess of Perak, in mind as she was pictured in this engraving.

The first thing that Doramin's wife does when the mud-bespattered Jim arrives is to put him into her bed: 'They put me into an immense bed—her state bed...' Conrad probably got this idea also from McNair who describes a visit he made to Princess Maida, wife of Nakhoda Trong, in which she showed him her state bed:

> The house...on the right is, as far as its principal apartment is concerned, fitted up with a bed which occupies about two-thirds of the room... Upon the introduction taking place between general and princess, the lady claimed the former as her guest, and with all the pride of an English country dame of the last century over her well-filled ticks, drew his attention to the bed... (p. 169).

The account in *Lord Jim* omits a detail recorded by Wallace, that a 'few [young women] were working at frames making sarongs'; and there is no mention of spittoon or sirih box. Perhaps one reason why Conrad left these details out of *Lord Jim* was that he had already used them in *An Outcast of the Islands*:

> Lakamba came out on the platform before his own house and sat down—perspiring, half asleep, and sulky—in a wooden armchair under the shade of the over-hanging eaves. Through the darkness of the doorway he could hear the *soft warbling of his womenkind, busy round the looms where they were weaving the checkered pattern of his gala sarongs.* Right and left of him on the flexible bamboo floor those of his followers to whom their distinguished birth, long devotion, or faithful service had given the privilege of using the chief's house, were sleeping on mats or just sat up rubbing their eyes...*A boy of about twelve*—the personal attendant of Lakamba—*squatted at his master's feet and held up towards him a silver siri box* [my italics] (p. 96).

Wallace, commenting on a Malay method of indicating rank and honour, writes:

> None can stand erect in his presence, and when he sits on a chair, all present...squat upon the ground. The highest seat is literally, with these people, the place of honour and the sign of rank. So unbending are the rules in this respect, that when an English carriage which the Rajah of Lombock had sent for arrived, it was found impossible to use it because the driver's seat was the highest, and it had to be kept as a show in its coach-house (p. 168).

In *An Outcast of the Islands*, we have Willems listing his achievements, and his last is described thus:

> ...the difficult business of the Rajah of Goak. He carried that last through by sheer pluck; he had bearded the savage old ruler in his council room, he had bribed him with a gilt glass coach, which, rumour said, was used as a hen-coop now... (p. 8).

The initial idea of a Rajah owning a carriage which could not be used as a carriage probably came from Wallace. But I think Conrad possibly added to this a piece of information he may well have seen in the *Straits Times* when he was in Singapore. On 12 January 1884 the paper published an account of a visit to the young Sultan of Sulu, who had a coach which was being used as a hen-coop.

So far as Dain Maroola in *Almayer's Folly* is concerned, I have not been able to find one definite prototype,* but then Conrad's picture of him is a very generalized one, the main emphasis being upon his status as a Rajah's son, and the fact that he is a gentleman. Almayer says to his daughter, 'It is bad to have to trust a Malay...but...this Dain is a perfect gentleman.'[48] I doubt very much whether Conrad had any intimate acquaintance with Malay nobility and I think it likely that his conception of Dain Maroola comes from Wallace. In his final chapter, Wallace makes some interesting comments upon the characteristics of the Malays generally, and Conrad seems to have transferred these characteristics rather woodenly to Dain Maroola; this in itself suggests that he was on uncertain ground. Wallace comments:

> The higher classes of Malays are exceedingly polite, and have all the quiet ease and dignity of the best-bred Europeans. Yet this is compatible with a reckless cruelty and contempt of human life, which is the dark side of their character (p. 448).
>
> The Malay is bashful, cold, undemonstrative, and quiet... (p. 450).
>
> In character the Malay is impassive. He exhibits a reserve, diffidence,

* Gordan, p. 49, tells us that Conrad took Dain Maroola's name from 'a Bugis who acted as Bornean agent for Syed Mosin Bin S. Ali Jaffree'.

and even bashfulness...His feelings of surprise, admiration, or fear, are never openly manifested...He is slow and deliberate in speech, and circuitous in introducing the subject he has come expressly to discuss* ...he is particularly sensitive to breaches of etiquette (pp. 447–8).

The impassivity and good manners of the Malay are seen when Dain Maroola visits Almayer for the first time. Almayer's wife and daughter scuffle nosily behind a curtain to get a view of the visitor:

He [Almayer] glanced at his Malay visitor, who was waiting silently for the end of the uproar in an attitude of amused expectation, and waving his hand contemptuously he murmured:

'It is nothing. Some women.'

The Malay nodded his head gravely, and his face assumed an expression of serene indifference, as etiquette demanded after such an explanation (p. 64).

And though Nina's beauty causes him to stare in 'open-mouthed admiration'[49] he is able 'the next minute' to shake 'Almayer's hand with grave courtesy, his face wearing a look of stolid unconcern as to any feminine presence'.[50]

Dain Maroola is a Brahmin from the island of Bali and Mrs Almayer says to Nina: 'A great Rajah has come to Sambir—a Son of Heaven.'[51] This term 'Son of Heaven', is repeated a number of times by different characters. Lakamba, the Rajah of Sambir in succession to Patalolo, says to Dain after his escape from the Dutch war-ship, 'Your refuge was with your father, the Rajah of Bali, the Son of Heaven, the "Anak Agong" himself'.[52] So far as is known Conrad never visited Bali but he is using the official title of the Rajah of Bali and it is likely that he took this also from Wallace. I have already quoted part of Wallace's account of his visit to Coupang. On that occasion, he made the mistake of visiting the village without a letter of introduction from the Rajah, and the Pumbuckle

* Lingard is made to say when in conference with Babalatchi: 'He had been living with Malays so long and so close that the extreme deliberation and deviousness of their mental proceedings had ceased to irritate him much' (*An Outcast of the Islands*, p. 222).

(Penghulu) asked him if he 'had brought a letter from the Anak Agong (Son of Heaven), which is the title of the Rajah of Lombock'.[53]

*

According to Jean-Aubry, the *Vidar* used to take on cargo at Dongala in Celebes. It is known from the bills of lading preserved in the Keating Collection at Yale that there was a trader called Babalatchi in Dongala. Though Conrad was not in the *Vidar* when she contracted to carry for Babalatchi fifty-eight bags of dammar from Dongala to Singapore, there can be no doubt that Conrad met this trader. The bill of lading is dated 12 August 1887 and the dammar was received in Singapore on 20 August 1887. Two days later Conrad joined the *Vidar* and the vessel left for Bulungan that same day. Lakamba, the Rajah of Sambir, was also a trader.* But we have no evidence that Conrad was doing more than using the names of these men in his stories. We cannot assume that the appearances, personalities, and histories of the two fictional characters have been taken from the actual men. My own view is that Conrad again used travel books as his source for the characters of Lakamba and Babalatchi, though I have not been able to find a convincing source for Lakamba.

In *Almayer's Folly* Babalatchi, 'that potentate's [Lakamba's] prime minister, harbour master, financial adviser, and general factotum...',[54] owes his origin more surely to details in travellers' books. For one thing his character, physique, and background are given much more fully by Conrad. He is a gentleman 'of Sulu origin'[55] is 'perfectly repulsive, possessing only one eye and a pock-marked face'. His single eye is often referred to. Dain Maroola calls him a 'one-eyed

* Jean-Aubry, I, 97–8. Before Lakamba succeeds the old Sultan Patalolo he is shown as a trader. In *Almayer's Folly* Conrad writes, 'Lakamba himself, then living as a private individual on a rice clearing, seven miles down the river' (p. 27), but writing of the same situation in *An Outcast of the Islands*, Conrad did not place Lakamba's clearing in the same area: 'Received coldly by the suspicious Patalolo, he persisted...in clearing the ground on a good spot some fourteen miles down the river from Sambir' (p. 50).

crocodile'[56] and he is also called 'the one-eyed statesman',[57] 'one-eyed Babalatchi'.[58] Before he came to the security of Sambir, he had been a pirate—a Lanun as opposed to a Balignini pirate (these were the two great pirate groups)—and he had fought with the Brunei rovers:

> Babalatchi had blundered upon the river while in search of a safe refuge for his disreputable head. He was a vagabond of the seas, a true Orang-Laut, living by rapine and plunder of coasts and ships in his prosperous days; earning his living by honest and irksome toil when the days of adversity were upon him. So, although at times leading the Sulu rovers, he had also served as Serang of country ships...He gathered experience and wisdom in many lands, and after attaching himself to Omar el Badavi, he affected great piety...He was brave and bloodthirsty without any affection, and he hated the white men who interfered with the manly pursuits of throat-cutting, kidnapping, slave-dealing, and fire-raising, that were the only possible occupation for a true man of the sea. He found favour in the eyes of his chief, the fearless Omar el Badavi, the leader of Brunei rovers, whom he followed with unquestioning loyalty through the long years of successful depredation (*An Outcast of the Islands*, pp. 51–2).

Babalatchi is fond of reminiscing about the old days when he was a pirate, fighting under Omar el Badavi, a man 'first in prayer and first in fight'. In the closing pages of *Almayer's Folly* he refers to the past and to Sir James Brooke, first Rajah of Sarawak, in a final remark to Captain Ford:

> Ah, Tuan!...the old times were best. Even I have sailed with Lanun men, and boarded in the night silent ships with white sails. That was before an English Rajah ruled in Kuching. Then we fought amongst ourselves and were happy. Now when we fight with you we can only die! (pp. 258–9).

In searching for the possible source of Babalatchi we have to remember that Conrad's method of building up an adequate background for a character is to take a passage from one work, a line from another, a hint from yet another. One source for the character of Babalatchi was Sherard Osborn's *My Journal in Malayan Waters*, but for other details he used Wallace's *The Malay Archipelago* and St John's *Life in the Forests of the Far East*.

Perhaps the most exhilarating character to appear in Osborn's *Journal* is a seaman called Jadee. Jadee is not physically like Babalatchi, though Conrad probably had in mind also 'a fine old one-eyed fellow called "Souboo" ', whom Osborn also mentions.[59] But Jadee's background fits Babalatchi's to a remarkable extent. '...the majority [of my crew]', Osborn writes, 'had...at various times been imprisoned in Singapore jail as pirates, the most notorious scamp being my serang, Jadee' (p. 33). Like Babalatchi, Jadee is fond of recollecting by-gone 'forays and skirmishes'.[60] Originally Jadee came from Sumatra but when he was very young he was sold to some Sulu slave-dealers and pirates. At first, he was only allowed to row and to bale water out of their prahus, but

> ...he gave such proofs of courage and address, that in a short time they advanced him to the rank of a fighting man. Jadee, however, did not like his masters, although he had an uncommon degree of respect for their enterprise and skill as sea-rovers; and after some years of strange adventures against the Chinese, Spaniards, and Dutch—the latter of whom he never spoke of without execrating the memory of their mothers—he escaped, and took service under the Rajah of Jehore...For a few years he led a chequered career: plenty one day—opium, curry and rice, and wives galore; then pulling at an oar like a galley-slave to win more; at last the white men spoilt his career. An expedition in which Jadee was engaged was attacked by a British man-of-war, and suffered a severe defeat. Jadee never bargained for fighting them...A Dutchman he did not mind, and a Spaniard he had often seen run; but the Orang-putihs*—there was no charm...which had ever been efficacious against pirates so mighty as they. Jadee had sailed with distinguished Malay 'Rajah Lauts', or Kings of the Sea, but their glory paled before the 'Rajah Lauts' of the white men; they were indeed rovers whom Malay men might envy but might not imtate (pp. 41–42).

And later he relates:

> Long before that action with the English man-of-war which drove me to Singapore, I sailed in a fine fleet of prahus belonging to the Rajah of Jehore. We were all then very rich—ah! such numbers of beautiful wives,

* A literal translation of Orang Putih is white man and its opposite is Orang Hitam, black man. The name of Lord Jim's servant, Tamb' Itam, means, literally, 'black messenger'.

and such feasting!—but, above all, we had a great many most holy men in our force!...Our thirteen prahus had all been fitted out...I wish you could have seen them, Touhan! [we would spell it Tuan as Conrad does] ...such brass guns; such long pendants; such creeses! Allah-il-Allah! our Datoos were indeed great men...Our cruise had been so far successful, and we feasted away,—fighting cocks, smoking opium, and eating white rice (pp. 86–8).

There are certain general similarities between the careers of Babalatchi and Jadee. Both were once notorious pirates and both had acted as serangs. Both knew prosperous days and also days of adversity when they had to live by 'honest irksome toil'. Both fought with the Sulus originally. Jadee was first their slave, but later 'a fighting man', Babalatchi led the 'Sulu rovers'. During this period Babalatchi 'gathered experience and wisdom in many lands', while Jadee had 'some years of strange adventures'. Babalatchi at last attached himself to Omar el Badavi and 'found favour in the eyes of his chief', a man 'first in prayer and first in fight', while Jadee, escaping from the Sulus 'took service under the Sultan of Jehore', and it is the fact that they 'had a great many most holy men' in their force that impresses Jadee. 'Long years of successful depredation' follow for Babalatchi, and Jadee 'led a chequered career' 'sailed in a fine fleet of prahus' and was 'very rich'. Both were eventually defeated by the white man. Babalatchi says, 'Then we fought amongst ourselves and were happy. Now when we fight with you we can only die!' and Jadee 'had sailed with distinguished Malay "Rajah Lauts"...but their glory paled before the "Rajah Lauts" of the white man; they were indeed rovers whom Malay men might envy but not imitate'.

Conrad would find in Spenser St John and Sherard Osborn several accounts of attacks upon piratical settlements and these no doubt gave him generally the background of such attacks, but I have not found any one which is a sufficiently exact parallel to be taken as a source for the attack on Omar el Badavi's stockade.[61]

Babalatchi's plans to take revenge for the destruction of Omar's stockade are rejected by the Sultan of Sulu:

For a short time he dreamed of vengeance, but his dream was dispelled by the cold reception of the Sultan of Sulu, with whom they sought refuge at first and who gave them only a contemptuous and grudging hospitality. While Omar...was recovering from his wounds, Babalatchi attended industriously before the exalted Presence that had extended to them the hand of protection. For all that, when Babalatchi spoke into the Sultan's ear certain proposals of a great and profitable raid, that was to sweep the islands from Ternate to Acheen, the Sultan was very angry. 'I know you, you men from the west,' he exclaimed, angrily. 'Your words are poison in a Ruler's ears. Your talk is of fire and murder and booty—but on our heads falls the vengeance of the blood you drink. Begone!'

There was nothing to be done. Times were changed. So changed that, when a Spanish frigate appeared before the island and a demand was sent to the Sultan to deliver Omar and his companions, Babalatchi was not surprised to hear that they were going to be made the victims of political expediency. (*An Outcast of the Islands*, pp. 53–4).

This comes from St John's account of an attack on the pirates by the British ship *Nemesis*:

Another story showed that the Sulu Government was in regular communication with the pirates; for when the miserable remains of the squadron, attacked by the *Nemesis* off the Brunei river in 1847, returned to Balignini, the families who had lost their husbands in the action, came in their grief to request leave of the Sultan to raise men or collect a force to revenge the death of their relations. The Sultan, of course, refused their request, and laughed at the absurdity of the idea (II, 195).

Omar and Babalatchi have to make a second escape, this time from the Sultan of Sulu:

And then began Omar's second flight. It began arms in hand, for the little band had to fight in the night on the beach for the possession of the small canoes in which those that survived got away at last (*An Outcast of the Islands*, 54).

This seems to correspond with St John's story of a 'well-known pirate chief' who escaped from the Spanish authorities:

The authorities kept a strict watch over him, knowing his enterprising character, but just before the rice harvest was ready to be gathered they became less vigilant, as they thought no one would abandon the result of a year's labour; but at dead of night, with a few companions to whom he had imparted his plan, he fled with his family to the sea shore, where, surprising a boat, he, though hotly pursued, escaped with them all to reach his old haunts... (II, 210).

It was not surprising that Conrad should introduce pirates into his Eastern stories, since Bulungan, which is slightly north of Berau and which he visited as often, was well known in his day as a pirate haunt and slave market. An article in the *Straits Times Overland Journal*, 31 October 1879 says:

The object of the Illanus is plunder, the speciality of Baligninis is kidnapping people for sale. Sugh [the capital of Sulu] used to be the best market,—now closed against them and since then they have taken their captives to Palawan, the Kina Batangan, Seeganan, *Booloongan* [my italics], and elsewhere, notably the last named place.

Conrad's attitude towards pirates is in accord with Mr Wyndham's view which St John quotes: 'Mr Wyndham describes these pirates as very fine men, brave, fierce, never giving quarter to Europeans.'[62]

*

I hope I have demonstrated that Conrad's 'dull, wise books' did more than refresh his memories of Borneo. They provided him with information about the East which he could not have obtained either from observation or hearsay during the short period he was at Berau and Bulungan. From them he was able to take not only Malay names, but suggestions for Malay characters and their histories and backgrounds, as well as obtaining information about the attitudes they would be likely to have towards each other, towards other races, and especially towards the white man. They also provided him with exciting incidents, necessary to the stories he was writing, and of which he would otherwise not have known.

'THE END OF THE TETHER'

8

AN EASTERN PORT: SINGAPORE

Where the naming of places in the East was concerned, Conrad seems to have had a settled policy—a policy of concealment. Either he gave no name and left the location of a story deliberately vague, as in the case of his 'Eastern' ports and the 'East' of 'Youth', or he provided a suitable fictional name, such as Sambir, or he transferred a name from another geographical area, such as Patusan.

He indicated the principle underlying this policy in a letter to Richard Curle. Expressing some irritation with Curle for mentioning, in the draft of an article, the name of the port at which he first landed in the East, Conrad wrote:

> Explicitness...is fatal to the glamour of all artistic work, robbing it of all suggestiveness, destroying all illusions...In 'Youth', in which East or West are of no importance whatever, I kept the name of the Port of landing out of the record of 'poeticized' sensations. The paragraph you quote of the East meeting the narrator is all right in itself; whereas directly it's connected with Muntok it becomes nothing at all. Muntok is a damned hole without any beach and without any glamour, and in relation to the parag. is not in tone. Therefore the par., when pinned to a particular spot, must appear diminished—a fake. And yet it is true![1]

This policy of non-explicitness is continued in 'Falk' and 'The Secret Sharer'. 'Falk' is set in Bangkok, but the port is never mentioned by name, though 'The Secret Sharer' has its initial setting given as the river Meinam on which Bangkok is situated. In *The Shadow-Line*, both Bangkok and the Gulf of Siam are mentioned by name, presumably since this was exact autobiography, though Singapore, the port from which the narrator begins his adventure, is not named. In *Lord Jim*,

Conrad gives the impression of a wide eastern background—the whole background against which Jim's story is played out—and of the distances covered by Jim in his 'retreat', by scattering Eastern place-names about the text—Bombay, Calcutta, Rangoon, Penang, Batavia, Bangkok, Aden, Hong Kong. But again he does not mention Singapore, the port to which the story constantly returns in the first part.

This vagueness as to the locality of the places with which he dealt no doubt allowed a more general application of the story and atmosphere. J. D. Gordan suggests that this was Conrad's intention in *Almayer's Folly*:

> Of the islands Conrad visited on the *Vidar* Borneo was the most important for *Almayer's Folly*, and it is revealed as the general setting of the story... Though Almayer lived on the east coast, the identification is not too exact, since Borneo is the second largest island in the world and the east coast some eight hundred miles long. The reader is able to associate with such a broad background all he may have imagined about the East Indies.[2]

On the other hand, even if Berau had been named specifically, the identification for the reader would have been as inexact as it is in the case of Sambir or Patusan. How many of Conrad's readers would know Berau, or Borneo, or Singapore, or any other Eastern area? They would depend for their impressions of the Eastern location upon traditions of Oriental mystery and romance and whatever other impressions Conrad chose to present. Conrad's attitude to the naming of specific places in his work, in spite of what he has to say about Muntok, would seem to evolve from something personal to himself. And since he was often dealing with actual places, people, and events, perhaps in not naming places he had the additional intention of concealing his sources. Yet though he achieved an unlocalized Eastern setting in his stories, he was often describing a specific—and narrow—area, and describing it exactly, even if he did not name it specifically.

Conrad's use of the Berau river is one example of his accuracy in this matter of setting, and his descriptions of the port of Singapore are another. Under the guise of 'an Eastern port', Singapore is the scene of the action in many of his Eastern novels, or at least of parts of these novels. Lord Jim goes into hospital in 'an Eastern port',[3] and later is involved in the Inquiry into the desertion of the *Patna* in 'the police court of an Eastern port';[4] the narrator in *The Shadow-Line* begins his story in 'an Eastern port';[5] 'The End of the Tether' is set, initially, in 'the *Sofala*'s port of registry on the great highway to the East'[6] where there is 'one of the most important post-offices of the East'.[7] Conrad's descriptions of the port of Singapore in these instances show that, in spite of the deliberate inexplicitness of location, he was writing with a specific setting in mind and recalling the details of this setting with remarkable fidelity. Where there are inaccuracies they can be accounted for by the fact that he was relying on memory, for no doubt this failed him in part; but in some instances the inaccuracies seem to be deliberate, resulting from a judicious selection of details to give a special effect.

His descriptions of the port are limited to one small portion of what was in those days a small city. That part of Singapore which Conrad knew was the oldest part, the area about the sea-front with which any sailor would become acquainted. (See Plates 14–16.) It became significant to Conrad because his interests as a sailor made it a part of Singapore which he must often have walked.

The most extended references to the topography and history of Singapore appear in 'The End of the Tether'. Captain Whalley, the hero of the story, is a man of about sixty-seven in the book's 'present' time, who has been in the East about forty years. Conrad places him in the Singapore he knew personally—the Singapore of the 1880's—and he describes accurately what Whalley would see at that time and the changes he would have experienced during his forty years in the East.

This description extends, with interruptions, from page 219 to page 258 and provides a background to Whalley's thoughts and feelings at a particular crisis in his life. In order to help his daughter and her husband through their financial difficulties, he has sold his ship, the *Fair Maid*, and has left himself without any means of earning a living. As he reflects upon his life and his present difficulties, he walks—at a specific time, late afternoon—through the quayside area of Singapore. The same walk, with much less descriptive detail, appears in *The Shadow-Line*, and I shall consider them together.

*

'It's a good step from the Officers' Home to the Harbour Office,' the narrator in *The Shadow-Line* remarks,[8] and he was quite right. It is the ground covered by this walk between these two points—the Harbour Office and the Officers' Sailors' Home—that appears in Conrad's stories. (See map on p. 177.) The main aspects of this walk that Conrad remembered were the 'small bridge' which crosses the Singapore river, the contrast between the west and east banks of the river, the large hotel on the Esplanade to the east of the river, and at the far end of the Esplanade the white spire of St Andrew's Cathedral. The same walk could be taken in Singapore today, from the quayside to the beginning of the city proper, among surroundings that have not changed so very much since Conrad's time, though the Sailors' Home which stood behind the Cathedral has now disappeared to make way for a cinema.

The Harbour Office in Singapore, with its 'portal of dressed white stone above a flight of shallow white steps',[9] was just as Conrad described it, and it stood in those days beside the post office (Plate 14*a*)—'the most important post-office in the East'—from which Captain Whalley, 'a lonely figure walking

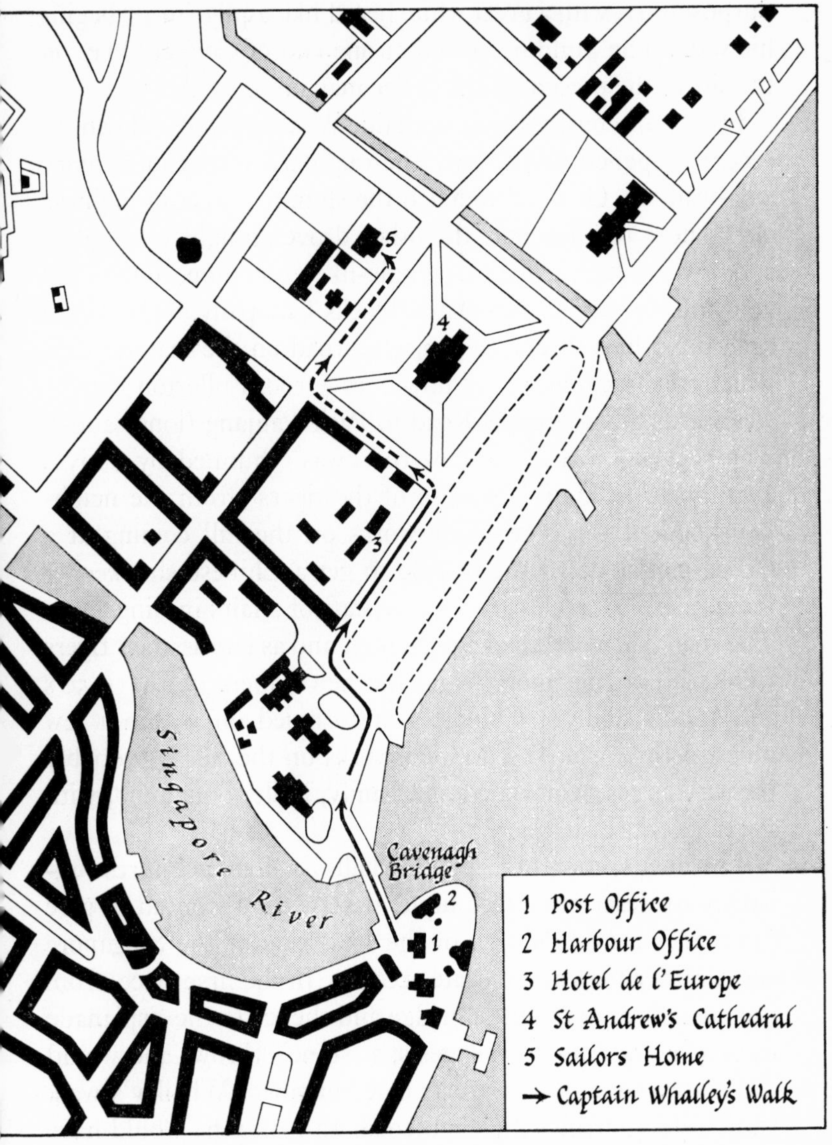

Captain Whalley's walk.

purposefully, with a great white beard like a pilgrim',[10] begins his walk. The buildings stood at one end of Collyer Quay on the site of the present G.P.O. (See map on p. 177.)

From the post office, Captain Whalley walks down 'a recently opened and untidy thoroughfare with rudimentary side-walks...One end touched the slummy street of Chinese shops near the harbour, the other drove straight on...for a couple of miles, through...jungle-like vegetation, to the yard gates of the new Consolidated Docks Company.'[11] This new road must have been the projected road on the map of 1884 which was to extend—and now does—from Fullerton Battery westwards along Keppel Road to Pasir Panjang (long sands). The suggestion that the new road was 'shunned by natives after business hours' because of the tigers 'from the neighbourhood of the New Waterworks on the hill coming at a loping canter down the middle to get a Chinese shopkeeper for supper'[12] was close to the true state of affairs in Singapore. The road had patches of jungle on it and as late as 1906 tigers were still in Singapore[13] and the newspapers of the 1850's and 1860's told 'of Chinese being carried off within a few miles of the town'.[14] The waterworks on the hill is probably the service reservoir on Mount Emily, built about 1878, with a waterworks at its foot.[15]

The next section of Captain Whalley's Walk is impressionistic in its descriptive technique, designed by Conrad to give the reader a general idea of the west side of the Singapore river, rather than an accurate account. In the first place, from the post office to the little bridge and thence to the Esplanade is, as *The Shadow-Line* suggests, a 'stone's throw' and would not involve one in the streets of Chinatown. Whalley's walk is, therefore, artificially lengthened. In reality he would have gone a few yards to the right, i.e. eastwards, to reach the bridge (Plate 14*a*). Instead he passes the 'crude frontages of the new Government buildings' and the new Courts of Justice and 'the pavilion wings of the new Colonial Treasury'.[16] Captain Whalley enters a crowded thoroughfare 'as narrow as a lane and absolutely riotous with life', where 'the tightly packed car of the cable tramways navigated cautiously up the human stream, with the incessant blare of its horn'.[17]

The riotous life of the west side of the river, 'the swarm of brown and yellow humanity', the shops of the Chinamen yawning 'like cavernous lairs' would certainly be true of the western part of Singapore as would be the tramway. Unoriental as it may seem for those days, steam trams were introduced in Singapore in 1885, and according to the *Straits Times* they ran at intervals of ten minutes. It will be remembered that later in the story Captain Whalley and the Master-Attendant hear 'the toot-toot-toot of the cable car beginning to roll before the empty peristyle of the Public Library on its three-mile journey to the New Harbour Docks'.[18]

The congestion of the streets and the noise of the trams which Conrad emphasizes, was the subject of a letter in the *Straits Times*, 13 July 1887, which Conrad may have read since he was in hospital in Singapore at that time:

> ...our streets are wholly insufficient for the immense traffic which struggles through our congested thoroughfares, therefore, we encourage a system of 'noiseless' tramways, which run Brobdignagian engines and cars up and down the town with a roar, jangle, and a rattle which defy description...

The particular aspects of this side of the river, which Conrad emphasizes—the crowded streets, the trams, the riotous life, the new government buildings visible across the river—were all aspects which he could not have helped noticing and remembering later.

Captain Whalley leaves behind the 'sweep of the quays', and stops on 'the apex of a small bridge spanning steeply the bed of a canalised creek with granite shores'.[19] Beneath, 'a sea-going Malay prau [boat] floated half hidden under the arch of masonry...and covered from stem to stern with a ridge of palm-leaf mats'.[20] This is Cavenagh Bridge (Plate 14*a*) which was built in 1868 across the Singapore river and is still in use today. A man standing on its apex midway between east and west banks could view, as Captain Whalley did, the noise and congestion of the business and commercial quarter, and, on the eastern bank, the government offices and the Esplanade with its 'avenues of big trees' and 'ordered grass plots'.

One thing Conrad does not mention, but which he must have seen from the bridge and been fascinated by, was not the single Malay prau, but the sweep of the boat quay, the thousand sampans and lighters which crowd the river just above the bridge, and form one of the most famous views of modern Singapore (Plate 15*a*). But Conrad describes this scene accurately in *The Rescue*, where Lingard and his friend Captain Jorgenson, do the same walk, and pause on the same bridge, as Captain Whalley:

> ...one evening about six months before Lingard's last trip, as they were crossing the short bridge over the canal where native craft lie moored in clusters...Jorgenson pointed at the mass of praus, coasting boats, and sampans that, jammed up together in the canal, lay covered with mats and flooded by the cold moonlight, with here and there a dim lantern burning amongst the confusion of high sterns, spars, masts, and lowered sails (pp. 123–4).

No doubt the single prau was more appropriate to Captain Whalley's feelings of isolation at that time than a crowded and thriving river.

Captain Whalley crosses the bridge to the 'unconfined spaciousness' of the Esplanade, bordering that roadstead to which he gives 'a long glance'. (See Plate 15*b*.) Apart from the changes in the type of shipping, the view from the Esplanade has not changed:

> It was a terraced shore; and beyond...an oblique band of stippled purple lengthened itself indefinitely through the gap between a couple of verdant twin islets. The masts and spars of a few ships far away, hull down in the outer roads, sprang straight from the water... (p. 230).

After a glance at the roadstead, Whalley walks on: 'The avenues of big trees ran straight over the Esplanade, cutting each other at diverse angles, columnar below and luxuriant above.'[21] Suddenly 'a succession of open carriages' come 'bowling along the newly opened sea-road'. They turn in 'an open space near the little bridge...in a wide curve away from the sunset'.[22]

R. St J. Braddell writes of the Esplanade that it 'was about seventy yards deep, much narrower than the present Esplanade, which has been extended by reclamation'.[23] And he goes on to report the fashionable hour for exercise round the Esplanade: '... the fashionable hour...was from five till dusk. The ride or drive was invariably finished off by a few turns on the Esplanade.' The 'succession of open carriages' which Captain Whalley sees 'bowling along' the sea-road and drawing up 'near the little bridge'[24] must have been a common sight in Singapore, especially in the late afternoon.

During his walk, Captain Whalley is joined by his friend the Master-Attendant of the port, and they continue walking east along the Esplanade towards the Cathedral: 'The sacred edifice, standing in solemn isolation amongst the converging avenues of enormous trees, as if to put grave thoughts of heaven into the hours of ease, presented a closed Gothic portal to the light and glory of the west' (p. 239). The same Cathedral is referred to in *Almayer's Folly*: '...they made love under the shadows of the great trees or in the shadow of the cathedral on the Singapore promenade.'[25] This is a description of St Andrew's Cathedral which still stands isolated among grass and trees. Built in 1861 by convict labour, it is in the Gothic style of the twelfth century (Plate 15*b*).

Captain Whalley turns back at this point and does not complete the walk which would have taken him to the Sailors' Home. He returns across the bridge and, reaching the jetty, calls for a sampan.

*

But since, for Conrad, and for the narrator in *The Shadow-Line*, the logical end of this walk would be the Sailors' Home —or Officers' Sailors' Home, to be more precise—we might as well consider what can be discovered about that building which lay just beyond the Cathedral and in which Conrad must have spent a good deal of his time in Singapore, sleeping there and taking his meals there when he was ashore.

Conrad describes the Officers' Home in *The Shadow-Line* as 'a large bungalow with a wide verandah and a curiously suburban-looking little garden of bushes and a few trees between it and the street'.[26] This building has long ago disappeared, but there is no doubt that Conrad was describing here the Sailors' Home and not the Officers' Home (Plate 16*a*). The Sailors' Home was 'a large bungalow' with a 'suburban-looking garden of bushes and a few trees'. According to an eighty-six year old sea captain still living in Singapore, the Officers' Home was in the same compound as the Sailors' Home, but close to the wall of the compound, being in fact rather a small annexe to the main building.

Lord Jim also stayed at the Sailors' Home: 'With Jim it was otherwise: the Government was keeping him in the Sailors' Home for the time being, and probably he hadn't a penny in his pocket to bless himself with.'[27] Lord Jim, as a mercantile marine officer, would cost the government $1.00 per day (*Singapore and Straits Directory*, 1877), and no doubt this is the sum that Conrad himself paid during his stay at the Sailors' Home (4 January to 19 January 1888) after he left the S.S. *Vidar*.

Conrad has much to say about the manager of the Sailors' Home and his irony is rather bitter:

> Its manager was officially styled Chief Steward. He was an unhappy, wizened little man, who if put into a jockey's rig would have looked the part to perfection. But it was obvious that at some time or other in his life, in some capacity or other, he had been connected with the sea. Possibly in the comprehensive capacity of a failure (*The Shadow-Line*, p. 8).

This is the man who, slapping his forehead, says, 'I always said you'd be the death of me.'[28] He is a 'miserable beggar', 'extremely wretched', a 'distressed cur', but one who, according to Captain Giles, is 'not a bad steward really. He can find a good cook...And, what's more, he can keep him when found.'[29] Also Giles tells the narrator, 'The confounded fool...tried to poison himself once—a couple of years ago.'[30] This is the man who does his best to get Hamilton, instead of the narrator, the command of the ship in Bangkok in *The Shadow-Line*. In the *Singapore and Straits Directory*, 1888, the Superintendent of the Home is listed as C. Phillips. Phillips is also listed in the Directories as an 'Inspector of Brothels'. He was also a Temperance worker. The *Straits Times*, 19 April 1888, records the holding of a Temperance Tea at the Sailors' Rest (not to be confused with the Sailors' Home): 'After the tea, Mr C. Phillips, being one of the oldest and most laborious Temperance workers, gave a talk on "Ten Thousand Wonderful Things".' (Conrad was then on his way to Sydney in the *Otago* and would miss this treat.) Phillips appears to be the person Conrad had in mind in *The Shadow-Line*, for he wrote to St Clair: 'The "Home" Steward's name (in my time) I don't remember. He was a meagre wizened creature, always bemoaning his fate, and did try to do me an unfriendly turn for some reason or other.'*

St Clair comments in his article:

> The steward of the Sailors' Home, originally Balestier's house, was a retired sergeant of artillery, who combined the supervision of the Sailors' Home with the job of instructor to the old Rifle Volunteers, disbanded about the time Conrad came to the East. His name was Phillips, really a very well-meaning person, whose evangelical activities were mainly devoted to Malay missions. He certainly did much work in translating hymns and portions of the New Testament into Malay. Perhaps his indigestion was strong upon him when he clashed with Conrad.

* See Appendix E, p. 317, below.

One other building in this part of Singapore makes its appearance several times in Conrad's Eastern novels. Much of Marlow's extended interview with Jim, during and immediately after the Inquiry into the desertion of the *Patna*, takes place in a hotel. And the narrator in *The Shadow-Line*, having gone through the formalities at the Harbour Office for giving up his berth in the 'Eastern ship' in which he had spent eighteen months, considers that since his connection with the sea is temporarily broken, he ought to stay in a hotel rather than in the Sailors' Home:

> There it was, too, within a stone's-throw of the Harbour Office, low, but somehow palatial, displaying its white, pillared pavilions surrounded by trim grass plots...I gave it a hostile glance and directed my steps towards the Officers' Sailors' Home. I walked in the sunshine, disregarding it, and in the shade of the big trees on the esplanade without enjoying it. The heat of the tropical East descended... (pp. 7–8).

This hotel was the Hotel de l'Europe which lay behind the Esplanade and which would certainly have been visible from the Harbour Office (Plate 16*b*). The narrator in *The Shadow-Line* looks at it with rejection. But Lord Jim observed the same view, perhaps not aware of it, as he contemplated his shame. Marlow, one fine morning, is 'standing in the shade by the steps of the harbour office' when he sees the captain and officers of the *Patna* arriving, among them Jim, who is described as '...that young fellow who, hands in pockets, and turning his back upon the sidewalk, gazed across the grass-plots of the Esplanade at the yellow portico of the Malabar Hotel'.[31] There has never been a Malabar Hotel in Singapore, though there was and is a Malabar Street. Conrad's description in both *The Shadow-Line* and *Lord Jim* indicates that he had the Hotel de l'Europe in mind. This hotel is no longer in existence but it had a big dining room,[32] its long 'front gallery' used for 'coffee and cigars', and the view from it would be the same as that from the Malabar Hotel: 'The riding lights of ships.'[33] Indeed, the Hotel de l'Europe was the only hotel in Singapore which faced the sea. In *Lord Jim*, there are tourists staying in the hotel: 'An outward-bound mail-boat had come in that afternoon, and the big dining-room...was more than half full of people with a-hundred-pounds-round-the-world tickets in their pockets.'[34] There is a further and more specific description of this hotel in 'The End of the Tether': 'The straggling building of bricks, as airy as a bird-cage...The rooms were lofty...the periodical invasions of tourists from some passenger steamer...flitted through the wind-swept dusk of the apartments...the draughty corridors and the long chairs of the verandahs.'[35]

The contiguity of the two buildings, the Harbour Office and the Hotel de l'Europe, is used again, obversely as it were, when Marlow is sitting with Jim on the verandah of the hotel and listening to his story of the desertion. In this instance, the reference is intended to add dramatic tension to the story:

> The lights had been put out in the dining-hall; our candle glimmered solitary in the long gallery, and the columns had turned black from pediment to capital. On the vivid stars the high corner of the Harbour Office stood out distinct across the Esplanade, as though the sombre pile had glided nearer to see and hear (p. 147).

And the distance from the Harbour Office to the hotel is recalled in *Lord Jim* for comic effect when Marlow, standing outside the Harbour Office, hears the Master-Attendant within giving the master of the *Patna* a dressing-down: 'No doubt the noise was great. I heard it down below, and I have reason to believe it was heard clear across the Esplanade as far as the bandstand.'[36] The bandstand used to be situated near the end of the long stretch of the Hotel de l'Europe.[37]

*

'The End of the Tether' in its first pages offers us a demonstration of Conrad's method of building up a character through a particular setting. The description is formed of the visual impressions Whalley, or anybody else, was likely to receive in Singapore, one evening in the 1880's, but it is also a blending with this of those aspects of Singapore's past history likely to be remembered by a seaman of Whalley's age and experience—or by a man like Captain Lingard, but certainly not by the young sailor Joseph Conrad Korzeniowski. And finally it is an accurate perception of the kinds of opinions and biases towards that period of history which a man of Whalley's background would have.

The appropriateness and accuracy of Captain Whalley's meditations is quite astonishing. It extends even to such passing references as his preference for his old Panama hat as opposed to the 'comparatively modern fashion of pipe-clayed cork helmets...he hoped he could manage to keep a cool head to the end of his life without all these contrivances for hygienic ventilation'.[38] But in the general backward drift of Whalley's reverie, the outstanding theme is the superiority of the early days of the colony to the present. This is natural, given Whalley's age—his youth seems a brighter period—and his present position, with little money and no ship.

His first memories of the colony are of 'muddy shores, a harbour without quays, the one solitary wooden pier...jutting out crookedly'.[39] A photograph I have of the Esplanade before river reclamation shows the early Singapore that Whalley remembered from his youth. But he remembers men also

> ...like himself; men, too, like poor Evans, for instance, with his red face, his coal-black whiskers, and his restless eyes, who had set up the first patent slip for repairing small ships, on the edge of the forest, in a lonely bay three miles up the coast...it was from that patent slip in a lonely wooded bay that had sprung the workshops of the Consolidated Docks Company [which could be seen] as you approached the New Harbour from the west.[40]

There was no Consolidated Docks Company in Singapore

when Conrad was here, but the new road he earlier described would have passed two Dock Companies—the New Harbour Dock Company and the Tanjong Pagar Company. The Tanjong Pagar Docks were not established until 1865, and since Whalley is going back to the 1850's it is apparent that Conrad had the New Harbour Dock Company in mind. Indeed, he uses the name of this company, probably unintentionally, on page 254 in his reference to the cable car 'on its three-mile journey to the New Harbour Docks'.

The history of the New Harbour Dock Company is given in an article by Walter Makepeace in *One Hundred Years of Singapore*. He writes:

> A place of honour should certainly be given to William Cloughton, master mariner, commonly known as Captain Cloughton, as the builder of the first dry dock at Singapore...Going backwards and forwards [between India and China], he saw that a dry dock was wanted at Singapore, and decided, with the aid of his friends and his own savings, to construct one, for which purpose he settled in Singapore about the year 1854, choosing his site in New Harbour, just opposite Pulo Hantu.[41]

Cloughton died soon after returning home to England in 1874, just as Evans had 'ended by dying at home'.[42] The New Harbour Dock Company, like Conrad's Consolidated Docks Company, was situated three miles up the coast to the west of Singapore, and would come into view as one approached the New Harbour from the west. And Whalley remembers also: '...the first coal-sheds erected on Monkey Point, that caught fire mysteriously and smouldered for days, so that amazed ships came into a roadstead full of sulphurous fog, and the sun hung blood-red at midday' (p. 236). This is a reference to a fire at Cloughton's yard at Sandy—not Monkey—Point: 'One afternoon a black cloud of smoke was seen going up from Sandy Point, and later news reached town that the New Harbour Dock Company's property there was on fire' (*One Hundred Years*, I, 588).

Whalley's reflections on his past are prompted by the passing of the Governor of the 'Eastern port' in his carriage along the Esplanade:

> But one carriage and pair coming late did not join the line.
>
> It fled along in a noiseless roll...It was a long dark-green landau, having a dignified and buoyant motion between the sharply curved C-springs, and a sort of strictly official majesty in its supreme elegance. It seemed more roomy than is usual, its horses seemed slightly bigger, the appointments a shade more perfect, the servants perched somewhat higher on the box. The dresses of three women...seemed to fill completely the shallow body of the carriage. The fourth face was that of a man, heavy lidded, distinguished and sallow, with a sombre, thick, iron-grey imperial and moustaches, which somehow had the air of solid appendages. His Excellency— (p. 233).

The Master-Attendant, who had also seen His Excellency pass, remarks to his friend, 'Sir Frederick looked well at the end of his time. Didn't he?'[43] This takes Whalley back to his early days in the colony when individuals were of some account...

> It struck him [Whalley] that it was to this port, where he had just sold his last ship, that he had come with the very first he had ever owned, and with his head full of a plan for opening a new trade with a distant part of the Archipelago. The then governor had given him no end of encouragement. No Excellency he—this Mr Denham—this governor with his jacket off; a man who tended night and day, so to speak, the growing prosperity of the settlement with the self-forgetful devotion of a nurse for a child she loves... (p. 234).

Conrad is again keeping close to historical fact here, and to contemporary likelihood, for it was indeed most likely that towards the end of the eighties the Master-Attendant of Singapore might remark upon the Governor's imminent departure from the port, and that that Governor should be 'Sir Frederick'. It is also likely that an old seaman like Captain Whalley, in his present misfortune, would look back nostalgically to the earlier Governor's rule.

Sir Frederick Weld was Governor of Singapore from 1880 to 1887. He was Governor at the time of the *Jeddah* disaster, just as Henry Ellis was then Master-Attendant. In fact, he was Governor on most of the occasions on which Conrad visited Singapore. He finally left Singapore for England in the S.S. *Orestes* on 17 October 1887. At this time Conrad was probably at Berau, for he had sailed in the *Vidar* on 30 September and did not return to port until 31 October 1887. The fact that Sir Frederick was still Governor before Conrad left Singapore on his second voyage to Berau, and had departed when he returned, must have impressed itself upon Conrad's memory. The retirement of Governor Weld must have been part of the talk of the port in any case.

'Sir Frederick' is contrasted with Governor Denham of 'five-and-thirty' years earlier. In the manuscript of 'The End of the Tether' the name 'Denham' had been written in above 'Bonham'. Samuel George Bonham was Governor of Singapore from 1837 to 1843,* and it is clear that Conrad had Bonham in mind here, though again without knowing a great deal about him. Whalley obviously prefers the earlier Governor to the later: 'No Excellency he—this Mr Denham—this governor with his jacket off', and he recalls going to see Governor Denham about

> an undertaking full of risk he had come to expound, but a twenty minutes' talk in the Government Bungalow on the hill had made it go smoothly from the start. And as he was retiring Mr Denham...called out after him, 'Next month the *Dido* starts for a cruise that way, and I shall request her captain officially to give you a look-in and see how you get on.' The *Dido* was one of the smart frigates on the China station... (p. 235).

Although Conrad is keeping generally to the history of the Colony here, he is not correct in his assessment of the two

* Conrad's dating is not quite accurate here, for if we take the date of Weld's retirement—1887—then thirty-five years earlier would be 1852, nine years after Bonham had himself retired. But it is accurate enough.

Governors. There is no doubt that Weld was a much better Governor than Bonham, superior on the very grounds for which Whalley prefers Bonham, i.e. he was concerned with the extension of British power outside Singapore and was a man who believed in dealing personally with affairs.* But it seems likely that Whalley's opinions here are the result of the influence of Conrad's reading rather than of his experience, and this might explain the inaccuracies. Bonham was a friend of Captain, later Admiral, Keppel, who discovered New Harbour, Singapore, and whose name remains in Singapore's extensive wharf road, Keppel Road, and in Keppel Harbour. In 1841 Keppel was appointed commander of the corvette, *Dido*, the same ship referred to by Denham in 'The End of the Tether', and in Keppel's book *A Sailor's Life Under Four Sovereigns* he gives an account of his voyages in the *Dido*.[44] On 7 May 1843, Keppel arrived in the port of Singapore, and a day later he records: 'Dined with Bonham. Nice quiet dinner in cool situation on the hill.'[45] Keppel had known Bonham for many years and they were good friends. But Conrad might also have obtained his impressions of Bonham from Sherard Osborn's book.[46] Osborn writes:

> ...on the top of the highest [hill]...stands Government House, tenanted by the present Sir Samuel Bonham—then governor of the Straits of Malacca—a most able civil servant of the Hon. East India Company, beloved by all classes, and always spoken of by the Malays with a mixed feeling of awe and affection, in consequence of the active part he took as a commissioner in the suppression of piracy in the Straits (p. 10).

And Whalley's impression that the earlier days of Singapore were better for the individual is perhaps an extension of Sherard Osborn's comments about the Singapore of the

* Whalley thinks that 'individuals were of some account then' (p. 235). But Weld wrote in a Government Dispatch to the Secretary of State: 'It is in native affairs that a mistake may lead to the most serious consequences...and all native races...look for personal government and may be guided by a man that has the gift when no abstraction of "government" will guide them' (General Dispatches from Singapore, GD/D no. 394, 19 September 1883). By contrast Bonham was undistinguished as a governor.

forties: 'There was an energy, a life, a go-aheadism about everything, that struck me much; everybody was in a hurry, everybody pushing with a will.'[47]

There is an implied contrast also, in Conrad's story, not only between the governors but between their residences. Conrad describes Denham and his residence in the following way:

> ...a lone bachelor who lived as in a camp with the few servants and his three dogs in what was called then the Government Bungalow: a low-roofed structure on the half-cleared slope of a hill, with a new flagstaff in front and a police orderly on the verandah (p. 234).

Conrad could not have seen this particular Government House himself since it no longer existed in his day, but it is probable that he needed, in order to write about it, no more than this comment from Keppel: 'Mar. 14 Anchored at Singapore. In the absence, and by permission, of Bonham—now Governor of the Straits Settlements—took possession of the Hill, a charming residence with flagstaff and native guard established' (1, 288). The situation on a hill, the possession of a flagstaff and native guard are all provided by Keppel, though he does not mention that it was merely a bungalow. Braddell gives this description: 'On the top of the hill stood Government House, which had been built by Raffles and added to by Crawfurd. It was one hundred feet long and fifty feet deep, a neat wooden bungalow with venetians and attap roof.'[48] This then is the Government House Whalley knew in the early days of Singapore's history. But Government House at the end of Captain Whalley's career was a palatial dwelling fit for more luxurious days. The Master-Attendant is said to dine 'once or twice every year at the Government House—a many-windowed, arcaded palace upon a hill laid out in roads and gardens'.[49] This is Conrad's description of the Government House which still stands today and is the home of the Singapore Head of State, the Yang di-Pertuan Negara.

*

'*The End of the Tether*'

Conrad writes in 'The End of the Tether' of the Master-Attendant, Captain Ellis:

> ...lately *he had been taking about a duke in his Master-Attendant's steam-launch* [my italics] to visit the harbour improvements. Before that he had 'most obligingly' gone out in person to pick out a good berth for the ducal yacht. Afterwards he had an invitation to lunch on board. The duchess herself lunched with them. A big woman with a red face. Complexion quite sunburnt. He should think ruined. Very gracious manners. They were going on to Japan... (p. 240).

Fifteen years later in *The Shadow-Line* Conrad again refers to the duke. The Master-Attendant says to the Shipping-Master:

> 'Mr R., let the harbour launch have steam up to take the Captain here on board the *Melita* at half-past nine to-night.'...R. was impressed... 'I say!' he exclaimed on the landing...'I say! His own launch...*the last person who had it before you was a duke* [my italics]. So, there!' (pp. 40–1).

Conrad's references were based on an actual duke who was in the vicinity of Singapore at the same time as Conrad. The Duke of Sutherland visited Singapore in his yacht just as Conrad was taking up his first command. Their paths crossed in such a way that Conrad was sure to remember him, and he might also have refreshed his memory of the occurrence by reading a book by Mrs Florence Caddy which is an account of the cruise she made with the Duke.[50]

On 19 January 1888 Conrad left Singapore on board the S.S. *Melita* on his way to Bangkok to take command of the barque *Otago*. The Duke of Sutherland was expected to arrive in Singapore on 18 January 1888 (*Singapore Free Press*, 7 January 1888). He did not arrive then, and on 23 January the same paper reports, 'The Duke of Sutherland is daily expected here in his yacht the *Sans Peur*. His destination is Bangkok.' The Duke's yacht actually arrived in Singapore on 6 February 1888, and Mrs Caddy recalls: 'A steam-launch' came 'for us at one o'clock...',[51] and 'After dinner, Mr Geiger ...came with a large steam-launch to convey us to the ball on board H.M.S. *Orion*'.[52]

The Duke of Sutherland stayed three days in Singapore, leaving on 9 February 1888. This was the date on which Conrad left Bangkok. The *Sans Peur* encountered no difficulties and arrived in Bangkok on 13 February, a journey of four days. She left Bangkok on 27 February,[53] reaching Singapore again on 3 March (*Singapore Free Press*, 6 March 1888), a journey of five days. Mrs Caddy writes: 'We anchored about five p.m. at Singapore.'[54]

Conrad, who had left Bangkok so much earlier than the Duke, had a much longer journey of twenty-one days, arriving in Singapore only three days before the *Sans Peur*. The *Otago* was still anchored outside the harbour limits of Singapore when the *Sans Peur* returned, with the Duke on board unconscious of the fact that he was earning himself a mention in two of Conrad's works.

*

This study of the 'Eastern port' of 'The End of the Tether' shows that Conrad described with a careful and conscious accuracy the impressions he retained of Singapore.* He made use of the past history of the colony and the opinions of other writers about it in order to build the character and background of Whalley, and to impress upon the reader the sense of Whalley's life drawing to a close, for Whalley seems a man out of the stream of the modern city of Singapore of the 1880's, and therefore a man doomed not to recover the success of earlier days.

Part of the history which Conrad introduces probably formed an ingredient in the gossip of the port. Cloughton, for example, had been an extremely eccentric character in his

* Gordan, p. 62, argues that Bombay is the setting for the Inquiry in *Lord Jim*, but see my article 'Conrad's Eastern Port', *REL* (October 1965).

time and was likely to have been remembered for this reason. Conrad may even have heard some old sea captain complaining that Governor Weld was not the governor Bonham had been. And it is almost certain, as I hope to show, that the Master-Attendant was a man much discussed in seafaring circles in the port at that time.

Conrad has been criticized for his too flamboyant descriptions of tropical nature in those books dealing with the remoter parts of the South-east Asian archipelago. But his fidelity to appearance and likelihood in his descriptions of Singapore and the Lingard settlement suggest that, however lush and romantic his descriptions may seem, they are, in fact, authentic.

9

THE DEPUTY NEPTUNE AND THE ARAB SHIPOWNER

Apart from A. P. Williams and William Lingard, there was one other man in the East who impressed Conrad particularly —Captain Henry Ellis, the Master-Attendant at Singapore, who gave Conrad his first command. All three men had strong connections with the sea, but whereas Williams's story inspired Conrad to write a heroic novel, Lingard and Ellis— and especially the latter—seem to have impressed him as 'characters', each in his own way an example of a particular 'type'. Both Ellis and Lingard (except in the case of *The Rescue*) remain in the background of the stories in which they appear, but they are, nevertheless, in certain ways 'prime movers'.

Ellis, as Master-Attendant, is in complete control of the Eastern port. His authority and knowledge of the seaport result in the narrators in *The Shadow-Line* and 'Falk', and Captain Whalley in 'The End of the Tether', finding berths which lead to adventures of one kind or another. As Captain Whalley's great friend in 'The End of the Tether', and in *Lord Jim*, he is called Captain Eliott; but in *The Shadow-Line* he is called Ellis. It may seem rather odd that Conrad, having disguised Ellis's identity by means of the fictional name of Eliott in two stories, should give the man's real name in *The Shadow-Line*. A possible reason is that Captain Ellis was alive when the first two stories were published. He died on 3 January 1908. By the time *The Shadow-Line* was published in 1917 there was no longer any danger of Captain Ellis recognizing himself in Conrad's work.

It is difficult to determine exactly how much Conrad knew

13-2

about the life and character of Captain Ellis. But I imagine he had no more information than was part of the common gossip of the harbour about the man in charge of it. Since Captain Ellis was a well-known character in Singapore at the time—as much a 'character' as Conrad makes him and more—the stories about him that formed this 'hearsay' were probably numerous. We do know that Conrad had one interview with Ellis when he was given command of the *Otago*.

Conrad's single interview with Ellis attains some prominence in his work, for it appears in different forms in two stories, and so is an example of Conrad's use of a very slight experience. In *Lord Jim* and *The Shadow-Line* the Master-Attendant is shown interviewing a seaman in his room at the Harbour Office. In *Lord Jim* the seaman is the renegade master of the *Patna* and in *The Shadow-Line* he is the narrator of the story, obviously Conrad himself. *The Shadow-Line* version is, consequently, the nearest to the facts of Conrad's experience of Ellis. In these instances we see very little of the Master-Attendant apart from the brief interview, though something of his reputation in the port is indicated.

In *The Shadow-Line*, the narrator finds himself 'before a portal of dressed white stone above a flight of shallow white steps'.[1] (See the Harbour Office in Plate 14*a*.) The narrator enters 'the dim cool hall' and ascends 'the broad inner staircase'. On 'the spacious landing about the curtained archway of the shipping office' lounged the 'crew of the harbour steam-launch'[2] and the Malay coxswain of the launch lifts the curtain so that the narrator can pass through into the office. He is met by the Eurasian shipping-master who hastily and deferentially ushers him through the 'tall and important-looking door' into the harbour master's room. Captain Ellis, we are told, 'pretended to rule the fate of the mortals whose lives were cast upon the waters'.[3] He was 'inquisitorial and peremptory', choleric in temperament, with a 'gruff, loud, authoritative voice'. The narrator in *The Shadow-Line* is, however, quite kindly treated by him. And after receiving the notification of his first command, Conrad writes that he 'went out, never to see him [Ellis] again in [his] life'.[4] This last statement was probably true, but contained within the brief portrait is the suggestion of Ellis's reputation of which Conrad had heard: 'Captain Ellis looked upon himself as...the deputy-Neptune for the circumambient waves', 'there were fellows who were actually afraid of him'.[5]

In *Lord Jim*, Conrad again makes use of this brief experience, expanding the character of Captain Ellis in his interview with the captain of the *Patna* along the lines of the stories he had heard of Ellis's reputation. But in its fundamentals, the interview follows that of *The Shadow-Line*. The scene is the same room in the Harbour Office in which the clerks work. The archway from the anteroom is mentioned, and the 'coxswain and crew of the harbour steam-launch',[6] on this occasion crowding in to watch the scene. The manner of the shipping-master[7] is more excitable, but the master of the *Patna* is also ushered by him into Ellis's private room, and we have a similar view in each case of Ellis looking up from his desk. Of the interview itself we are given only an outsider's impression which leads into a description of Ellis:

> No doubt the noise was great. I heard it down below, and I have every reason to believe it was heard clear across the Esplanade as far as the bandstand. Old father Elliot had a great stock of words and could shout—and didn't mind who he shouted at either. He would have shouted at the Viceroy himself. As he used to tell me: 'I am as high as I can get; my pension is safe. I've a few pounds laid by, and if they don't like my notions of duty I would just as soon go home as not. I am an old man, and I have always spoken my mind. All I care for now is to see my girls married before I die.' He was a little crazy on that point. His three daughters were awfully nice, though they resembled him amazingly, and on the mornings he woke up with a gloomy view of their matrimonial prospects the office would read it in his eye and tremble, because, they said, he was sure to have somebody for breakfast (pp. 46–7).

This interview indicates the limits of Conrad's personal contact with Captain Ellis. By the time he returned from Bangkok in the *Otago*, Ellis had retired, just as Weld, a few months earlier, had retired during one of Conrad's visits to Berau. At the end of *The Shadow-Line* he writes:

> ...when I inquired if I could see Captain Ellis for a moment, I was told in accents of pity for my ignorance that our deputy-Neptune had retired and gone home on a pension about three weeks after I left the port (p. 163).

Six days before Conrad returned from Bangkok with his fever-ridden crew, Ellis had left Singapore for the last time: 'Captain Ellis after long and valued service as Master Attendant at Singapore has retired, sailing for Europe by the S.S. *Orestes* on Thursday' (*Singapore Free Press*, 28 February 1888). The *Orestes* sailed on 23 February 1888, and the *Otago* came into harbour at the end of February. The narrator's remark about the Master-Attendant in *The Shadow-Line*—'So I suppose that my appointment was the last act, outside the daily routine, of his official life'[8]—could almost be said of Captain Ellis's appointment of Conrad as commander of the *Otago*.

But this was not the end of Ellis's usefulness to the novelist. He reappears in 'The End of the Tether', this time a much fuller portrait, not based on Conrad's own experience of him but on the hearsay of the port. A great deal of the man's character is presented in his conversation with Whalley, and a great deal of his biography through the narrative.

> Captain Eliott was fairly satisfied with his position, and nursed no inconsiderable sense of such power as he had. His conceited and tyrannical disposition did not allow him to let it dwindle in his hands for want of use. The uproarious, choleric frankness of his comments on people's character and conduct caused him to be feared at bottom; though in conversation many pretended not to mind him in the least, others would only smile sourly at the mention of his name, and there were even some who dared pronounce him 'a meddlesome old ruffian'. But for almost all of them one of Captain Eliott's outbreaks was nearly as distasteful to face as a chance of annihilation (pp. 237–8).

His topics of conversation are limited to his pension—'He only hung on to his berth so long in order to get his pension on the highest scale before he went home';[9] his daughters—'Lawn-tennis and silly novels from morning to night...as ill-luck would have it, there did not seem to be any decent young fellows left in the world...[to make] a good woman happy';[10] his poverty—'Extreme indigence stared him in the face'; and 'the Marine Office, the men and the ships of the port'.[11]

Captain Eliott's concern for the matrimonial prospects of his three girls is not based on fact. Captain Henry Ellis married twice, and when Conrad met him he was living in Singapore with his first wife. They then had one daughter. She was born in 1878 and would be only ten when Conrad knew Ellis and clearly unlikely to indulge in 'lawn-tennis and silly novels from morning to night'.

But the loudness of Ellis's voice, his sudden outbreaks of temper, his sense of power, his bluntness and yet essential goodness come through every account of him I have read. In a letter dated 5 July 1963 his grandson, the Reverend Henry Ellis Briscoe, wrote:

> Captain Henry Ellis was my grandfather...He was a big broad shouldered man with a powerful voice that struck terror into all his subordinates, whether oriental or occidental; his word was law and he always spoke with the authority of a man who was not accustomed to having his opinions controverted. He ruled with a rod of iron. He had a horror of red tape and did not take kindly to interference from government officials. Henry Ellis had a very violent temper and shouted and roared when things did not go his way...He died of a broken leg because he would not let the doctor put it in splints. He was offered a very good appointment in Venezuela after his retirement in Singapore but was advised not to take it because of his violent temper. This would have eventually led to his being knifed.

An article about Ellis, published in the *Singapore Free Press* 5 December 1907 and entitled 'Port Admiral

Gamp', confirms some of the aspects of Conrad's fictional portrait:

He was an Irishman of intensity, a real good man and kindly, but with a quickness of temper that almost set the river on fire. One minute he would be a stately and dignified official, courteous and gentlemanly; the next he was boiling over with temper and hardly knew what he was doing. Next morning he was all right again and never omitted to make amends for the havoc he had wrought in his haste.

Ellis's obituary gives a brief account of his life:

...As Lieutenant Ellis of the Indian Marine he came to this Colony a year or two before the transfer from the Indian Government to the Colonial Office. His duties then were connected with the tiny navy of this Colony, two small steamers being maintained as guardships and to keep down piracy in the Straits of Malacca, no easy job in those days when most of the navigation locally was carried on in small sailing craft. Lieutenant Ellis's first command was the small steam paddle gunboat 'Mohr', of 95 tons and 50 h.p. stationed at Penang, the other Government vessel being the 'Pluto', also a paddle gunboat, of 450 tons, stationed at Singapore. Lieutenant Ellis commanded the 'Rainbow', a screw gunboat of 100 tons. Soon afterwards Lieutenant Ellis became Harbour-Master at Penang for a short time, coming to Singapore as Harbour-Master and Marine Magistrate, an appointment he held continuously until his departure in 1888...

Captain Ellis was a strong official, blunt and straightforward, standing no nonsense, with a good deal of Irish humour about him and some national touchiness as well. He was by virtue of his office, one of the best known men in Singapore, although in private life he mixed little in Society... (*Singapore Free Press*, 20 February 1908).

Eliott's 'staying on' in order to receive the highest possible pension may be based on fact. Ellis's pension, according to the Civil List, was higher than those of other Civil Servants, even including retired governors. He received the pension of $2,780 which Governor Sir Frederick Weld had recommended for him.*

* This was probably given in return for his excellent service. Sir Cecil Clementi Smith, who succeeded Weld, recorded in a dispatch sent ten days before the Master-Attendant left Singapore that 'during the whole of his long service of over 21 years he had shown untiring energy in the responsible duties of his appointment...it is impossible to speak too highly of the strict integrity of his conduct' (*Straits Settlement Dispatches*, 13 February 1888).

According to Captain Pavitt, the present Master-Attendant at Singapore, Conrad's description of the powers of the Master-Attendant in the 1880's was accurate. Conrad writes:

A master-attendant is a superior sort of harbour-master; a person, out in the East, of some consequence in his sphere; a Government official, a magistrate for the waters of the port, and possessed of vast but ill-defined disciplinary authority over seamen of all classes ('The End of the Tether', p. 237).

Governor Cecil Clementi Smith, in asking for someone to replace Ellis on his retirement, lists the Master-Attendant's functions in the following paragraph, a comparison of which with Conrad's description shows that the latter was well aware of these functions, including magisterial duties:

The post is a very important one, and requires special qualifications in its occupant...Besides the General Supervision over the Port and its shipping the Master-Attendant has magisterial functions to perform and is in charge of the light houses belonging to the Colony.[12]

Eliott's desire to build 'himself a little house in the country —in Surrey—to end his days in'[13] was certainly achieved by Ellis, though he did not build it in Surrey but in the place of his birth,* to which he returned on his retirement from Singapore as Master-Attendant. The Town Clerk of Bundoran, with whom I have corresponded, wrote as follows: 'The subject of your inquiry returned to Bundoran, Co. Donegal and built a house known as Ellismere on an Estate known still as Ellismere Estate' (letter of 9 April 1963).

*

Captain Whalley as a character seems to lack conviction. He says little and does less. He is described in such terms as: 'had something of a grand air',[14] 'tranquil bearing',[15] 'a temper carelessly serene'.[16] While he is listening to the

* He was born at Bundoran, County Donegal, Ireland in 1835, and when he was made Master-Attendant at Singapore on 15 October 1873 he was only thirty-eight. When Conrad met him he was fifty-three.

Master-Attendant, Captain Eliott, he is almost entirely negative in attitude: 'Captain Whalley could not say',[17] 'Captain Whalley...assented as if in a dream',[18] 'Captain Whalley, who seemed lost in a mental effort...gave a slight start',[19] 'Captain Whalley stroking his beard slowly, looked down on the ground without a word'.[20] Later in the story he is described by Van Wyk:

His very simplicity (amusing enough) was like a delicate refinement of an upright character. The striking dignity of manner could be nothing else, in a man reduced to such a humble position, but the expression of something essentially noble in the character...the serenity of his temper at the end of so many years, since it could not obviously have been appeased by success, wore an air of profound wisdom. Mr Van Wyk was amused at it sometimes. Even the very physical traits of the old captain of the *Sofala*, his powerful frame, his reposeful mien, his intelligent, handsome face, the big limbs, the benign courtesy, the touch of rugged severity in the shaggy eyebrows, made up a seductive personality (p. 351).

Eliott in 'The End of the Tether' on the other hand is seen almost in terms of caricature:

He beheld then, waddling towards him autocratically, a man of an old fashioned and gouty aspect, with hair as white as his own, but with shaved, florid cheeks, wearing a necktie—almost a neckcloth—whose stiff ends projected far beyond his chin; with round legs, round arms, a round body, a round face—generally producing the effect of his short figure having been distended by means of an air-pump as much as the seams of his clothing would stand. This was the Master-Attendant of the port (p. 237).

And in his loquaciousness and bounce he is the exact opposite of Whalley. This contrast is necessary to Conrad's artistic purpose in the book, but I would suggest that the inspiration for these two antithetical characters stemmed from one source and that source was Captain Henry Ellis.

Ellis seems to have had two sides to his character, and Captain Whalley would appear to be based on Ellis's more dignified characteristics. According to the Reverend Henry

Ellis Briscoe, his grandfather was 'big, broad-shouldered, had a moustache and beard, was a good living man, not given to drink, went to church and read his bible regularly'. Captain Whalley was also a regular bible reader.[21] But Mr Briscoe also states that his grandfather 'had a very violent temper and shouted and roared when things did not go his way'. The article in the *Singapore Free Press*, 5 December 1907, also refers to this duality: '...one minute...stately and dignified ...courteous and gentlemanly; the next...boiling over with temper...'. Conrad himself says in a letter to J. M. Dent: 'Captain E. was...big but not a raw-boned Irishman. He was a fine, dignified personality, an ex-Naval officer.'[22] Conrad, in creating Captain Whalley, had in mind the dignified side of Ellis's character and reserved the bombastic and choleric side for Captain Eliott. This would account for the obviously exaggerated (and false) description of the Master-Attendant's appearance in 'The End of the Tether', and for the negativeness of Captain Whalley as a character.

Conrad also transferred part of the history of the actual Henry Ellis to the fictional Captain Whalley. Captain Ellis's wife, according to Mr Briscoe, died on the voyage home from Singapore in 1888, and was buried at sea. She was only thirty-nine. Conrad seems to have transferred this information about Ellis's wife to Captain Whalley—'She went away from under the ensign like a sailor's wife, a sailor herself at heart.'[23]

Conrad gives us quite a lot of information about the friendship between Whalley and Eliott. It is based on long years in Eastern waters:

> They had been good comrades years ago, almost intimates. At the time when Whalley commanded the renowned *Condor*, Eliott had charge of the nearly as famous *Ringdove* for the same owners; and when the appointment of Master-Attendant was created, Whalley would have been the only other serious candidate. But Captain Whalley, then in the prime of life, was resolved to serve no one but his own auspicious Fortune (p. 239).

Whalley in his early days had been known as:

> ...Dare-devil Harry Whalley, of the *Condor*, a famous clipper in her day. [He had] sailed famous ships...had made famous passages, had been the pioneer of new routes and new trades...had steered across the unsurveyed tracts of the South Seas... (p. 204).

During their conversation in 'The End of the Tether', Eliott suddenly realizes that perhaps his friend is 'hard up' and it is Eliott's casual remarks about the *Sofala* which bring about Whalley's last employment as her master.

It might be supposed that Conrad was inventing this relationship, but in fact Captain Ellis did have a friend of long-standing with a background similar to Whalley's. It was a friendship which was well known in Singapore, and it was extremely likely that the meeting described by Conrad, where the two old friends discussed the affairs of the port on the Esplanade in the evening, was one which had taken place many times. It was very likely also that they reflected on such occasions that conditions were 'not so in our time' and that Ellis might have remarked, 'Of all the people on it [the island of Singapore] there seems only you and I left to remember this part of the world as it used to be.'[24]

The actual friendship is described in the article, 'Port Admiral Gamp' (see p. 199, above):

> The Admiral [nickname for the Master-Attendant] and an old ship-mate had both been officers in the Royal Indian Marine Service, and were both warm-hearted and hasty-tempered Irishmen. B. joined the merchant service about the same time that E. became Master Attendant, and their old friendship was renewed as the former came into port—he then in command of a three-masted schooner trading between Singapore and the southern ports of China...Eventually he left the sea, very poorly off, and was practically supported by the Board of Trade, through the recommendation of the Admiral, who was still a warm friend and many a crack the two old shipmates had.

Here we have the Whalley–Eliott relationship—Whalley no longer wealthy, meeting his friend Eliott in port. Indeed

Whalley, at one point, recalls the earlier days of their friendship: 'Not a bad fellow the pleasant, jolly Ned Eliott; friendly, well up to his business—and always a bit of a humbug...When the *Condor* and the *Ringdove* happened to be in port together, she [Whalley's wife] would frequently ask him to bring Captain Eliott to dinner. They had not met often since those old days.'[25]

It seems likely, therefore, that Conrad knew of this long-lasting friendship and of the different fortunes of the two men and made use of it in 'The End of the Tether'.

Captain Eliott/Ellis is an excellent example of Conrad's use of scattered gossip, which he heard in the port of Singapore, to create a substantial fictional figure.

*

In *The Shadow-Line*, Conrad gives certain information about the owner of the 'Eastern ship' in which the narrator of the story has had a berth for 'the past eighteen months'. This short inset biography was founded upon what Conrad knew of the owner of the *Vidar*:

> He was the head of a great House of Straits Arabs, but as loyal a subject of the complex British Empire as you could find east of the Suez Canal. World politics did not trouble him at all, but he had a great occult power amongst his own people...He had to employ white men in the shipping part of his business, and many of those he so employed had never set eyes on him from the first to the last day. I myself saw him but once, quite accidentally on a wharf—an old, dark little man blind in one eye, in a snowy robe and yellow slippers. He was having his hand severely kissed by a crowd of Malay pilgrims to whom he had done some favour, in the way of food and money. His almsgiving, I have heard, was most extensive, covering almost the whole Archipelago. For isn't it said that 'the charitable man is the friend of Allah'? (p. 3).

The *Singapore and Straits Directory* for 1883 records Syed Mohsin Bin Salleh Al Jooffree as a merchant and ship-owner of 36 Raffles Place, owner of the steamers *Eastern Isles*, *Vidar*, *Tlang Wat Seng*, *Emily I*, and with branch houses in 'Brow and Bulungan* and agencies at Samarang, Soerabaya, Bally, Macassar, Pulo Laut, Saigon, Penang, Galle, Karical, Aden, Jeddah and Suez'. By the time Conrad joined the *Vidar* the trading situation for Syed Mohsin was not so prosperous. The *Singapore and Straits Directory* for 1887 shows that by 30 September 1887 Syed Mohsin was owner of only two ships, the *Vidar* and the *Emily I*.

Members of two leading Arab families living in Singapore today have confirmed that Syed Mohsin was well known as a merchant and a famous owner of ships. He is said to have been known as far afield as Jeddah, Java, Celebes, India and Burma. He was, as Conrad puts it, 'head of a great House of Straits Arabs', and as a Syed, or male descendant of Fatimah, daughter of Mohammed, would be held in reverence and considered by the Malays to have occult powers.

Charles Burton Buckley writes that Syed Mohsin was 'very well known and liked in Singapore by many of the European community',[26] whilst J. H. Drysdale, onetime chief engineer in the S.S. *Vidar*, recalls in 'Awakening of Old Memories'[27] how he once encountered the owner, Syed Mohsin, about to come down the engine-room ladder to have a look round. This seems to disprove Conrad's report that 'many of those he...employed had never set eyes on him [the owner] from the first to the last day', but we have to take into account that Drysdale first came to Singapore in 1872. Perhaps by 1887 Syed Mohsin had given up this custom.

Drysdale makes no reference to Syed Mohsin being 'blind in one eye' but Syed Mohsin's obituary in the *Singapore Free Press* on 22 May 1894, as well as providing us with much

* Compare *Almayer's Folly*: '...the up-country canoes glided past the little rotten wharf of Lingard & Co., to paddle up the Pantai branch, and cluster round the new jetty belonging to Abdulla' (p. 32), 'Syed Abdulla was the great man and trader of the Pantai' (p. 31). Syed Abdulla was the elder son of Syed Mohsin.

information about the trader, confirms what Conrad has to say:

Another of the old faces of Singapore has passed away to-day in Syed Massim bin Sallie Al Jeoffrie, an Arab merchant who twenty or thirty years ago had a large business and owned several steamers in this place. He first came to Singapore about 1840, as the Nakodah, or master, of an Arabian trading vessel, and having then saved a few dollars he opened a small shop in Arab Street. In time he amassed a good deal of money and bought some steamers, and was a rich man; but his business did not continue to prosper, for times changed and the old systems of thirty or forty years before were no longer successful after the many changes which the opening of the Suez Canal and speedy steamer communication to all the native countries round Singapore brought about. In 1891 he was compelled to place his affairs in the hands of trustees for his creditors, and about that time his eye-sight, which had been failing for some time, failed almost completely. His office for many years was in the building next to the former Oriental Bank premises which are just being pulled down. There was, perhaps, no native merchant better known in Singapore in the old days than Syed Massim was, but of late years, in his misfortune, he has been little known except to the older residents. He has been very ill for some weeks and his death was expected. The funeral took place this afternoon at 2 o'clock and there was a very large crowd of persons. All the principal Arabs, and many of the old European residents were present. He was close upon 80 years of age.

His death was registered by his eldest son, Syed Abdulla of *Almayer's Folly*.

‘THE SHADOW-LINE’

EXACT AUTOBIOGRAPHY

10

FIRST COMMAND

The Shadow-Line, because of Conrad's own claims for the book, involves us in a different kind of quest. Unlike *Lord Jim*, which depends on the experience of others, *The Shadow-Line* is autobiographical. Its source lies, therefore, in Conrad's direct experience, of which he is the only chronicler. We cannot turn to extensive reports in official documents or in newspapers, or to references in travel books. And so the difficulties in reaching his actual experience are immense. He subtitles this story 'A Confession', and while one would not claim that structure in Conrad's work is an unfailing test, one must remark that the simplicity of form, the straightforwardness of the narrative, the lack of the more complex techniques of story-telling which he uses elsewhere suggest the autobiographical influence. And we have Conrad's own word for its accuracy.

In 1917 Conrad wrote two letters on the subject of *The Shadow-Line*, one to his agent, J. B. Pinker, the other to his friend, Sidney Colvin. Both letters emphasize that this story is exact autobiography. To Pinker he wrote of 'that piece of work—which is not a story really but exact autobiography',[1] and to Colvin he stated, 'The very speeches are (I won't say authentic—they are that absolutely) I believe, verbally accurate. And all this happened in March–April, 1887.'[2] This would appear to settle the matter except for one or two discrepancies. For example, the main episode with which he deals in *The Shadow-Line*, and which forms the background to 'Falk'—his first command—took place not in March–April 1887, but in January–March 1888. This might well be a slip of memory on Conrad's part, but as a result of these assurances it has been accepted[3] that what Conrad had written in *The Shadow-Line* and in parts of 'Falk' gave an accurate account of his first command. The rediscovery of the facts of Conrad's experience at this time shows that *The Shadow-Line* cannot be accepted in *all* its details as 'exact autobiography', and this applies with greater force to 'Falk', which is subtitled 'A Reminiscence'.

I have no doubt that Conrad began to write *The Shadow-Line* as autobiography. His Author's Note here is most interesting:

> Perhaps if I had published this tale...under the title of *First Command*, no suggestion of the Supernatural would have been found in it... Primarily the aim of this piece of writing was the presentation of certain facts which certainly were associated with the change from youth...to the more self-conscious and more poignant period of maturer life...it *is* personal experience seen in perspective with the eye of the mind...The effect of perspective in memory is to make things loom large because the essentials stand out isolated from their surroundings of insignificant daily facts...[4]

This reveals his awareness that what was begun as biography had been caught up by the imaginative process and turned into something else. The change had involved the introduction of the supernatural element which bothered some readers so much; but this did not invalidate the theme of the maturing process—rather it heightened and enlarged it.

*

The Shadow-Line begins with the narrator suddenly and inexplicably giving up his berth on the ship in which he has sailed for eighteen months. Probably, just as inexplicably, Conrad, on 4 January 1888, gave up his berth as first mate in the *Vidar*. He describes this ship at the beginning of *The Shadow-Line*:

> She was an Eastern ship, inasmuch as then she belonged to that [an Eastern] port. She traded among dark islands on a blue reef-scarred sea, with

the Red Ensign over the taffrail and at her masthead a house-flag, also red, but with a green border and with a white crescent in it. For an Arab owned her, and a Syed at that (pp. 2–3).*

After leaving the *Vidar*, Conrad stayed at the Sailors' Home in Singapore until 19 January, when he went to Bangkok to take command of the *Otago*. This is also the situation of the narrator in *The Shadow-Line*, who is staying at the Officers' Sailors' Home in an Eastern port, waiting for a passage home, when he is offered the command of a ship which is then at Bangkok. The same basic situation from his own experience involving the ship in Bangkok and the finding of a new commander for her appears also in 'Falk' and 'The End of the Tether', but there are some differences of detail in each of the three versions of the incident and it is intriguing to attempt to determine what was the truth of the matter so far as Conrad was concerned.

In *The Shadow-Line* the narrator is told by the Master-Attendant that he is to take command of a sailing ship whose master had died at Bangkok. The Consul-General there had telegraphed to him to find a replacement. The narrator later learns from the first mate of the ship, however, that the master died at sea and was buried in the Gulf of Siam. In this version, a sailor called Hamilton tries to obtain the command intended for the narrator. In 'Falk' the narrator is appointed 'ex officio' by the British Consul, to take over from a captain who had died suddenly. In 'The End of the Tether' the Master-Attendant forces the reluctant loafer Hamilton to take over a ship after he has received a cable from Her Majesty's Consul-General in French Cochin-China asking him to fill the place of a master who had died in Saigon.

Conrad is certainly making use here of his own appointment to the command of the *Otago*, but we cannot be certain

* And if we are thinking in terms of the 'exactness' of the story, then these facts about the *Vidar* are all accurate. See my article 'Conrad and the *Vidar*', *RES* (May 1963).

which of these versions is the closest to the facts, so far as the sailor Hamilton is concerned. Certainly, the version in *The Shadow-Line*, in which Hamilton tries to get the berth for himself, is the most dramatic, but it may be that the version in 'The End of the Tether' in which Hamilton is offered the job and objects that 'he did not think the berth was good enough' is closer to the truth. Perhaps the berth *was* offered to another sailor who refused it, and was then offered to Conrad. Conrad must have been very much a foreigner in speech at this time, and it is possible that a properly qualified Englishman might have been offered the position first, particularly if, as Conrad stresses in two of the versions, that Englishman had been running up bills at the Officers' Home. In support of this theory, there was a C. Hamilton in the East who is mentioned in the *Singapore and Straits Directory*, 1883, the year of Conrad's first visit to Singapore. In 1883 Hamilton was first mate of the S.S. *Martaban*. There is no way of determining, since most marine records have been destroyed, whether this was the Hamilton of Conrad's novels, but First Officer Hamilton would know the sea route from Singapore to Bangkok very well, for the regular run of the *Martaban* was from Singapore to Bangkok.[5] Therefore, if Hamilton had left the *Martaban* by 1887 the Master-Attendant would probably have offered him the command of the *Otago* first. This must remain speculation, but certainly the grounds on which the command is refused in 'The End of the Tether' might have been considered valid ones by a sailor accustomed to a steamship. The Master-Attendant's outburst: 'Afraid of the sails. Afraid of a white crew. Too much trouble. Too much work', could be applied to the *Otago*, which was a sailing ship and which carried a white crew.

It is interesting to note the different ways in which Conrad introduces this experience of his into three different tales. In *The Shadow-Line*, obtaining the command is a major motif of the first part of the story—a significant introduction of a young sailor about to cross 'the shadow-line' into a new area involving the intrigues and machinations of men. In 'Falk', the appointment is put briefly away in a paragraph in order to explain the narrator's presence in the Eastern capital and his meeting with Captain Falk, the hero of the tale. In 'The End of the Tether', it is introduced as part of the Master-Attendant's gossip with his old friend Captain Whalley. The latter use is perhaps most interesting, as Conrad has put part of his own story into the fictional gossip of the port in which it occurred.

The telegram from Her Majesty's Consul-General in Bangkok announcing the need for a master has never been discovered and, therefore, it is not possible to find out whether there was, between its arrival and the appointment of the new master to the *Otago*, a lapse of time during which the berth might have been offered first to another sailor. But it is certain that the Master-Attendant was in a hurry to bring about Conrad's departure for Bangkok. The memorandum from Ellis found in Conrad's papers and now in the Keating Collection at Yale does not give Conrad any time for second thoughts: 'This is to inform you that you are required to proceed today in the S.S. *Melita* to Bangkok and you will report your arrival to the British Consul and produce this memorandum which will show that I have engaged you to be Master of the *Otago* in accordance with the Consul's telegram...'[6] This memorandum shows that Conrad, when he wrote *The Shadow-Line*, did not change the name of the ship that took him from Singapore to Bangkok—it was the *Melita* in fact as well as in the story. No record has survived of Conrad reporting to the Consul in Bangkok, but I have discovered a letter, preserved in the Public Record Office, London, from Henry Ellis, the Master-Attendant in Singapore, to the Consul in Bangkok (Plates 8 and 9). Like the memorandum it is dated 19 January 1888, and there is a discrepancy in the name of the ship in which Conrad was to travel, which suggests that the letter preceded the memorandum by some hours.

Sir,

I have the honor to acknowledge the receipt of your telegram 'can you engage Master to take "Otago" from Bangkok to Melbourne salary £14 a month to come here by first steamer and sail at once' to which I replied 'Master engaged proceed "Hecate"'.

The person I have engaged is Mr Conrad Korzeniowski, who holds a certificate of Competency as Master from the Board of Trade. He bears a good character from the several vessels, he has sailed out of this Port. I have agreed with him that his wages at £14 per month to count from date of arrival at Bangkok, ship to provide him with food and all necessary articles for the navigation of the vessel. His passage from Singapore to Bangkok to be paid by the ship, also on his arrival at Melbourne if his services be dispensed with, the owner to provide him with a cabin passage back to Singapore.

I consider the above terms are cheap, reasonable, and trust will meet with your approval.

I have the honor to be
Sir
Your Obedient Servant
HENRY ELLIS
Master Attendant S.S.

Conrad did not travel from Singapore to Bangkok in the *Hecate*, though obviously the Master-Attendant had originally intended that he should. The reason for the change of plan seems to have been that the *Hecate* was late in arriving at Singapore. The *Singapore Free Press*, weekly edition, 23 January 1888, gives the arrival and departure dates of both the *Hecate* and the *Melita*. The *Hecate* did not arrive from Bangkok until 19 January, whereas the *Melita* arrived on 17 January. Both ships stayed two days in Singapore before being cleared for Bangkok. According to the newspaper they both did the Bangkok–Singapore run regularly, and Conrad is keeping to the facts of his experience when he says, 'I... refrained from questioning him [the captain of the *Melita*] as to the appearance of my ship, though I knew that being in Bangkok every month or so he must have known her by sight.'[7] Since Conrad went on board the *Melita* on 19 January, her master had probably last seen the *Otago* when he left Bangkok on 12 January (*Bangkok Times*, 14 January 1888).

There is one further circumstance which seems to confirm that the *Hecate* had been expected earlier in Singapore and that Ellis was not prepared to wait for her arrival when she was delayed. It also suggests that Conrad was dealing with fact when he describes the displeasure of the master of the *Melita* at having to carry a passenger: '"You are the first passenger I ever had in my life, and I hope to goodness you will be the last."...For the four days he had me on board he did not depart from that half-hostile attitude.'[8] There is no record in the *Straits Times* of passengers listed for the *Melita* during the period January 1887 to January 1888. On her previous voyage she had carried 93 bullocks from Bangkok to Singapore. If she was accustomed to carry only cargo, the master's irateness over his passenger would be accounted for and Ellis's desire to get Conrad to Bangkok as quickly as possible confirmed. The name of the master—'the first really unsympathetic man I had ever come in contact with'[9]—was given in the *Singapore Free Press* as Morck, though there is some doubt about this since the *Bangkok Times* gives his name as Moretz.

Conrad states in *The Shadow-Line* that the journey to Bangkok took four days, which is exact. The *Bangkok Times*, 28 January 1888, reported under arrivals: 'Jan. 24th *Melita* Gr. Steamer 389 tons Capt. Moretz.' The *Melita* departed again for Singapore three days later, leaving Conrad to his first command.

II

CONRAD'S PREDECESSOR ON THE 'OTAGO'

The Shadow-Line celebrates Conrad's pride in his first command, the 'little barque' of which he always wrote affectionately:

> At the first glance I saw that she was a high-class vessel, a harmonious creature in the lines of her fine body, in the proportioned tallness of her spars. Whatever her age and her history, she had preserved the stamp of her origin...she looked like a creature of high breed—an Arab steed in a string of cart-horses (pp. 60–1).*

But his joy in the first sight of his ship is soon marred by 'the bitter flavour' of his interview with Mr Burns, the mate, when he is told the fate of the previous captain, and receives Mr Burns's hints as to who ought to have taken over the command.

A central motif of *The Shadow-Line* evolves from the contrast between the previous captain of the barque and the narrator who takes over the command. The previous master, suffering from some form of insanity, brought his vessel close to destruction, and the ship was kept 'loafing' at sea and had to weather a typhoon. Conrad's fictional account of the previous master and of the difficulties the ship underwent as a result of his behaviour have been accepted by biographers as an account of the master of the *Otago* and the history of the barque before Conrad took over. In the absence of any documentary evidence this was understandable. But I have been able to discover enough fresh evidence to allow us to reconstruct the true history of the *Otago* before Conrad

* See Appendix G, p. 320, below, for the history of the *Otago*.

became master and this shows that we can no longer take the fictional account in *The Shadow-Line* as fact.

The previous master in *The Shadow-Line*:

...was a peculiar man—about sixty-five—iron-grey, hard-faced, obstinate, and uncommunicative. He used to keep the ship loafing at sea for inscrutable reasons. Would come on deck at night sometimes, take some sail off her, God only knows why or wherefore, then go below, shut himself up in his cabin, and play on the violin for hours—till daybreak, perhaps...It came out that this stern, grim, wind-tanned, rough, sea-salted, taciturn sailor of sixty-five was not only an artist, but a lover as well... in Mr Burns's own words, 'mixed up' with some woman. Mr Burns had had no personal knowledge of that affair, but positive evidence of it existed in the shape of a photograph taken in Haiphong. Mr Burns found it in one of the drawers in the captain's room.

In due course I, too, saw that amazing human document...There he sat, with his hands reposing on his knees, bald, squat, grey, bristly, recalling a wild boar somehow... (pp. 71–2).

In the earlier story 'Falk', Conrad provides us with substantially the same situation:

I found besides a large account-book, which, when opened, hopefully turned out to my infinite consternation to be filled with verses—page after page of rhymed doggerel of a jovial and improper character, written in the neatest minute hand I ever did see. In the same fiddle-case a photograph of my predecessor, taken lately in Saigon, represented in front of a garden view, and in company of a female in strange draperies, an elderly, squat, rugged man of stern aspect in a clumsy suit of black broadcloth, and with the hair brushed forward above the temples in a manner reminding one of a boar's tusks (p. 177).

There are slight differences between the two physical descriptions of the deceased captain in *The Shadow-Line* and 'Falk'. In *The Shadow-Line* he is 'hard-faced, obstinate, and uncommunicative...bald, squat, grey, bristly, recalling a wild boar'. His age is given as sixty-five. In 'Falk' he is also 'squat' and of 'stern aspect', 'elderly', but instead of being bald he has hair which is 'brushed forward above the temples in a manner reminding one of a boar's tusks'.

Through the *Otago*'s registration certificate, I discovered that the captain previous to Conrad was a Captain John Snadden, and inquiries in Australia eventually put me in contact with his descendants, who were able to provide a photograph of him taken just before he left Australia for Haiphong on his last voyage in the *Otago* (Plate 10). He sailed from Newcastle, New South Wales, on 6 August 1887 with a cargo of 548 tons of coal (*Newcastle Morning Herald and Miners' Advocate*, 6 August 1887).*

I may say I was eager to get a photograph of Snadden because of Conrad's description of the one left in the fiddle-case. This photograph must have preceded the one Conrad mentions by only a few months and it shows that Conrad had most probably seen a photograph of Snadden and had it in mind at least while writing his description in *The Shadow-Line*. Snadden is a man of stern, even fierce aspect. Though only fifty at the time, he looks more, and sixty-five would be a reasonable assessment of his age. He is bald and has what might be described as a bristly beard, and even the analogy 'recalling a wild boar' might seem to be apt.

Conrad may actually have found a large account-book 'filled with verses—page after page of rhymed doggerel of a jovial and improper character' though it is unlikely to have been written 'in the neatest minute hand' the narrator had ever seen. A specimen of Snadden's writing shows that on the contrary his was a large sprawling hand. One of Snadden's sons also became a shipmaster and was a poet in his own right, most of his poetry being nautical verse, and Mrs Harvey, a

* Some twenty-seven years before his death Snadden had presented himself for an examination in order to gain his certificate of competency as mate of foreign-going ships. This gives the following information: John Snadden was born at Kirkcaldy, Fifeshire, on 9 May 1837. At the time he took the examination he was living at Little Bedford Street, North Shields, Northumberland, and he received his mate's certificate on 29 October 1860 when he was twenty-three. He had served at Shields as cook, seaman, boatswain and boatswain's mate. A. T. Saunders stated in a letter to the *Nautical Magazine* in June 1921 that he had known Snadden for 'twenty-five years'. If this is so, Snadden must have left England within two years of taking his certificate.

granddaughter of Snadden's, has stated that there is a family tradition that her grandfather wrote verse.

A certain mystery surrounds the death of the *Otago*'s former master. Conrad gives different versions of his death in *The Shadow-Line* and 'Falk', but he also presents the whole incident so vividly that it would seem that he must have been given a description of Snadden's illness and the details of his death.

Mr Burns, the first mate, tells the narrator in *The Shadow-Line* of the previous captain's death. The captain having got himself mixed up with a woman in Haiphong, the ship 'was kept sweltering at anchor for three weeks'. After vanishing for a week, the master reappeared and took the ship out to sea. Having bumped her on a reef, he 'informed Mr Burns that he had made up his mind to take the ship to Hong-Kong and dry-dock her there'. This meant beating it up to Hong-Kong against a fierce monsoon, 'an insane project'. The captain 'shut up in his cabin...played the violin...It was obvious that he was ill in some mysterious manner...The water-tanks were low, they had not gained fifty miles in a fortnight.' In desperation, Mr Burns tells the captain '...you haven't many days left in [the world]...One can see it by your face...I've shaped a course for Pulo Condor...When we make it...you'll tell me into what port you wish me to take the ship...' The captain died and was buried at the entrance of the Gulf of Siam, latitude 8° 20′. Mr Burns then 'stuck the ship's head north and brought her in [to Bangkok]'.

Not all of this story is based on the actual experiences of the *Otago*. I have discovered three documents—the crew list of the *Otago*, indorsements attached to this, and a letter from Snadden to his wife—which show that Captain Snadden was not so irrational as the master in the story and that the events leading to the ship's arrival in Bangkok were not as Conrad describes them.

The *Otago* was, as Conrad records in *The Shadow-Line*, in Haiphong for three weeks. An indorsement by the Consul at Haiphong attached to the crew list shows that the *Otago* arrived in Haiphong on 29 October 1887 and departed for Hong Kong on 22 November. (See back end-papers.) Obviously then, Captain Snadden had decided to sail to Hong Kong before leaving Haiphong and this was *not* the 'insane project' of a sick man, for it was a journey of only 482 miles. At that time of year Captain Snadden would not expect his ship to meet with such a fierce monsoon that she made less than 'fifty miles in a fortnight'. December is outside the season of typhoons. If the *Otago* encountered one, it was exceptional,* but certainly the ship put back before she reached Hong Kong, and certainly Captain Snadden was taken ill.

On 5 December he was so ill as to be unable to write, and on that day he dictated a letter to his wife and children, which was taken down by the mate Born (Conrad's Burns). In this letter (Plates 10 and 11) he says that he has been ill for over a week. His illness, therefore, must have dated from 28 November 1887 at least, six days out from Haiphong. He died on 8 December 1887, according to a further indorsement to the crew list by the Consul at Bangkok, which states:

> I hereby certify that the mate on entering [the port of Bangkok] reported the death on December 8/87 of the Master John Snadden to H.M. Consul and that the entries in the Official Log Book regarding the occurrence were shown to H.M. Consul and signed by him. Agreement deposited December 20/87 and returned Feb 1/88. C. E. W. Stringer, for H.M. Consul (dated 1 February 1888).

The *South Australian Register*, 1 February 1888, reports that John Snadden died of heart disease, and this is confirmed by Snadden's letter: 'The worry...has at last affected my heart so much that I am compelled to resign shortly to nature...'

* The typhoon in *Typhoon* is also exceptional for it occurs in December in the same area. Conrad may have had in mind the typhoon encountered by the *Otago*.

Conrad must have known from the ship's log and from his chief mate that the captain died from heart trouble and not from some 'mysterious illness'.

But Captain Snadden *was* buried at sea, though the precise position of the ship at the time is not given in any document. In *The Shadow-Line*, the mate, in his delirium, insists that the captain was 'buried in latitude 8° 20′...ambushed at the entrance of the Gulf [of Siam]'.[1] The truth, so far as Conrad knew it, is likely to be found in manuscript form, since Conrad frequently began by writing the facts of his sources and later modified them. In the 'Falk' manuscript, Conrad writes: '... the remains of his captain [were shot] overboard somewhere off Cap St Jacques.' Cap St Jacques might very well have been the place of Snadden's burial. It is some distance from the Gulf of Siam, on the route to Pulo Condor—off the coast of Cochin-China, in fact. This might account for Conrad's mention of Saigon and French Cochin-China when he refers briefly to the *Otago* story in 'The End of the Tether'. Snadden died on 8 December and his barque arrived at Bangkok on 20 December (see indorsements by Consuls) which suggests a longer journey than that from the mouth of the Gulf. It seems certain that Snadden was *not* buried at the mouth of the Gulf of Siam and that therefore Conrad could not have been harassed by his first mate's superstitious fears in this matter as is suggested by *The Shadow-Line*, since the *Otago*, on her way to Singapore, would not pass near Snadden's burial place.

Moreover, the letter dictated by Snadden (Plates 10 and 11) and part of the mate's covering letter* suggest that relations between the two men were not as they are represented in *The Shadow-Line*, or in the text of 'Falk'. Snadden writes: '...the Chief Mate, Mr Chas Born...has been very kind during my illness.' It is more likely that the version of the relationship

* See Appendix F, p. 319, below.

presented in the 'Falk' manuscript but excised from the published text is the true one:

The mate who had brought the ship into harbour, after shooting the remains of his captain over-board somewhere off Cap St Jacques turned sulky on my joining...He either gave me underhand gloomy glances as though I had been a sort of gloomy ghoul or else wearying me with a persistent scrutinising stare would keep on in a low and monotonous voice through every meal relating the story of my predecessor's last moment, he referred to him as the Captain. What the Captain said. What he said. How the Captain looked lying there on that couch where I was sitting then. How all hands were called into the cabin to see the captain die, and so on, and so on, over and over again with the same minute and horrible details. Whether he wanted to bore me to death or only was trying to scare me out of the ship I can't tell; but it came to this at last that when I saw him approaching me I felt ready to howl. Shivers ran down my back every time he opened his mouth. I lost my appetite and shirked coming to table (MS, p. 7).

Since Captain Snadden knew for some days that he was dying—'I may linger on a little longer but finally in a few hours or days I must say good bye to all'—it was very likely that he took leave of his men in the manner suggested here, and that Conrad had this from Born (Burns).* Conrad may have made use of this excised passage to refresh his memory of the incident when he came to write *The Shadow-Line* fourteen years later. In that story the young master asks:

'Where did he die?'

'In this saloon. Just where you are sitting now,' answered Mr Burns...

His tale was that at seven bells in the forenoon watch he had all hands mustered on the quarter-deck, and told them that they had better go down to say good-bye to the captain.

Those words, as if grudged to an intruding personage, were enough

* The narrator in *The Shadow-Line* describes the final hours of the late master: 'That night he used the last of his strength to throw his fiddle over the side. No one had actually seen him in the act, but after his death Mr Burns couldn't find the thing anywhere. The empty case was very much in evidence, but the fiddle was clearly not in the ship. And where else could it have gone to but overboard?' (p. 76). According to Mrs Harvey, John Snadden's granddaughter, he did play the violin and he had his instrument on board the *Otago*, but he did not throw it overboard since it was 'sent home with his belongings' (letter of 31 July 1963).

for me to evoke vividly that strange ceremony: The barefooted, bare-headed seamen crowding shyly into that cabin, a small mob pressed against that sideboard, uncomfortable rather than moved, shirts open on sunburnt chests, weather-beaten faces, and all staring at the dying man with the same grave and expectant expression (pp. 69–70).

The previous master of the barque is contrasted most strongly with the narrator in *The Shadow-Line*, and the contrast is dramatically effective. The previous captain's dying speech was:

'If I had my wish, neither the ship nor any of you would ever reach a port. And I hope you won't.'...the end of his life was...the betrayal of a tradition which seemed to me as imperative as any guide on earth could be (pp. 75–7).

Burns exclaims:

He wouldn't write to his owners, he never wrote to his old wife either—he wasn't going to. He had made up his mind to cut adrift from everything. That's what it was. He didn't care for business, or freights, or for making a passage—or anything. He meant to have gone wandering about the world till he lost her with all hands (p. 76).

Jean-Aubry concludes from the evidence of 'Falk' and *The Shadow-Line*: 'The new captain must have been profoundly shocked by the evidences of his predecessor's complete disregard of the principles and traditions of the position he himself was about to fill for the first time.'[2]

But Conrad's portrayal of this character was not exact biography where Captain John Snadden was concerned. In a letter to the *Nautical Magazine*, Saunders, clerk in the firm of Henry Simpson and Sons, part owners of the *Otago*, objected:

The account of Captain Snadden in the *Shadowline* is absurd, but I do not blame Joseph Conrad for it. Captain Snadden was not an uncommunicative man; he was rather loquacious and never kept his ship loafing at sea.*

The fact that the *Otago*, a very small sailing vessel, left Newcastle, Australia, for Haiphong on 6 August 1887 and arrived there on 29 October of the same year does not suggest

* See Appendix H, p. 322, below.

that the captain was 'loafing'. Moreover, he did write to his wife, and there is no suggestion that he was not concerned for the safety of his ship and her crew. Charles Born wrote to Mrs Snadden, 'He told me to look after the vessel as well as I could.'*

A letter to Conrad from James Simpson of the firm of Henry Simpson and Sons has been taken to confirm Conrad's portrayal of Snadden:

> The accounts which you enclosed are no doubt at all in order but I have no means of comparing them with other documents as the late Captain never favoured me with a scratch of the pen from the time of leaving Newcastle in August last and the acting Master Mr Born only wrote me a brief note acquainting me with his Captain's death. Therefore, I am at loss to know what business was done by the ship after she arrived at Haiphong, whether she earned or whether she lost money. In fact, other than your documents, I have no record whatever of receipts and expenditure. Will you, therefore, please inform me whether any freight was obtained between Haiphong and Bangkok and if so, how much and generally what business was done by the ship for the ten months previous to your assuming command? (5 April 1888.)

This letter seems to me to distort the facts of the case. Simpson could hardly have expected any communication from Captain Snadden until the ship reached Haiphong, since her cargo of coal was destined for this port. He might legitimately complain that he had not heard from her master since her arrival at Haiphong, but Snadden was taken ill six days after leaving Haiphong and states in his last letter that his illness is caused by the worry over the Simpson Agency. I think there was a disagreement between Simpson and Snadden which is reflected in the tone of Simpson's letter, but, far from being negligent, Snadden was extremely concerned about his ship. It must be remembered also that Snadden and Simpson were joint owners of the *Otago*.† The

* See Appendix F, p. 319, below.

† According to Simpson's letter Snadden had two shares in the *Otago*; these could not have been negligible since he was able to force the sale of the ship: 'As to what will

Registrar of British Ships, Customs House, Adelaide, shows that J. Snadden and J. L. Simpson were registered as the *Otago*'s owners on 12 November 1886, and presumably Snadden had as much say as Simpson in the business done by the ship.

Snadden's concern for his business interests after his death seems to reflect his worry over this partnership, and hence his detailed instructions to his wife in his last letter: 'My business matter[s] are in the hands of J. P. Hodge as Agent Port Adelaide and should you require further advice consult D. Bews Esq. J. Taylor and A. F. Taylor.' And hence also his statement: 'No doubt they [the Simpsons?] will jump on you now, as it has been in all cases nearly.'

The Shadow-Line does not, therefore, give a true account of Captain Snadden. Conrad must have found an account of the ship's journey from Haiphong to Bangkok in her log and possibly knew something of the true story of her master. Born must have added his version, and Conrad probably heard Simpson's point of view when he visited the Simpsons' home in Australia. I have obtained a letter which James Simpson's wife wrote to Saunders on 2 May 1917 in which she says:

> Your letter giving Joseph Conrad's message and address reached me yesterday—Thank you very much for it—We all remember with pleasure Capt Korsenowskis' [*sic*] visits to us at Woodville—The boys used to enjoy him as much as my husband and I did. I will write to him.

But dramatically, the story Conrad gives of the previous captain's character and last days is more effective than the true one in that the contrast between the old master and the new is more striking. It also serves to complicate the predicament of the new master in taking over his first command, but it cannot be claimed as exact autobiography.

be done later on, nothing has yet been determined, but probably the late Captain's executors will wish the vessel sold in the interest of the widow and mortgagees.' Simpson finally bought these two shares from the Snadden family but not until 18 December 1889.

12

THE DELAY IN BANGKOK

Conrad stresses in both *The Shadow-Line* and 'Falk' the difficulties and delays which the respective narrators encountered in trying to get their vessels out of harbour: 'The word "Delay" entered the secret chamber of my brain, resounded there like a tolling bell which maddens the ear...'[1] And it is true that the *Otago* was delayed for a considerable time in Bangkok before Conrad was able to get her out of port and on her way to Singapore. A letter to Conrad from William Willis, physician to the British Legation in Siam, seems to be referring to these delays: 'I can speak of my own knowledge that you have done all in your power in the trying and responsible position of Master of the ship to hasten the departure of your vessel from this unhealthy place.'[2] And the letter from Messrs Henry Simpson and Sons confirms that Conrad was unable to leave Bangkok until 8 February: 'Your favours dated Bangkok 2nd and 6th February, latter with P.S. dated 7th on the eve of sailing...'[3] This suggests that Conrad had first hoped to leave about the second and then on the sixth, and was finally delayed until 8 or 9 February. The *Bangkok Times*, because it gives the wrong departure date for the *Otago*, would seem to confirm that Conrad made efforts to get the ship out earlier. On 4 February 1888 the newspaper records in its Shipping Departure list: 'Feb. 1. *Otago* Br. Bk. for Sydney.'

Conrad was in Bangkok, therefore, from 24 January to 9 February 1888; if we combine the accounts given in *The Shadow-Line* and 'Falk', we find that several reasons are given for this delay. In 'Falk' the narrator says: 'The crew was sickly, the cargo was coming very slow; I foresaw I would have lots of trouble with the charterers, and doubted whether they would advance me enough money for the ship's expenses' (p. 178). And there is further delay because Captain Falk refuses to tow him out of the river. In *The Shadow-Line*, the narrator 'foresaw trouble ahead unless the people of the other part were quite exceptionally fair-minded and open to argument'[4] about the charter-party signed by Mr Burns, and 'the men ailed'.[5] If we can accept these fictional accounts, the delay seems to have been due to difficulties with the charterers and in getting cargo, difficulty in getting towage out of the river, and sickness among the crew. For fictional purposes, Conrad emphasizes the towage difficulties in 'Falk' and the sickness in *The Shadow-Line*.

Undoubtedly there was severe sickness among the crew of the *Otago*. William Willis refers to the condition of the crew in his letter to Conrad: '...the crew of the sailing ship *Otago* has suffered severely whilst in Bangkok from tropical diseases, including fever, dysentery and cholera.' The Master-Attendant, Henry Ellis, could hardly have concealed this from the prospective master. But Conrad sets great store by the simple virtue of courage. He had travelled in the derelict *Palestine* which had been deserted by many of her crew; he had travelled up the difficult and little-known Berau river; and he was prepared to take command of a cholera-infected vessel.

However, sickness among the crew was not, I think, quite the dramatic reason for delay that Conrad makes it in *The Shadow-Line*. Conrad tells us that his steward died: 'The first member of the crew fairly knocked over was the steward—the first man to whom I had spoken on board. He was taken ashore (with choleraic symptoms), and died there at the end of a week' (p. 83). This is related slightly differently in the earlier story 'Falk':

> ...and when the steward had to be taken to the hospital ill with choleraic symptoms I felt bereaved of the only decent person at the after end of the

ship. He was fully expected to recover, but in the meantime had to be replaced by some sort of servant. And on the recommendation of a certain Schomberg, the proprietor of the smaller of the two hotels in the place, I engaged a Chinaman... (pp. 178–9).

This incident of the steward's sickness and death has been accepted as a part of Conrad's experience in Bangkok.[6] But a study of the *Bangkok Times* and the Protestant Register of Deaths in Bangkok for the early months of 1888 disproves this. It is true that one of the crew of the *Otago* died in Bangkok, but he died eight days before Conrad's arrival. The entry in the Protestant Cemetery Record is as follows: 'January 16, 1888 John Carlson, age 29, Sweedish [*sic*], sailor bark "Otago"...Cholera.' Included in the crew list is a certificate dated 26 January 1888, stating: 'that John Carlson died in the Bangkok Hospital on Jan. 16 of cholera, that his effects have been burnt at this Cons. Genl. and that the balance of his wages has been paid to me (123.80 dollars). (Sgd.) C. E. W. Stringer for H.M. Consul.' For dramatic purposes, therefore, Conrad made use of the death of Carlson *of which he must have heard* but which was not directly part of his experience.

John Carlson was taken on, as the agreement of crew shows, as 'Cook and Steward' of the ship, and he is mentioned in Captain Snadden's last letter: 'Steward...has been also very kind.' The crew list shows that Conrad had tried to find someone to replace Carlson. He signed on a W. Davis on 27 January 1888 but the engagement was cancelled. I have a copy of a letter from the Consul-General in Bangkok to Saunders which states that in a book at the Consulate offices there are entries for 30 January and 3 February 1888 concerning the engagement of seamen for the *Otago*. These men are not mentioned in the crew list and therefore we can be reasonably certain that the new members of crew refused duty once they discovered that there was cholera on board. We can conclude that the *Otago* was forced to sail without a cook-steward.

Before the departure of the vessel in *The Shadow-Line* the narrator has trouble with his first mate, Burns. Burns also goes down with fever and has to be taken to hospital—actually 'to a sort of sanatorium, a pavilion of bricks which the doctor had in the grounds of his residence'.[7] Burns had said earlier to the young captain, 'If I hadn't a wife and a child at home you may be sure, sir, I would have asked you to let me go the very minute you came on board',[8] and the narrator remarked, 'Before many days had elapsed it was Mr Burns who was pleading with me anxiously not to leave him behind...'

> Then one day, suddenly, a surge of downright panic burst through all this craziness.
>
> If I left him behind in this deadly place he would die. He felt it, he was certain of it...
>
> He produced his wasted forearms from under the sheet which covered him and clasped his fleshless claws. He would die! He would die here...
>
> Next day he upset me thoroughly by renewing his entreaties...The day after...he attacked me at once in a much stronger voice, and with an abundance of argument which was quite startling. He presented his case with a sort of crazy vigour, and asked me finally how would I like to have a man's death on my conscience? He wanted me to promise that I would not sail without him...'But don't ask that doctor, sir. You and I are sailors'...again he pleaded for the promise that I would not leave him behind...That prostrated man, with hardly strength enough to breathe, and ravaged by a passion of fear, was irresistible. And, besides, he had happened to hit on the right words. He and I were sailors (pp. 85–7).

It is important for Conrad's story that the narrator should take his first officer back on board and have to tolerate his morbid fancies about the power of the previous captain: 'And it was not comforting in the least to hear him begin to mutter crazily about the late captain, that old man buried in latitude 8° 20′, right in our way—ambushed at the entrance of the Gulf.'[9]

It is of course possible that the first mate of the *Otago* also went down with fever, but a passage in the 'Falk' manuscript which does not appear in the published text casts doubts on this. The passage in 'Falk' does not refer to the first mate but to the steward, who was taken 'ill with choleraic symptoms' ('Falk'), and who died (*The Shadow-Line*). The passage in the manuscript is as follows:

> He was the nearest approach to the dumb slave of romance I've ever come across. The way he folded my pyjamas in the morning expressed a devotion too profound for words. I took him up myself in a steam launch and the parting was peculiarly harrowing. The poor man in the intervals of his writhing while they were putting him to bed, entreated me not to leave him there. He would rather die on board, he said—anywhere, on the main hatch, in the scuppers. I felt as sorry as though he had been a personal attendant from boyhood (p. 10).

Though Conrad did not himself witness the sickness and death of John Carlson of the *Otago*, he must have had it described to him, and this may well be an authentic account of what happened. When he came to write *The Shadow-Line*, almost twenty-seven years after the event, he had a means of recalling this incident by looking at the 'Falk' manuscript, and he must have seen how much more effective it would be if he transferred the account he had written of the steward's desire to return and die on the ship to Burns. He is most probably making this one example of hearsay do double duty in *The Shadow-Line*.

*

The lack of documents for the period Conrad spent in Bangkok makes it difficult to discover precisely what was the situation with regard to the towage on the river Meinam, the trouble with the charterers, and such incidents in 'Falk' as the affair of the Chinese 'boy' who turned out a thief. But by indirect means we can discover sufficient of the facts to make some suggestions about the actual situation in Bangkok.

The Delay in Bangkok

In the manuscript of Conrad's story 'Falk'[10] there is a description of a newspaper, which does not appear in the published text: 'The dingy, spongy sheet sprinkled thinly with advertisements and edited by the haughty little gentleman in nose nippers called it a "crying shame" and an "impediment to civilisation"' (p. 45). The 'Eastern seaport ...capital of an Eastern kingdom, lying up a river...'[11] in which the story is set is, of course, Bangkok, and the 'crying shame' referred to in this passage is the nuisance caused by a shallow bar at the mouth of the Meinam river on which Bangkok is situated. But this excised passage is of interest to us because the newspaper it describes must have been a Bangkok newspaper, and when Conrad was in Bangkok only one English newspaper was being published—the *Bangkok Times*. Conrad had obviously read this, and his description of it corresponds with the appearance of those copies which I have in my possession. Each issue consists of a single folded sheet carrying, apart from news reports, a number of advertisements.

A study of this newspaper for the period of Conrad's stay in Bangkok gives us an accurate account of certain events which Conrad made use of in his stories, and it also shows that, as they appear in his fiction, these events cannot be taken, as they have been, as facts of Conrad's biography.

Conrad relates in the published text of 'Falk' how, on the death of the steward of his ship, the narrator was forced to employ a Chinese 'boy', which he did on the recommendation of the hotel-keeper Schomberg. The 'boy' proves to be an opium-smoker and a thief and departs with 'thirty-two golden sovereigns' of the narrator's 'hard-earned savings'. Jean-Aubry comments that 'the Chinaman who replaced him [the steward] disappeared after three days with thirty-two pounds, the whole of Conrad's painfully accumulated economies set aside against serious emergencies'.[12] But a report in the

Bangkok Times shows that Conrad was making use of something which happened not to himself but to one of his crew:

> A chinese 'boy' employed on the barque *Otago* managed the other day to steal 15 gold mohurs from a sailor on board, and then to abscond. The captain and mate, however, met the juvenile thief a few hours afterwards in Mr Clarke's compound and arrested him. Whilst being conducted to the Bang Rak Police Station, he unfortunately managed to bolt and has not since been seen. But Mr Clarke's cook, a man named Kam Kow, at once offered a cattie of silver if the matter was quashed and this fact, coupled with his being found in possession of 15 ticals, raised suspicion, so Kam Kow is now in jail. He appears to have been a friend of the 'boy' and thus probably knows his present whereabouts... (*Bangkok Times*, 1 February 1888).

The passage ends with an ironic comment by the editor on the fact that an ordinary seaman should have 15 golden mohurs. As one mohur is worth 15 rupees, the sum involved was about £16 17*s.* 6*d.*, a much smaller sum than that mentioned by Conrad. But the important fact is that the money was not Conrad's own and so Conrad did not lose his 'own hard-earned savings' and could not have felt, as he writes in 'Falk', 'as poor and naked as a fakir'.

A passage in the manuscript of 'Falk' which is not included in the published text shows, I think, Conrad in the process of transferring this experience to himself—or rather to his narrator. In the manuscript he writes, 'to go and face the broken drawer in the cabin on board'.[13] There is nothing personal in this, it is simply the action he would have to take as master of the *Otago*. This passage is crossed out and replaced by references to 'my cabin' and 'my drawer'.

The report's reference to the captain and mate of the *Otago* having 'met' the 'juvenile thief' in 'Mr Clarke's compound' must be a facetious account of the incident. The play on the words 'boy' and 'juvenile thief'—a 'boy' being of course a servant and not a juvenile—suggests this, and it is likely that Conrad and his first mate had actually gone in search of the thief and caught him in Mr Clarke's compound. In 'Falk', the narrator goes in search of a man called Johnson, 'formerly captain of a country ship, but now spliced to a country wife and gone utterly to the bad',[14] hoping that he will give him 'assistance in getting' his 'ship down to the sea, without steam'.[15] In this way the narrator hopes to by-pass the tug-boat master's refusal to tow him out of port. The description of the captain's search for Johnson, with the help of the Consulate's constable, exploring together 'an infinity of infamous grog shops, gambling dens, opium dens', and finally finding Johnson in a 'very clean native compound', where Mrs Johnson, a 'big native woman, with bare brown legs as thick as bed-posts, pursuing on all fours a silver dollar that came rolling out from somewhere',[16] is probably based on Conrad's search for the Chinese steward, and not on his search for a pilot to take him out of the river.

It is interesting to note, as a sidelight on Conrad's re-use of material, that he had already, in writing *Lord Jim*, transferred the search for the Chinese 'boy' to the search for Gentleman Brown:

> I had found him out in Bankok through that busybody Schomberg, the hotel-keeper, who had, confidentially, directed me where to look. It appears that a sort of loafing, fuddled vagabond—a white man living amongst the natives with a Siamese woman—had considered it a great privilege to give a shelter to the last days of the famous Gentleman Brown. While he was talking to me in the wretched hovel...the Siamese woman, with big, bare legs and a stupid, coarse face, sat in a dark corner chewing betel stolidly (pp. 427–8).

In the manuscript of 'Falk' there is a scene set in a police station during which a Eurasian police inspector makes what seems to be a sarcastic remark at the narrator's expense: 'They would catch the chinaman', he said, 'if I liked' (p. 22). This scene appears only in the manuscript version. Perhaps Conrad felt that he did not come out of the episode too well in catching the thief and then allowing him to escape, and therefore did not include the scene in the final text.

Jean-Aubry thought that Falk himself was 'a real person, a Scandinavian captain, who actually refused Conrad the loan of his tug...'.[17] At first it seemed to me, however, that there could be no basis in fact for the story of Falk's refusal to tow the narrator's vessel, since the *Singapore and Straits Directory*, 1887, lists at a date earlier than Conrad's arrival in Bangkok two tugboats as operating on the Meinam river. But the *Directory* was a little premature in this announcement, and Conrad was dealing with fact to some extent, as the *Bangkok Times* proves. Up to 15 February 1888 there was only one tugboat on the Meinam, the *Bangkok*, and her master was a Captain Saxtrop. Three days before Conrad arrived in Bangkok the following item appeared in the newspaper:

> The new steam lighter and tugboat the *Chamroen* passed Port Said safely on the 11th instant, all well. She is intended for service on the Meinam and is owned by Messrs Windsor Rose, & Co., for three-quarter shares, whilst Messrs Jucker, Sigg and Co., hold the rest.

Conrad had already left Bangkok six days before the *Chamroen* arrived. She is reported in the *Bangkok Times* as arriving on 15 February 1888.*

The name Falk, though not the character, was almost certainly taken from the firm of Falck and Beidek, which existed in Bangkok at this time. They ran two stores, one in the upper and one in the lower part of the town (*Singapore and Straits Directory*, 1888). Previous to this date there had been a Falck hotel. In the *Bangkok Times Supplement*, 4 January 1888, there is a report of an attempt to burn down some stables

* Hermann, owner of the *Diana* in 'Falk', is German, and, although there was no *Diana* in Bangkok during Conrad's stay there, there was, according to the *Bangkok Times*, a German steamer called the *Hermann*. Conrad may be recalling this steamer in his description of the *Diana* and transferring the name Hermann to her fictional owner. The master of the *Hermann* was a Captain Traulsen and he may be the original of Falk.

and it is stated that this happened 'not far from where Falck's hotel formerly stood'.

In order to get round Falk's refusal to tow him out of port, the narrator goes to see his firm of charterers, Messrs Siegers, and he interviews the head of the firm. Schomberg had earlier told him that Falk received money from old Mr Siegers—'a good bit of money from the start' for 'it suited their business that there should be good towing facilities on the river'.[18] The narrator interviews the son, the father having 'retired from business on a fortune and got buried at sea going home',[19] but gets no satisfaction, Siegers only reiterating that they 'had... been acquainted with Captain Falk for very many years, and never had any reason...'.[20] The narrator admits there was no love lost between him and the younger Siegers and that they had several passages of arms. 'It took me all I knew to guard the interests of my owners—whom, *nota bene*, I had never seen—while Siegers (who had made their acquaintance some years before, during a business tour in Australia) pretended to the knowledge of their innermost minds...'[21]

It seems more likely that this was the real situation than that the captain of the *Bangkok* refused to tow the *Otago*. The owners of the *Bangkok*—a vessel of 100 horse-power—were Windsor, Rose and Co., and it is difficult to imagine that Saxtrop, the master of the tug-boat, would be allowed to refuse towing facilities to any ship.

The firm of Siegers appears to have been based on an actual firm. In the manuscript of 'Falk', Conrad had originally written the name Yucker and then crossed it out and put Siegers. But Yucker is given as the name of the firm which employed Lord Jim after he had deserted the *Patna* and had had his certificate cancelled:

> ...in Bangkok, where he found employment with Yucker Brothers, charterers and teak merchants...I heard Siegmund Yucker (native of Switzerland), a gentle creature ravaged by a cruel dyspepsia, and so

frightfully lame that his head swung through a quarter of a circle at every step he took, declare...he was 'of great gabasidy'...'Why not send him up country?' I suggested anxiously. (Yucker Brothers had concessions and teak forests in the interior.) (pp. 241–2.)

An exhaustive check of the *Bangkok Directories* has not revealed any Siegers, but there was a Jucker, Sigg and Co., and it is quite clear that Conrad has had these two names in mind in writing *Lord Jim* and 'Falk'. He has used the name of the first partner in the manuscript of 'Falk' and the text of *Lord Jim*, spelling it as it would be pronounced—'Yucker'.* This firm was closely related to Windsor, Rose and Co., important charterers in Bangkok, having shares in the second tug-boat with them. When I visited Bangkok on my Conrad quest, I learnt from Mr E. Jucker (born 1882 and son of Albert Jucker who died 1885) that Jucker, Sigg and Co. were teak merchants. In *Typhoon* Conrad makes use of the name of the second partner Sigg: 'She (the *Nan-Shan*) had been built in Dumbarton less than three years before, to the order of a firm of merchants in Siam—Messrs Sigg and Son.'[22] The use of these names in three consecutive stories—*Lord Jim*, *Typhoon* and 'Falk'—proves that Conrad had Jucker, Sigg and Co. specifically in mind when he came to write these stories.†

By the time Conrad arrived in Bangkok, Albert Jucker himself was dead. The last record of him is in the *Singapore and Straits Directory*, 1885. Conrad's reference to 'Siegers' retiring 'from business on a fortune' and getting 'buried at sea going home'[23] may be a reference to the fate of Gustav

* Conrad does the same kind of thing in *Almayer's Folly*: 'Nina, brought up under the Protestant wing of the proper Mrs Vinck' (p. 49). This is an unusual name, but according to Mrs Oehlers of Singapore, daughter of Jim Lingard, there was a family of Fincks many years ago living here and they took in a few boarders.

† My speculations about Jucker, Sigg and Co. were born out by the St Clair article. The relevant passage is in the letter from Conrad: 'In Bangkok when I took command, I hardly ever left the ship except to go to my charterers (Messrs Jucker, Sigg and Co.).' The firm still exists in Bangkok but its name has changed to Berli, Jucker and Co. Unfortunately they have no old records.

Falck. According to the *Straits Times*, 3 June 1888, Falck arrived in Singapore in the S.S. *Borneo* from Bangkok. That same day his death is recorded in the Register of Deaths, Singapore: 'Gustav Falck, aged 40, German, Dysentery.'*

*

It has been supposed that Conrad met the original of his character Schomberg, the hotel-keeper, in Bangkok, since he introduces him in *Lord Jim* and 'Falk' as living in that port. Jean-Aubry writes: 'It was also at Bangkok that Conrad met that hotelkeeper to whom he gave the name of Schomberg...'[24] Baines also holds this view, though his statement is qualified: 'Here also he apparently came across the preposterous hotel keeper, with his famous *table d'hôte*.'[25]

In following Schomberg from his first appearance in *Lord Jim*, through the manuscript and later versions of 'Falk', until his final appearance in *Victory*, where he is most fully developed, we can see Conrad expanding his initial and limited conception of Schomberg's character. In *Lord Jim* he receives a bare mention:

> Schomberg, the keeper of the hotel where he [Jim] boarded, a hirsute Alsatian of manly bearing and an irrepressible retailer of all the scandalous gossip of the place, would, with both elbows on the table, impart an adorned version of the story to any guest who cared to imbibe knowledge along with the more costly liquors. 'And, mind you, the nicest fellow you could meet,' would be his generous conclusion; 'quite superior' (p. 241).

At this stage, Schomberg is a gossip but in no way an evil person. In 'Falk' he is treated less kindly. Malice becomes a characteristic of his. It gathers momentum when he discusses Captain Falk, and it has its origin in nothing more important

* Other names Conrad may have owed to his stay in Bangkok are: Tesman—'Mr Tesman of Tesman Brothers, a Sourabaya firm—tip-top house' (*Victory*, p. 7), from S. Tisseman, an importer and committee member of the Gymkhana Association; Captain Kent in *The Shadow-Line* from Captain J. Kent of the *Impregnable* in Bangkok harbour at that time.

than that Falk rarely uses his hotel.* Conrad also reveals Schomberg's brutality to his wife: ' "Sit still," he hissed at her, and then, in a hospitable, jovial tone, contrasting amazingly with the angry glance that had made his wife sink in her chair, he cried very loud: "Tiffin still going on in here, gentlemen." '[26] In *Victory*, this attitude towards his wife is developed, and he is introduced into far more of the action of *Victory*. He joins forces with the villain Jones against Heyst, partly because Heyst has taken Lena, a possible mistress for Schomberg, away from his hotel.

Conrad himself, in his Author's Note to the first edition of *Victory*, mentions this development: 'Schomberg is an old member of my company. A very subordinate personage in *Lord Jim* as far back as the year 1899, he became notably active in a certain short story of mine published in 1902. Here he appears in a still larger part...'[27] I suspect that Conrad's use of Schomberg in 'Falk' was an afterthought and that initially he had not thought of developing him as a character. We see this by comparing the manuscript version of 'Falk' with the published text, that part where the narrator is describing the employment of a Chinese steward. In the manuscript he does not at first mention Schomberg: 'Then when the Chinese I engaged (had to engage) of one of the two hotels in the place' (MS, p. 10). This is then crossed out and Schomberg is made to bear the responsibility for the recommendation. In the published text it becomes:

> And on the recommendation of a certain Schomberg, the proprietor of the smaller of the two hotels in the place, I engaged a Chinaman. Schomberg, a brawny, hairy Alsatian, and an awful gossip, assured me that it was all right. 'First-class boy that. Came in the *suite* of his Excellency Tseng the Commissioner—you know...' At the time, however, I did not know what an untrustworthy humbug Schomberg was (p. 179).

* Perhaps both Falk and Heyst have their source in one person and not two separate persons, since Heyst earns Schomberg's hatred for the same reason as Falk—his failure to patronize his hotel.

Schomberg's business difficulties are based upon an actual situation in Bangkok at this time. His antagonism towards Falk shows itself in business terms: 'He makes ten times the money I do. I've another hotel to fight against, and there is no other tug on the river.'[28] In 1888, when Conrad was in Bangkok, there were only two hotels, the Universal and the Oriental. The Universal was the smaller hotel and was owned and managed by Schumaker and Ulrich, while the Oriental, a much larger hotel which is still in existence today, had three proprietors, N. Andersen, P. Andersen, and P. Satorph (*Singapore and Straits Directory*, 1888). Assuming that Schumaker was the active proprietor at the Universal, he could well have been the model for the fictional 'Schomberg, the proprietor of the smaller of the two hotels in the place'.[29] And yet I think not. My own view is that Conrad had another hotel and hotel-keeper in mind.

In *Victory*, Conrad describes Schomberg as a sort of peripatetic hotel-keeper: '...a certain Schomberg, a big, manly, bearded creature of Teutonic persuasion...he was by profession a hotel-keeper, first in Bangkok, then somewhere else, and ultimately in Sourabaya' (p. 20). Even if we could assume that Conrad based Schomberg's character on a hotel-keeper he met in Bangkok at this time, he did not take his name from that port, for I have found no record of the name Schomberg. There was, however, a respectable and respected German broker living in Singapore named Schomburgk, who, when he died in 1911, had had 42 years' continuous residence in Singapore. His establishment was in Bonham Street, a street named after Governor Bonham. Conrad knew this street and introduces it and Governor Bonham into 'The End of the Tether', changing the name to Denham. In the manuscript version of 'The End of the Tether', as I have stated, the name Bonham is written and then crossed out and replaced by Denham. The reference in the printed text is on p. 253: 'Not a single one of that contemptible lot ashore at the "Home" had twopence in his pocket to bless himself with..."They are much more likely one and all to owe money to the Chinamen in Denham Road..."' Conrad no doubt had frequently walked down Bonham Street which is close to the water-front of Singapore and noticed the firm of 'Schomburgk and Co., est. 1867'. Moreover, Conrad must have known of Schomburgk by reputation since he had been a senior partner of the Labuan Trading Company. The men involved in this company were John Dill Ross, a friend of William Lingard's, Captain Cowie and Karl Schomburgk. This company was engaged in running the Spanish blockade of the Philippines in the late 1870's. Also Schomburgk was a friend of Captain Schuck, a well-known mariner in Eastern waters, who died in the Singapore hospital on 24 July 1887. Conrad had been in hospital some eighteen days by then. Conrad, indeed, may have been introduced to Schomburgk who was likely to have visited his great friend Schuck in the white man's ward.

In *Victory*, Schomberg's hotel seems larger than the hotel in 'Falk' because much is made of the ladies' orchestra playing there. Captain Davidson is described as looking at a poster outside Schomberg's hotel which reads:

> 'Concerts Every Evening,'...He...was struck by the fact—then not so very common—that it was a ladies' orchestra; 'Zangiacomo's eastern tour—eighteen performers.' The poster stated that they had had the honour of playing their select repertoire before various colonial excellencies, also before pashas, sheiks, chiefs, H.H. the Sultan of Mascate, etc., etc. (p. 38).

No ladies' orchestra appeared in Bangkok during Conrad's stay, but there was a concert every evening and lady as well as gentleman performers took part. The *Bangkok Times*, 21 January 1888, carried the following advertisement:

> The Old Oriental Hotel
> Grand Concert
> The greatest combination of vocal and musical talent that has ever appeared in Bangkok

Nevertheless, I do not think Conrad had the Oriental Hotel or its concerts in mind when he was writing *Victory*. He himself said in his letter to St Clair: 'In Bangkok when I took command, I hardly ever left the ship except to go to my charterers...I was really too busy ever to *hear* much of shore people', and this statement is probably accurate. Here is the description of Schomberg's hotel and the ladies' orchestra, supposedly situated in Sourabaya:

> He [Axel Heyst] spent his evenings sitting apart on the verandah of Schomberg's hotel. The lamentations of string instruments issued from the building in the hotel compound, the approaches to which were decorated with Japanese paper lanterns strung up between the trunks of several big trees...One evening...in his desperate mood Heyst ascended three steps...and went in [to Schomberg's concert-hall].
>
> The uproar in that small, barn-like structure, built of imported pine boards, and raised clear of the ground, was simply stunning. An instrumental uproar, screaming, grunting, whining, sobbing, scraping, squeaking some kind of lively air; while a grand piano, operated upon by a bony, red-faced woman with bad-tempered nostrils, rained hard notes like hail through the tempest of fiddles. The small platform was filled with white muslin dresses and crimson sashes slanting from shoulders provided with bare arms, which sawed away without respite. Zangiacomo conducted...
>
> When the piece of music came to an end, the relief was so great that he felt slightly dizzy...When he raised his eyes, the audience, most perversely, was exhibiting signs of animation and interest in their faces, and the women in white muslin dresses were coming down in pairs from the platform into the body of [the place]...This was the interval during which, as the astute Schomberg had stipulated, the members of the orchestra were encouraged to favour the members of the audience with their company (*Victory*, pp. 66–9).

German hotel-keepers were a regular feature in the East during Conrad's time and such information therefore helps us little in establishing the original hotel and manager Conrad had in mind. But the fact that this hotel had an all-ladies' orchestra, uncommon then and now in the East, made it a much more distinctive hotel. And though I could find no evidence for such a hotel having existed in either Bangkok or Sourabaya,

I did find one in Singapore itself, though the hotel has long since disappeared.

The first reference appears in *One Hundred Years of Singapore*, II, 183, in an article by Walter Makepeace:

> ...at the corner of North Bridge Road there was a concert and dancing hall—the original Tingel-tangel—owing its origin to a Mr Finkelstein [actually a Mr Goldenberg]. Later the Tingel-tangel was removed along North Bridge Road, and lasted for many years under Austrian control, there being a very decent string band, the lady-performers being allowed to dance with visitors.

The next reference appears in E. A. Brown's *Indiscreet Memories*,[30] which deals with his experiences (hardly ever indiscreet by modern standards) in the Singapore of 1901–4:

> In North Bridge Road, just past Bras Basah Road, on the left hand side going out, was the celebrated 'Tingel Tangel'. This was, in fact, a local edition of a continental dance hall. It was kept by an old Austrian named Hackmeier, and sported a ladies orchestra. The girls in the orchestra were Austrian and Poles...One went there, drank beer, and paid fifty cents a time to dance with one of the band girls (p. 42).

The fact that this hotel sported Polish girls must have been of some interest to Conrad, a lonely Polish gentleman serving in the British mercantile marine. I felt certain that the 'Tingel Tangel'—this was a nickname and is not found in the Singapore Directories—was Schomberg's hotel. But I was to find further evidence to endorse this view.

On 9 May 1886 Otto Ziegele, a young man of 22 years, arrived in Singapore to work for Brinkmann and Co. During the next four years he kept a diary and portions of this have now been published by the British European Association in its magazine *The Beam*. It is a unique record of the Singapore Conrad himself experienced. On 16 July 1886 there is the following entry: 'We then drove to the Hotel de Louvre and heard some music. After every piece the girls come down to sit among the gentlemen ready to drink any amount of beer etc. We stayed till 12.30 p.m.' The editor of *The Beam*, John Gauntlett, added a footnote: 'This is believed to have been what was known as "The Tingel Tangel" where Austrian girls played in a string band and danced for the guests wearing white muslin frocks and blue sashes.' Here was the final piece of the jigsaw, the reference to the frocks of the ladies' orchestra —Conrad could quite easily have changed the colour of the sashes from blue to crimson—and when I interviewed the editor on 12 August 1965 I learnt that the source was an oral one, from the lips of a very old lady, Miss Gunn, who died in Singapore some months previously.

Finally, I met a vigorous eighty-year-old lawyer, René Eber, who was able to recall going to the Tingel Tangel for violin lessons in 1895—only seven years after Conrad's departure from the East. These were given by the band-master. His description of the Tingel Tangel, the building, concert hall and courtyard, tallied with Conrad's. A year before Eber visited the hotel, the management had changed and thus Eber did not meet the man whom I believe to be the original of Schomberg. In Conrad's day the manager was one H. Zerner, as the *Singapore and Straits Directory*, 1888, shows.

*

This reconstruction of the environment Conrad experienced in Bangkok and the numerous suggestions he obtained there for his later stories is necessarily tentative since it has been done by oblique means. But it is worth stressing that Conrad retained these details for later use. The details are of such a kind that they lead one to conclude either that Conrad had a prodigious memory for such details or that he kept a notebook which was later destroyed, for thirteen years elapsed before he wrote 'Falk' and another fourteen years before he wrote *The Shadow-Line*.

13

THE GULF OF SIAM

'The *Otago* took three weeks to reach Singapore, a passage of about eight hundred miles', says Jean-Aubry,[1] and Baines describes it as a nightmarish voyage and by the end all 'except for Conrad and the cook, Ransome, who had been his mainstay throughout, had succumbed to fever. At Singapore a fresh crew was provided, except for Mr Born.'[2] Both Jean-Aubry and Baines take Conrad at his word about losing the whole of his crew and having to recruit others at Singapore:

> As we had a signal for medical assistance flying on the mizzen it is a fact that before the ship was fairly at rest three steam-launches from various men-of-war arrived alongside; and at least five naval surgeons clambered on board. They stood in a knot gazing up and down the empty main-deck, then looked aloft—where not a man could be seen either...One of the surgeons had remained on board. He came out of the forecastle looking impenetrable, and noticed my inquiring gaze.
>
> 'There's nobody dead in there, if that's what you want to know,' he said deliberately. Then added in a tone of wonder: 'The whole crew!'
>
> 'And very bad?'
>
> 'And very bad,' he repeated...
>
> When I returned on deck everything was ready for the removal of the men. It was the last ordeal of that episode which had been maturing and tempering my character...It was awful. They passed under my eyes one after another (*The Shadow-Line*, pp. 159–62).

Conrad is again, for dramatic purposes, exaggerating here. It is true that there were, when Conrad came into the port of Singapore, 'various men-of-war' in port. There were five, to be exact, one British, one German, and three Dutch (*Singapore Free Press*, 6 March 1888). But it seems unlikely either that three steam launches would come alongside, or that at least five naval surgeons came on board, especially since Conrad was not in such serious trouble as *The Shadow-Line* suggests. In the *Singapore Free Press* there are two references to the *Otago*. The first, in the Shipping Arrivals column, is as follows: '*Otago*, Brit. bk., 349, Korgemourki [*sic*], Bangkok, Feb. 9. Rice, Master—Put in for medical advice. Outside Harbour Limits.'

The second report is also tantalizingly short but it gives more information.

> The British bark *Otago*, bound from Bangkok to Sydney with a cargo of rice, put into port here last evening for medical advice as several of the crew are suffering from fever and the Captain wished to get a further supply of medicine before he proceeded on his journey. Dr Mugliston went on board and ordered *three* of the crew [my italics] to be sent to Hospital. The vessel is outside the Harbour limits.

In *The Shadow-Line* the narrator discovers that the bottles in the medicine kit contained a 'white powder' instead of quinine and the reference to 'a further supply of medicine' in the newspaper report may be confirmation of this. On the other hand, it may have been that because of sickness on board the *Otago* the supply of medicine had been used up.

Conrad obviously did not lose his whole crew at his 'Eastern port'. As the newspaper report shows, three men were ordered to hospital by the doctor. According to the crew agreement these were A. W. Leonard, J. Scarfe, T. Nils Krisfran. They left on 1 March and one of them was too ill to sign the crew agreement.

This does not account for the 'unfailing Ransome', 'the housekeeper of the ship', who is devoted to the captain in *The Shadow-Line*:

> Even at a distance his well-proportioned figure, something thoroughly sailor-like in his poise, made him noticeable. On nearer view the intelligent, quiet eyes, a well-bred face, the disciplined independence of his manner made up an attractive personality. When, in addition, Mr Burns

told me that he was the best seaman in the ship, I expressed my surprise that in his earliest prime and of such appearance he should sign on as cook on board a ship.

'It's his heart,' Mr Burns had said. 'There's something wrong with it. He mustn't exert himself too much or he may drop dead suddenly.'...

After the poor steward died, and as he could not be replaced by a white man in this Oriental port, Ransome had volunteered to do the double work (p. 84).

His devotion continues to the very end, for, in spite of being ill himself, he agrees to stay on the deserted ship to look after the mate until the master returns from a trip ashore:

The first thing I saw when I got back to the ship was Ransome on the quarter-deck sitting quietly on his neatly lashed sea-chest...I listened to him going up the companion stairs cautiously, step by step, in mortal fear of starting into sudden anger our common enemy it was his hard fate to carry consciously within his faithful breast (pp. 166–7).

Just as in *The Shadow-Line* Ransome is the last to leave, so in the case of the *Otago* on 3 March 1888—two days after the sick men had left and the day on which the *Otago* sailed—a fourth member of crew left the ship and he also was too ill to sign. His name was Pat Conway and he received more pay than either Scarfe or Krisfran though he was the same age as they (nineteen) and joined the ship at the same time. This suggests that he had undertaken extra duties and he may well be the original of Ransome though probably it was not heart trouble that took him away from the ship, as in the case of Ransome, but fever.

Conrad writes in *The Shadow-Line* that 'the Marine Office let me off the port dues, and as there happened to be a shipwrecked crew staying in the Home I had no difficulty in obtaining as many men as I wanted'.[3] In his letter to St Clair, Conrad wrote: 'Yes, I remember Bradbury. It was he who let me off port-dues when I put into Singapore in distress with *all* my crew unfit for duty (1888).' The crew list of the

Otago shows that Conrad took on five men in Singapore to make up the full complement of crew. There was the crew of a shipwrecked vessel, the *Anne Millicent*, in the port of Singapore, and an account of her loss is given in the *Singapore Free Press*. Conrad did take one man from the crew of the *Anne Millicent*, but did not, as he implies, obtain a full crew from the shipwrecked vessel.*

One would not wish to deny that Conrad's experiences in taking up his first command were in many ways nightmarish. He certainly struggled against sickness, lack of crew, and calms in the Gulf of Siam. The memory of these trials was strong enough to inspire *The Shadow-Line* as a tale of trial in extreme circumstances. But it is not 'exact autobiography' in the sense Conrad claims. The creative instinct in Conrad was too strong to allow him to set down unvarnished facts, and I shall deal more fully with this fictional distillation in the conclusion.

* Conrad says of his second officer that 'all I can say [is] his name was Tottersen, or something like that. His practice was to wear on his head, in that tropical climate, a mangy fur cap. He was, without exception, the stupidest man I had ever seen on board ship. And he looked it too. He looked so confoundedly stupid that it was a matter of surprise for me when he answered to his name' ('Falk', p. 178). This is not a reference to Jackson who was second mate when the ship left Bangkok, as the crew agreement shows. But Jackson must have left the *Otago*, for on her return from Mauritius the Certificate of Release at the Termination of a Voyage (10 January 1889) shows that the second mate was then an F. Totterman. In the manuscript of 'Falk' Conrad writes the name of the second mate as Totterman and only in the published text is it changed to Tottersen.

CONCLUSION

THE WORK OF THE IMAGINATION

14

'THE SECRET SHARER': THE BASIC FACT OF THE TALE

The foregoing chapters set out what I have discovered of the nature of Conrad's Eastern world and of those incidents and people within it which inspired his Eastern novels. It remains to consider the processes by which this raw material from life became the completed fiction.

One aspect of this imaginative transformation in Conrad's case is his complex, yet economical, use of his source material. This resulted in different aspects of the same source appearing in different novels; we have seen something of this already at a minor level in Conrad's use of Captain Ellis, the Master-Attendant, who appears in *Lord Jim*, *The Shadow-Line* and 'The End of the Tether'. But a more significant example of this complex utilization of source material can be seen if some of the strands of experience are disentangled in three stories—'The Secret Sharer', *Lord Jim* and *The Shadow-Line*.

There is a basic similarity in the nature of the main source stories of *Lord Jim* and 'The Secret Sharer', and in the way in which Conrad came into contact with them. Like *Lord Jim*, 'The Secret Sharer' has its origins in an actual sea-crime—the murder on the *Cutty Sark*—which took place at the same time as the *Jeddah* disaster; the story again reached Conrad via seamen's gossip and newspaper reports. The main difference is that, so far as I can judge, there was no meeting of any kind between Conrad and the protagonist of the *Cutty Sark* incident as there may have been between Conrad and Williams.

Conclusion: The Work of the Imagination

Conrad acknowledged the main source of 'The Secret Sharer' in his Author's Note to *'Twixt Land and Sea*:

The origins of the middle story, The Secret Sharer, are quite other. It was written much earlier and was published first in *Harper's Magazine*, during the early part, I think, of 1911. Or perhaps the latter part?... The basic fact of the tale I had in my possession for a good many years. It was in truth the common possession of the whole fleet of merchant ships trading to India, China, and Australia...The fact itself happened on board...[the] *Cutty Sark*...I do not know the date of the occurrence on which the scheme of The Secret Sharer is founded; it came to light and even got into newspapers about the middle eighties, though I had heard of it before, as it were privately, among the officers of the great wool fleet in which my first years in deep water were served. It came to light under circumstances dramatic enough, I think, but which have nothing to do with my story (pp. viii–ix).*

His references to the date of the *Cutty Sark* incident are confusing. He first denies all knowledge of the date and then, admitting that the incident found its way into the newspapers, states that he had heard of it earlier—'as it were privately'. In one of his letters to A. T. Saunders, Conrad's references to the date of the incident are more confusing. Since he recognized that Saunders was something of a literary detective —'You are a terror for tracking people out'—Conrad was probably trying to put him off the track:

The *Secret-Sharer* in the same vol: also does in a way [belong to the *Otago* cycle]—as far as the Gulf of Siam setting goes. The swimmer himself was suggested to me by a young fellow who was 2nd mate (in the '60) of the *Cutty Sark* clipper and had the misfortune to kill a man on deck. But his skipper had the decency to let him swim ashore on the Java coast as the ship was passing through Anjer Straits. The story was well remembered in the Merchant Service even in my time.†

* 'The Secret Sharer' (London: Dent, 1947). Conrad's statements must be accepted with reservations. 'The Secret Sharer' was not 'published first in *Harper's Magazine*, during the early part...of 1911', but from August to September 1910. Conrad can have had nothing to conceal here, and his memory must have been genuinely at fault.

† See Appendix A, p. 295, below.

The story would be 'well-remembered' because the incident took place not in the 'sixties, nor in the mid eighties, but in September 1880 during Conrad's service in the Merchant Navy. At that time he was an officer in the wool clipper *Loch Etive*, bound for Sydney.* The incident was no doubt discussed among the officers of the *Loch Etive*, and when he returned to London in April 1881 he probably read of it in the newspapers.

Conrad must have become acquainted with the story of the *Jeddah* and the story of the *Cutty Sark* at the same time. In the *Straits Times* editorial column, 20 September 1880, there is a report of the motion 'touching the abandonment of the S.S. *Jeddah* in open sea by her master and officers when she had over 1,000 souls on board' which was discussed in the Singapore Legislative Assembly. In the same column is the report of the arrival in Singapore of the chief officer of the *Jeddah*, A. P. Williams, followed immediately by the following paragraph:

> Another painful story from the sea. The British barque *Cutty Sark*, formerly a tea clipper, arrived here on Saturday morning from Anjer, and the second officer, in whose charge she arrived, reports that while at Anjer the chief officer struck a seaman who died from the effects of the blow. The Chief Officer, alarmed at the consequences of his act, made his escape...

Undoubtedly the two incidents must have been connected in seamen's gossip and were probably linked in Conrad's memory because of this.

A full account of the *Cutty Sark* incident appears in Basil Lubbock's book *The Log of the Cutty Sark*.[1] He drew his information from the ship's log, and also from the narratives

* Conrad did spend his first years as a seaman sailing in deep waters among 'the officers of the great wool fleet'. He embarked as an ordinary seaman in the wool clipper *Duke of Sutherland* on 12 October 1878 and travelled from London to Sydney. On 21 August 1880 he got a berth as an officer in the wool clipper *Loch Etive*, bound for Sydney. It was at this time that he would hear the *Cutty Sark* story discussed.

of sailors on board at the time, and therefore it is likely that he was, in this last instance, drawing upon the kind of hearsay Conrad would have access to.

The incident in the *Cutty Sark* was as follows. Sydney Smith, the chief mate, gave an order to John Francis, a Negro seaman, which Francis did not obey. Because of the man's insolence and the fact that he threatened Smith with a capstan bar, there was a struggle, the mate got possession of the capstan bar and brought it down on Francis's head, knocking him unconscious. Francis never regained consciousness and died three days later. According to Lubbock's account of the incident, the mate retired to his cabin for the rest of the passage. When the *Cutty Sark* arrived at Anjer, the mate persuaded his skipper, Captain Wallace, to help him escape and he was eventually smuggled aboard an American ship, the *Colorado*. The mate was not heard of for two years but was then found and arrested and tried in London, being sentenced to seven years' imprisonment for manslaughter.

In 'The Secret Sharer' the chief mate of the *Sephora*, Leggatt, commits a murder and escapes to the narrator's ship. Baines commented that, in using this incident,

> ...Conrad softened the crime...and also softened the character of the mate. The mate of the *Cutty Sark*...was apparently a despotic character with a sinister reputation...Leggatt was, however, clearly an exemplary sailor, and his provocation was greater; it was in the middle of a storm when the fate of the ship was at stake and the captain had lost his nerve (p. 357).

Baines took his assessment of the character of the mate of the *Cutty Sark* from Lubbock's account, but Sydney Smith was given a good character at his trial by his employer John Willis who also helped him to find a berth when he came out of prison. Conrad mentions John Willis in his Author's Note to *'Twixt Land and Sea* and may have known, from the accounts of the trial, Willis's opinion of the mate. Nevertheless, it would be true to say that Conrad does make excuses for Leggatt and tries to gain the reader's sympathy for him.

*

Lord Jim and 'The Secret Sharer' both depend upon an amalgam of the same three sources—the *Jeddah* case, the murder on the *Cutty Sark*, and Conrad's experiences on the *Otago*— for although he insisted that, in spite of its autobiographical form, 'The Secret Sharer' was not a record of personal experience, personal experience *is* one of his sources here, in a definite sense.

Lord Jim contains the first suggestions of several later stories and the initial conception of the relationship between the narrator in 'The Secret Sharer' and Leggatt lies unobtrusively in this novel. The narrator sees Leggatt in some ways as his double: 'The shadowy, dark head, like mine, seemed to nod imperceptibly above the ghostly grey of my sleeping-suit. It was, in the night, as though I had been faced by my own reflection in the depths of a sombre and immense mirror.'[2] He hides Leggatt in his cabin and takes him away from Bangkok. Thus the mate escapes imprisonment and becomes 'a fugitive and a vagabond on the earth'.[3] In *Lord Jim*, Captain Marlow describes how he took Jim away from Bangkok after another unsuccessful start, this time in the employ of Yucker Brothers, charterers and teak merchants:

> I took him away from Bankok in my ship, and we had a longish passage. It was pitiful to see how he shrank within himself. A seaman, even if a mere passenger, takes an interest in a ship, and looks at the sea-life around him with the critical enjoyment of a painter, for instance, looking at another man's work. In every sense of the expression he is 'on deck'; but my Jim, for the most part, skulked down below as though he had been a stowaway. He infected me so that I avoided speaking on professional matters, such as would suggest themselves naturally to two sailors during a passage. For whole days we did not exchange a word; I felt extremely unwilling to give orders to my officers in his presence. Often, when alone with him on deck or in the cabin, we didn't know what to do with our eyes (pp. 244–5).

There is a definite connection here between the two situations, which have their origins in the *Otago*'s voyage from Bangkok to Singapore. Conrad is grafting on to that journey the idea of the captain taking on board a seaman as passenger. Jim, feeling his disgrace, takes no interest in the ship and 'skulked down below as though he had been a stowaway'; Leggatt remains out of sight and is a kind of official stowaway. It is easy to see the development of the initial minor incident in *Lord Jim* to the major situation in 'The Secret Sharer'.

An entry in the crew list of the *Otago*, during the time Conrad was in Bangkok, gives rise to some interesting speculation on the subject of this twice-repeated idea of the seaman who remains in concealment, or semi-concealment, below decks. At present I have no evidence to make my theory more than speculation, but it might be of some interest to the reader who has wondered whether Conrad had on board some stowaway when the *Otago* left Bangkok, or whether some incident which occurred there gave Conrad such an idea.

The entry in the crew list concerns a seaman from Hamburg called Davis. Davis was signed on to the crew of the *Otago* as an able seaman on 27 January and at a wage of £3.10*s*. per month. He was not kept on, however, for a note against his name shows that he had not been discharged from his former ship.

His previous ship, the Norwegian *Emilie*, was in port on 28 January, and it would appear that the sailor had absconded from her and tried to leave Bangkok by signing on the *Otago*. I have no information about him or about what happened to him, but I suspect that Conrad's own musings on the possibility of taking Davis illegally out may have been the starting point for his inspiration for 'The Secret Sharer'.

There are other similarities between Lord Jim and Leggatt which show that Conrad is again making use of A. P. Williams as a source. Jim, we know, originally came from a parsonage, but when 'his vocation for the sea had declared itself, he was sent at once to a "training-ship for officers of the mercantile marine"'.[4] During the Court of Inquiry into the desertion of the *Patna*, Jim tells Marlow about his father: 'I can never face the poor old chap...I could never explain. He wouldn't understand.'[5] I have already shown that Conrad probably had in mind the actual relationship between Williams and his father here. But he returns to the same situation in 'The Secret Sharer':

> 'A pretty thing to have to own up to for a Conway boy,' murmured my double, distinctly.
>
> 'You're a Conway boy?'
>
> 'I am,' he said, as if startled. Then, slowly...'Perhaps you too—'
>
> It was so; but being a couple of years older I had left before he joined. After a quick interchange of dates a silence fell...My double gave me an inkling of his thoughts by saying: 'My father's a parson in Norfolk. Do you see me before a judge and jury on that charge?' (p. 101).

As in *Lord Jim*, we have here a sailor confessing his transgression against the code to another sailor, and concerned about the effect his action will have upon his father who is a parson. In *Lord Jim*, the parsonage is in Essex. Here it is in Norfolk. Since in the case of A. P. Williams his father's parsonage was at Porthleven in Cornwall, the difference in place is of no importance.

We have seen that Conrad deliberately rejected some conditions in the *Jeddah* when writing *Lord Jim*, and turned to his own experience in the *Palestine*. But in 'The Secret Sharer' he appears to be making use of the material he rejected, for the conditions on board the *Sephora* in 'The Secret Sharer' at the time of the murder are similar to those on the *Jeddah* at the time of her desertion. To begin with, the murder on the *Sephora* takes place during a storm:

> I tell you I was overdone with this terrific weather that seemed to have no end to it. Terrific, I tell you—and a deep ship...And the ship running for her life, touch and go all the time, any minute her last in a sea fit to turn your hair grey only a-looking at it (pp. 102–3).

Captain Clark of the *Jeddah* reported:

> After this [29 July] the weather became very heavy the wind increasing almost to hurricane force at times with a very high cross sea, the ship rolling, pitching and straining heavily (*Straits Times Overland Journal*, 8 September 1880).

In each case the mate dealt with a difficult situation, different though those situations were, and in each case the captain panicked. The Assessor at Aden said of the *Jeddah* case that the first mate advised the master 'to leave the ship, telling him his life was in danger, also his wife's life; that he, the master, was sure to be killed if he remained on board; and that he, the first mate, did thrust the master into the boat'. Leggatt commits the murder while a reefed foresail was being set: 'You know, that foresail saved the ship. She was too deep to have run long under bare poles. And it was I that managed to set it for him [the master].'[6] He says of the master of the *Sephora*:

> ...the skipper, too, started raving like the rest of them. The man had been deprived of sleep for more than a week, and to have this sprung on him at the height of a furious gale nearly drove him out of his mind... Devil only knows what the skipper wasn't afraid of (all his nerve went to pieces altogether in that hellish spell of bad weather we had)—of what the law would do to him—of his wife, perhaps. Oh, yes! she's on board (pp. 103–7).

It is a surprising fact that while in *Lord Jim* Conrad used his knowledge about Williams almost unchanged he did not use the character of the master of the *Jeddah*, Captain Joseph Lucas Clark. Instead he created a new figure as master of the *Patna*, the grotesque German. But Conrad did not forget Clark and he makes his appearance as Captain Archbold of the *Sephora*. The description of Archbold, his plain speaking, and his references to his wife seem to link this character to Captain Clark of the *Jeddah*. Conrad describes Archbold in this way:

The skipper of the *Sephora* had a thin red whisker all round his face, and the sort of complexion that goes with hair of that colour; also the particular, rather smeary shade of blue in the eyes. He was not exactly a showy figure; his shoulders were high, his stature but middling—one leg slightly more bandy than the other...Never took liquor (pp. 115–16).

This could be accounted an accurate description of Captain Clark. The two photographs I have of him show that he had whiskers all round his face, that his eyes—one of the photographs is coloured—are blue, that his chest is high and that he is of middling height. Clark's grandson, James Beeson of New Zealand, has confirmed that Conrad's Captain Archbold is in appearance the same as his grandfather. When I sent him a description of Archbold, he replied telling me that it 'afforded my wife and myself great amusement', because it was 'a very apt description of me, i.e. dark-blue eyes, shortish, big-chested and "bandy". Even my beard has a reddish-gold streak' (letter of 13 June 1963). And he is very like his grandfather in appearance. He also commented on the fact that his grandfather had been a consistent teetotaler. An old nurse in Auckland, New Zealand, wrote of Captain Clark's home there: 'I never saw or heard of any drinking in their home and it was the type of good N.Z. house of that period' (letter of 10 June 1963).

Captain Archbold's 'wife aboard, too', twice repeated in the short interview that the narrator records in 'The Secret Sharer', would surely be characteristic remarks of Clark if Conrad spoke to him of the *Jeddah* incident. It was stated by the Assessor at Aden that Clark deserted the ship because he had his wife aboard and was concerned for her safety. Clark was in fact married only twelve days before the *Jeddah* sailed.

*

The story of Brierly in *Lord Jim* is one of those inset pieces of marine gossip with which Marlow punctuates his story, and which extend and give conviction to the background of *Lord Jim*. In this case the anecdote also provides a contrast to Jim's story, since Brierly, like Jim, has some dark secret, but while Jim seeks his salvation in Patusan, Brierly commits suicide. I think that Conrad, in writing Brierly's history, again had in mind the story of the *Cutty Sark*—not the case of murder which provides the basis for 'The Secret Sharer', but the suicide of her master, Captain Wallace. Wallace was a very young and successful skipper. He took his second mate's certificate when he was twenty-one, his first mate's when he was twenty-three, and his master's when he was twenty-four.[7] At twenty-seven he was commander of the famous clipper *Cutty Sark*, and in the same year he committed suicide by walking over the side of the ship. The only reason that could be adduced for his suicide was that he had helped his mate, Sydney Smith, to escape to the *Colorado* after the murder of John Francis. The death of this famous skipper at such an early age when he was at the height of his career and when there was no strong reason for such an act must have caused a great deal of speculation. Brierly, like Wallace, is an extremely successful skipper. He is 'captain of the crack ship of the Blue Star line' who, it seemed:

> ...never...made a mistake, never had an accident, never a mishap, never a check in his steady rise, and he seemed to be one of those lucky fellows who know nothing of indecision, much less of self-mistrust. At thirty-two he had one of the best commands going in the Eastern trade...his self-satisfaction presented to me and to the world a surface as hard as granite. He committed suicide very soon after (pp. 68–70).

Brierly's first officer, a 'grey-headed mate, a first-rate sailor... but in his relations with his commander the surliest chief officer I've ever seen', adds: '...I couldn't stand poor Captain Brierly, I tell you with shame...He had been promoted over too many heads, not counting my own, and he had a damnable trick of making you feel small' (p. 71).

The parallels between Wallace's suicide and that of Brierly are strong. Wallace was very upset by the mate's escape:

Ever since the escape of the mate he had been unable to sleep...Night and day he stood gazing out to sea or walked with bowed head up and down the poop...On the fourth day after leaving Anjer, the watch had just been called at 4 a.m., when the captain, who was standing at the break of the poop with the carpenter, turned to his faithful petty officer and asked if the second mate was on deck.

'Chips' replied that he was just coming up. Whereupon Captain Wallace left the carpenter and walked aft: called the helmsman's attention to the course; then deliberately stepped on to the taffrail and jumped overboard.[8]

The details of Brierly's death are similar:

It appears that when he [the mate] came on deck in the morning Brierly had been writing in the chart-room. 'It was ten minutes to four,' he said, 'and the middle watch was not relieved yet, of course. He heard my voice on the bridge speaking to the second mate, and called me in. I was loth to go, and that's the truth, Captain Marlow...Says he, "... Come in here, Mr Jones," in that swagger voice of his...In I went. "We'll lay down her position," says he, stooping over the chart, a pair of dividers in hand... he marked off the ship's position with a tiny cross..."Thirty-two miles more as she goes," says he, "and then we shall be clear, and you may alter course twenty degrees to the southward."...Then he calls out to me from the dark, "Shut that dog up in the chart-room, Mr Jones—will you?" This was the last time I heard his voice...' (pp. 71–3).

The time is the same in both cases—four o'clock in the morning— as is the sense of deliberation on the part of both Wallace and Brierly, their interest in the course of the ship, and the fact that immediately afterwards, without a word, both step over the side.

The report in the *Singapore Daily Times*, 18 September 1880, of the *Cutty Sark* incident suggests reasons for Wallace's suicide:

The Captain appears to have assisted the chief officer to escape on board an American ship bound for Saigon and afterwards whether from pangs of conscience or fear of future trouble he threw himself overboard and was drowned.

Lubbock gives support to the latter suggestion when he states:

> Captain Wallace...saw an official investigation looming ahead at Yokohama, in which there was little doubt but that he would be held responsible for the mate's escape, and the very least that he could expect was the suspension of his certificate.[9]

Conrad seems to have this in mind in the case of Jim when he has Brierly say to Marlow:

> 'This infernal publicity is too shocking: there he sits while all these confounded natives, serangs, lascars, quartermasters, are giving evidence that's enough to burn a man to ashes with shame. This is abominable. Why, Marlow, don't you think, don't you feel, that this is abominable?' (p. 81).

And the conversation between Jones and Marlow suggests that fear of publicity and loss of reputation were the reasons for the suicide:

> 'Why did he commit the rash act, Captain Marlow—can you think?' asked Jones, pressing his palms together. 'Why? It beats me! Why?' He slapped his low and wrinkled forehead. 'If he had been poor and old and in debt—and never a show—or else mad. But he wasn't of the kind that goes mad, not he. You trust me. What a mate don't know about his skipper isn't worth knowing. Young, healthy, well off, no cares...I sit here sometimes thinking, thinking, till my head fairly begins to buzz. There was some reason.'
>
> 'You may depend on it, Captain Jones,' said I, 'it wasn't anything that would have disturbed much either of us two,' I said; and then, as if a light had been flashed into the muddle of his brain, poor old Jones found a last word of amazing profundity. He blew his nose, nodding at me dolefully: 'Ay, ay! neither you nor I, sir, had ever thought so much of ourselves' (p. 78).

*

Apart from making use of the *Jeddah* and the *Cutty Sark* incidents in 'The Secret Sharer', Conrad also drew upon his own experience. The description of the Meinam river at the beginning of the story confirms that the setting is the Gulf of Siam which Conrad knew from his command of the *Otago*.

That Conrad has in mind his first command is shown by what the narrator says:

> In consequence of certain events of no particular significance, except to myself, I had been appointed to the command only a fortnight before. Neither did I know much of the hands forward. All these people had been together for eighteen months or so, and my position was that of the only stranger on board (p. 93).

But Conrad is, I think, drawing upon another aspect of his experience in the *Otago* for the character of Brierly's mate, Jones.

The chief mate of the *Otago*, called Burns in *The Shadow-Line*, but actually named Charles Born, had brought the ship into Bangkok after the death of her captain. Conrad took over the command from him at Bangkok, and it may be that Born had hoped to get it himself. This is reflected by Conrad's comment in *The Shadow-Line*: 'He took the ship to a port where he expected to be confirmed in his temporary command from lack of a qualified master to put over his head' (p. 78). Born's antagonism as a result of his disappointment seems to be reflected in several stories, as does Conrad's uneasy relationship with him and his ambiguous attitude to him.

In *Lord Jim* Jones expected to get command of the *Ossa* and Brierly, in spite of Jones's dislike of him, had recommended him as his successor:

> He had written two letters in the middle watch, one to the Company and the other to me. He gave me a lot of instructions as to the passage—I had been in the trade before he was out of his time—and no end of hints as to my conduct with our people in Shanghai, so that I should keep the command of the *Ossa*...In his letter to the owners...he said that he had always done his duty by them—up to that moment—and even now he was not betraying their confidence, since he was leaving the ship to as competent a seaman as could be found—meaning me, sir, meaning me! He told them that if the last act of his life didn't take away all his credit with them, they would give weight to my faithful service and to his warm recommendation, when about to fill the vacancy made by his death. And

much more like this, sir. I couldn't believe my eyes...What with the shock of him going in this awful rash way, and thinking myself a made man by that chance, I was nearly off my chump for a week. But no fear. The captain of the *Pelion* was shifted into the *Ossa*—came aboard in Shanghai—a little popinjay, sir,...'Aw-I am-aw-your new captain, Mister-Mister-aw-Jones.'...He mumbled something about my natural disappointment—I had better know at once that his chief officer got promotion to the *Pelion*—he had nothing to do with it, of course—supposed the office knew best—sorry...Says I, 'Don't you mind old Jones, sir; damn his soul, he's used to it.' I could see directly I had shocked his delicate ear, and while we sat at our first tiffin together he began to find fault in a nasty manner with this and that in the ship...I set my teeth hard, and glued my eyes to my plate, and held my peace as long as I could; but at last I had to say something...'You'll find you have a different person to deal with than the late Captain Brierly.' 'I've found it,' says I, very glum, but pretending to be mighty busy with my steak. 'You are an old ruffian, Mister-aw-Jones; and what's more, you are known for an old ruffian in the employ,' he squeaks at me...'I may be a hard case,' answers I, 'but I ain't so far gone as to put up with the sight of you sitting in Captain Brierly's chair.' With that I lay down my knife and fork. 'You would like to sit in it yourself—that's where the shoe pinches,' he sneers. I left the saloon, got my rags together, and was on the quay with all my dunnage about my feet before the stevedores had turned to again. Yes. Adrift—on shore—after ten years' service—and with a poor woman and four children... (pp. 74–6).

Echoes of this appear in *The Shadow-Line*. The narrator, on taking over command, says, 'I am your new captain',[10] which reflects the statement that the 'Popinjay' makes above with the omission of the '*aw*'s. In *The Shadow-Line*, Burns considers leaving the vessel: 'If I hadn't a wife and a child at home you may be sure, sir, I would have asked you to let me go the very minute you came on board.'[11] Here we have the same reference to wife and children as Jones makes in *Lord Jim*. Marlow says of Jones: 'I often wondered how Brierly could put up with his manners for more than half a voyage',[12] and this ambiguous attitude towards Jones is true of Conrad's attitude towards Born. Conrad deals with Born and his relationship with him in *The Mirror of the Sea*.

On examining now, after many years, the residue of the feeling which was the outcome of the contact of our personalities, I discover, without much surprise, a certain flavour of dislike. Upon the whole, I think he was one of the most uncomfortable shipmates possible for a young commander...His eternally watchful demeanour, his jerky, nervous talk, even his, as it were, determined silences, seemed to imply—and, I believe, they did imply—that to his mind the ship was never safe in my hands...there were moments when I detested Mr B— exceedingly. From the way he used to glare sometimes, I fancy that more than once he paid me back with interest...then, on our first leaving port (I don't see why I should make a secret of the fact that it was Bangkok), a bit of manœuvring of mine amongst the islands of the Gulf of Siam had given him an unforgettable scare. Ever since then he had nursed in secret a bitter idea of my utter recklessness. But upon the whole, and unless the grip of a man's hand at parting means nothing whatever, I conclude that we did like each other at the end of two years and three months well enough (pp. 18–19).

I think we can take it that the 'bit of manœuvring...amongst the islands of the Gulf of Siam' which gave Born 'an unforgettable scare' is the basis for the incident in 'The Secret Sharer' when the captain takes the vessel extraordinarily close to the islands in order to allow Leggatt to escape:

The strain of watching the dark loom of the land grow bigger and denser was too much for me...The black southern hill of Koh-ring seemed to hang right over the ship like a towering fragment of the everlasting night...

'My God! Where are we?'

It was the mate moaning at my elbow...He clapped his hands and absolutely cried out, 'Lost!'

'Be quiet,' I said, sternly.

He lowered his tone, but I saw the shadowy gesture of his despair. 'What are we doing here?'

'Looking for the land wind.'

He made as if to tear his hair, and addressed me recklessly.

'She will never get out. You have done it, sir. I knew it'd end in something like this. She will never weather, and you are too close now to stay. She'll drift ashore before she's round. O my God!'

I caught his arm as he was raising it to batter his poor devoted head, and shook it violently.

'She's ashore already,' he wailed, trying to tear himself away.

'Is she?...Keep good full there!'

'Good full, sir,' cried the helmsman... (pp. 139–41).

At the end of 'A Smile of Fortune', Conrad writes:

> At breakfast I informed Mr Burns that I had resigned my command.
>
> He dropped his knife and fork and looked at me with indignation.
>
> 'You have, sir! I thought you loved the ship.'
>
> 'So I do, Burns,' I said. 'But the fact is that the Indian Ocean and everything that is in it has lost its charm for me. I am going home as passenger by the Suez Canal.'
>
> 'Everything that is in it,' he repeated angrily. 'I've never heard anybody talk like this. And to tell you the truth, sir, all the time we have been together I've never quite made you out...'
>
> He was really devoted to me, I believe. But he cheered up when I told him that I had recommended him for my successor (p. 87).

In both 'Falk' and *The Shadow-Line*, Conrad tells us that though Burns (Born) hoped to get the command of the barque after the death of the previous master he was not properly qualified: 'The old mate, who had acted as chief mourner at the captain's funeral, was not particularly pleased at my coming. But the fact is the fellow was not legally qualified for command, and the Consul was bound, if at all possible, to put a properly certificated man on board.'* The fact is that soon after the *Otago* arrived at Australia from Bangkok, Born took his master's certificate. The certificate I have in my possession is dated 29 June 1888 and the examination was sat at Melbourne.† Thus he was 'legally qualified' at last and I think the narrator's statement in 'A Smile of Fortune' that when he resigned command of his vessel he recommended his first officer, as Brierly did in *Lord Jim*, and with the same result, was based on Conrad's own action. For just as Jones failed to gain command of the *Ossa* so Born failed in spite of the recommendation to get the command of the *Otago* and it was given to Captain Edward Trivett. I have no proof that Born

* 'Falk', p. 178. Born was not an old man at all, but Conrad makes him so, as he makes Jones old also.

† The *Otago* arrived from Bangkok and berthed at Sydney on 7 May 1888 and left Sydney for Melbourne on 19 May. She remained at Melbourne until 7 July during which time Charles Born took his master's certificate.

left the *Otago* quite as dramatically as Jones left the *Ossa*, but he did leave. He had been first mate of the *Otago* for some years, yet when she arrived in Sydney on 16 August 1890 the Inwards Crew List shows that Born had left the ship by that date. The new chief mate was a Charles Hopkinson.

The work of Conrad's imagination involved an intricate transference of sources, as this chapter has shown. He had already made use of the *Cutty Sark* story in *Lord Jim* for the incident of Brierly, and of his own experience on the *Otago* for the character of Jones. When he came to write 'The Secret Sharer', he grafted the story of the *Cutty Sark* on to the basis of his experience on the *Otago* by placing himself, as narrator, in the situation of the captain who took the mate of the *Cutty Sark* on board after his escape. His imagination provided him with the narrator's reactions to this situation, and he added to this the likeness between the narrator and Leggatt and their common bond as *Conway* boys. He took from the *Jeddah* case Captain Clark and the conditions under which the *Jeddah* was deserted. But he also returned to A. P. Williams in order to provide more sympathy for the guilty Leggatt.

15
JUSTICE TO THE VISIBLE UNIVERSE

In the selection of his source material, two major influences, it seems to me, were at work in Conrad's mind. The first was his conception of the nature of his art, the second his conception of life's predicaments. And in his conception of the nature of his art, two ideas stand out: the first his own lack of the inventive faculty, the second the importance of 'truth'. These led him to return constantly to his past—and to the details of that past—for inspiration.

In this sense, truth is fact for Conrad, and this brings about the accuracy of setting in those of his Eastern stories that I have considered. The setting may be elaborate and extended as in 'The End of the Tether', or consist of hints only, as in 'Falk', but it is as close to the facts of the original setting as could be expected in any work of fiction. Then there is the truth to historical event, which appears in the history of Singapore colony in 'The End of the Tether' and the history of Borneo in the Bornean novels. There is the truth to a man's work and existence, such as the accurate presentation of the Master-Attendant's duties, including the taking round of a visiting Duke, the details of the trading post on the Berau river, the duties of a ship-chandler's water-clerk in *Lord Jim*. There is a strong fidelity where names are concerned. The *Lord of the Isles* in *An Outcast of the Islands*, the *Nan-Shan* in *Typhoon*, the *Bonito*, *Neptun* and the *Bohemian Girl* in 'Freya of the Seven Isles', *Ringdove* and *Condor* in 'The End of the Tether', the *Ly-e-moon* in *The Rescue*, and the *Patna* in *Lord*

Jim— all these were names of actual ships which sailed in Eastern waters during Conrad's period of service in the mercantile marine. The names of places and men were also important to him—they often appear in their true form in the manuscript even though they may be altered or erased in the final draft. There is the reliance upon the truth to men's lives and situations, so that, even though his knowledge depended upon gossip, or a brief knowledge, or the written word, the life of Lingard, of Almayer, of Captain Ellis, appears true in its essentials. And there is the truth of atmosphere, so that the gossip of the sea-ports he knew, the tales of men and ships, appears often in its original form of the seaman's tale, as in 'Falk', *The Shadow-Line*, and *Lord Jim*.

Conrad's fidelity to fact extends so far towards accuracy as a man's age, and appearance, or a ship's tonnage, or the exact distance up a river of a particular settlement. It is this kind of exactitude which must have been an important part of his recall of those brief months in Eastern waters. And including them in his stories must have enhanced the sense of reality for him just as it does for the reader, providing the solidity of a concretely imagined world.

That he was accurate in these respects, I hope I have shown. That he had this accurate sense of recall after a period of many years was probably due to his having been a seaman. His words in the MS of *The Rescue* might be applied also to him:

> ...He seemed to dole out facts, to disclose with sparing words the features of the coast, but every word showed the minuteness of his observation, the clear vision of a seaman able to master quickly the aspect of a strange land and of a strange sea; the professionally wideawake state of mind of a man confronted by rapid changes of circumstance.[1]

But constantly in what he writes of the nature of his work, he refers to the importance of another kind of 'truth', and in some cases this appears as a defence of his art. To

A. T. Saunders, the shipping clerk engaged in discovering the basic facts of the people and incidents Conrad wrote about, he explained:

> ...I need not point out that *I had to make material from my own life's incidents arranged, combined, coloured for artistic purposes* [my italics]. I don't think there's anything reprehensible in that. After all I *am* a writer of fiction; and it is not what actually happened, but the manner of presenting it that settles the literary and even the moral value of my work. My little vol: of autobiography of course is absolutely genuine. *The rest is a more or less close approximation to facts and suggestions. What I claim as true are my mental and emotional reactions to life, to men, to their affairs and their passions as I have seen them. I have in that sense kept always true to myself* [my italics].*

And this necessity for a particular kind of truth is stressed also in the Note to *The Nigger of the Narcissus*:

> A work that aspires, however humbly, to the condition of art should carry its justification in every line. And art itself may be defined as *a single-minded attempt to render the highest kind of justice to the visible universe, by bringing to light the truth, manifold and one, underlying its every aspect....* sometimes, by the deserving and the fortunate, even that task is accomplished. And when it is accomplished—behold! all the truth of life is there...[my italics][2]

His work is 'truly imagined from hints of things that really happened and of people that really existed', and 'imagined' in a special sense for, as he said, 'that sort of work is of course of a creative (not reminiscent) nature'.[3]

The result of this is that his work is 'true' in the Aristotelian sense, in the likelihood and possibility of its action, '...it is not the poet's province to relate such things as have actually happened, but such as might have happened—such as are possible, according either to probable or necessary consequence' (Aristotle's *Poetics*). Conrad's 'probable or necessary consequence' exists in his bringing together in one work many incidents and characters, all 'true' in that they had

* See Appendix A, p. 295, below.

existed, not all together as they do in his work, but at some time. He felt free to bring together incidents and characters scattered initially in space and time, into one piece of fiction. And he felt free also, to move from the original 'true' incident, such as the *Jeddah* case or his experiences in the *Otago*, by the addition of some disparate experience, or by the enhancing of one aspect of the original, or by the invention of a new aspect not in the original source but a possible consequence of the action described. Dickens's method, Humphry House tells us, was to have his characters grow fictionally from the small original seed in life,[4] and we can often see this growth happening in a novel. This is not Conrad's method. His characters and incidents grow by means of an amalgamation with other characters and incidents, by the addition of further 'truths'.

Conrad's ability was not, as he said, 'inventive' in the sense of creating fictions. His advice to Norman Douglas is significant here—'make it a novel of *analysis* on the basis of some strong situation'[5]—for this is essentially his method. And this leads us to his conception of life's predicaments, for a 'strong' situation for Conrad was one which trapped his hero in some predicament.

Again, the comparison with Dickens is useful. Dickens as a novelist was concerned with society and with social evils. The material he chose from life was suited to his social purpose—Sadleir the financier became Merdle the financier, both involved with speculations ultimately ruinous to large sections of society. The Grants became the Cheeryble Brothers to demonstrate Dickens's belief in benevolence within a social framework. But Conrad chose incidents from life in which the single individual's reaction to circumstances was the important thing. One aspect of the circumstances would be some accepted code, such as that of the merchant marine, and the individual's situation would be complicated by the need to act according to such a code when such action was difficult. A. P. Williams was an example of an individual caught in circumstances aboard the *Jeddah* which caused him to act against the accepted code of the sea. The 'Geordie skipper' of the *Palestine*, on the other hand, expended himself in staying with his ship until the last possible moment. The captain and mate of the *Cutty Sark*, caught up in the circumstances of murder, turned in one case to suicide, in the other to flight, in order to escape the consequences of their actions. To transgress the code involves 'failure' at one level; at another level it involves living according to one's dream—the supreme egoism of Lord Jim and of Kurtz. Conrad, in transforming such incidents from life into fiction, stressed man's isolation in such predicaments, the part played by chance, the possibility of self-betrayal, and the impossibility of finally judging a man. As Marlow says: 'I was made to look at the convention that lurks in all truth and on the essential sincerity of falsehood.'[6]

Conrad's own sense of isolation must have been strong—most of his life was spent as a kind of outcast from society. As a boy he was exiled with his father, and as a young man, speaking a strange tongue, he was an exile in the sense that any sailor is. There would be the temporary, yet strong, community of the ship and her business, but beyond that the isolation of language and nationality, the isolation of ports, the constant change from ship to ship. Even in England, Conrad lived exiled from the social world. This sense of isolation was probably responsible for the number of 'outcasts' who appear in Conrad's work, especially in his Eastern novels—Almayer, Jim, Willems, Leggatt, Axel Heyst, Falk, the mad captain in *The Shadow-Line* (Razumov and the Professor in his Western novels). And this sense of sympathy with the outcast must have caused Conrad to choose from the people he met and heard of in the East— Williams, Olmeijer, the mate of the *Cutty Sark*, Jim Lingard, Captain William Lingard—as models for his characters. And where the isolation was lacking in the original, as in Snadden's case, Conrad added it.

*

Conrad must have seen in the *Jeddah* story an example of what he considered to be, at that period of his writing career, life's predicament. In the first place, it was a sea story and appealed because of his knowledge of sea life. But more important, it presented an example of close, isolated circumstances in which an important choice of action had to be made, with an accepted code on the one hand as one aspect of the choice, and on the other the pressure of circumstances which made allegiance to a code seem impossible. The circumstances on board the *Jeddah* which must have attracted Conrad as examples of the curious workings of fate or destiny or chance were the danger of her sinking, the fact that there were not nearly enough boats to take off her crew and passengers, and the fact that the captain had his newly married wife on board, which made him susceptible of breaking the code, not only of the merchant service, but of humanity itself. In this situation the mate, A. P. Williams, was involved in the ultimate choice, which must have seemed to be either that they stayed on board to die amidst scenes of terrible panic, or that they deserted and left the pilgrims to what would have been their fate in any case.

It was a situation which allowed Conrad to 'doubt of the sovereign power enthroned in a fixed standard of conduct'.[7] And it was made worse in this instance by the extraordinary action of the captain and officers in not only abandoning the 953 pilgrims, but making no effort to have them rescued when the opportunity arose.

Finally, it raised an interest in the kind of man who acted in this way in these circumstances, and who could live with this act later. It invited an analytical, a psychological inquiry.

Conrad brings out in the novel the idea that the face of the facts was different from the emotions beneath it:

> Whether they knew it or not, the interest that drew them there was purely psychological—the expectation of some essential disclosure as to the strength, the power, the horror, of human emotions. Naturally nothing of the kind could be disclosed...Its [the official inquiry's] object was not the fundamental why, but the superficial how of this affair (p. 67).

Desertion and cowardice were the key-notes of the *Jeddah* affair, where the heroic virtues of self-sacrifice and bravery ought to have been demonstrated, and—the final irony—might *safely* have been demonstrated, since the ship did not sink. This final working of destiny must have attracted Conrad particularly.

But a further influence must have been at work in his choice of the *Jeddah* story, since he himself was at that time being accused of desertion and betrayal. While he was writing the novel, a compatriot of his, Eliza Orzeszkowa the novelist, accused him of being 'a shameless careerist, betraying for money his country and his language'. Conrad made a refutation of this in *A Personal Record*:

> ...why should I...undertake the pursuit of fantastic meals of salt junk and hard tack upon the wide seas? On the kindest view it seems an unanswerable question. Alas! I have the conviction that there are men of unstained rectitude who are ready to murmur scornfully the word desertion. Thus the taste of innocent adventure may be made bitter to the palate. The part of the inexplicable should be allowed for in appraising the conduct of men in a world where no explanation is final. No charge of faithlessness ought to be lightly uttered (p. 35).

He was deeply hurt by the accusation, and while the parallels between his case and that of Williams are slight—Williams, after all, *did* desert—it may have been Conrad's awareness of the extenuating circumstances in his own case that caused him to introduce some extenuating circumstances in the case of Jim. For the original source was altered in order to provide different circumstances which might at least provide some sympathetic explanation of such a crime, and the analytical treatment of the source in the novel served to bring out the complexities of such a predicament.

Conrad must have known four facts about Williams with reference to the *Jeddah* incident. Williams did not lose his head in the *Jeddah* incident—he was, in fact, brutally in command of the situation, as the Court of Inquiry shows. He was also a product of a typically English background—good family, good training, the type of the gentleman. He had an ability to rationalize his situation—his letter shows that he has not, or is concealing from himself, a true understanding of his action. And finally, he faced up to the situation by remaining in Singapore as a water-clerk.

It must have been easy to judge Williams because his action was so clear—this was the crime and here was the self-confessed criminal. It demanded, and received, severe public criticism. The Court of Inquiry stated: 'The Court consider it very probable that, but for Mr Williams's officious behaviour and unseamanlike conduct, the master would (*by the first mate's own showing*) have probably done his duty by remaining on the ship.' And in the Assessor's report we have the statement: 'The first mate of the *Jeddah*, *according to his own statement*, is greatly to blame in doing what he could to demoralize the master.' And Williams's reaction was the kind of aggressiveness at which Conrad hints at the beginning of the manuscript version. But Conrad obviously felt that such a case was too simple. Jim had to be a different person, a more sensitive person, in order that the complex matter of loyalty, desertion and betrayal in certain given circumstances could be fully explored. Williams's background was appropriate, and the situation on the *Jeddah* remained that of the *Patna*, but pressure on Jim was added to by the straightforward cowardice of the captain and other officers. In this situation,

Jim had to be at once as simple as Williams, and also complicated by qualities of sensitivity, romantic idealism, and extreme youth. As Marlow says of Jim (almost as though he is Conrad working out the necessary nature of his hero):

> He was not—if I may say so—clear to me. He was not clear. And there is a suspicion he was not clear to himself either. There were his fine sensibilities, his fine feelings, his fine longings—a sort of sublimated, idealised selfishness. He was—if you allow me to say so—very fine; very fine—and very unfortunate. A little coarser nature would not have borne the strain; it would have had to come to terms with itself—with a sigh, a grunt, or even with a guffaw; a still coarser one would have remained invulnerably ignorant and completely uninteresting (pp. 216–17).

Williams was not so coarse that he remained 'invulnerably ignorant and completely uninteresting'. He is totally different from the fictional character Chester in *Lord Jim*: 'What's all the to-do about? A bit of ass's skin...Look at me. I made it a practice never to take anything to heart.'[8] Chester is an example for Conrad of the 'invulnerably ignorant'. Conrad does write of simple characters such as McWhirr and Tom Lingard to whom the issues are plain and who act on them immediately. But he was aware that to some people, especially those afflicted by strong imagination, a situation could not be simple. Jim in this sense is very like the narrator in *The Shadow-Line* and therefore like Conrad: '...I have nothing to do to keep my imagination from running wild amongst the disastrous images of the worst that may befall us...I am shrinking from it. From the mere vision.'[9] Perhaps therefore Conrad is adding something of his own nature, in addition to his own experience, in the creation of Jim.

The novel begins at the point at which Conrad may have met Williams, that is, when he was working as a ship-chandler's water-clerk in Singapore. And it is also from this point onwards that Conrad abandons the facts of Williams's life for the fiction of Jim. The work of a water-clerk, as Conrad makes clear, is not easy. The inset story of little Bob Stanton illustrates this:

> He used to tell us his experiences in that line. He made us laugh till we cried, and [was] not altogether displeased at the effect... 'It's all very well for you beggars to laugh, but my immortal soul was shrivelled down to the size of a parched pea after a week of that work' (p. 184).

And Marlow comments: 'You can't imagine a mode of life more barren of consolation, less capable of being invested with a spark of glamour—unless it be the business of an insurance canvasser' (p. 183). Yet Jim 'did it very well. He shut himself in, put his head down, said never a word.'[10] This is, perhaps, a tribute to Williams, on Conrad's part.

The fact of Jim's sensitivity forced Conrad to find another area in which he could flourish. It is at this point that another aspect of fate or chance enters into Conrad's scheme of things —the importance of character as part of one's destiny. It became necessary for Jim to be given a further opportunity so that his sensitivity, his romantic aspirations, might be tried in a more appropriate arena. Jim is not aware that his opportunity which 'sat veiled by his side like an Eastern bride'[11] is partly his own character. 'I always thought that if a fellow could begin with a clean slate...',[12] he tells Marlow, who reflects, 'A clean slate, did he say? As if the initial word of each our destiny were not graven in imperishable characters upon the face of a rock!'[13] No doubt, had Conrad been able to know the later history of Williams he would have seen in it confirmation of his belief in this form of destiny. As it was, he could not see Jim remaining within the bounds of a society that knew his past because of his sensitivity to his own actions. Yet he had to be tried again, he had to be given further opportunities to try out his character, his destiny. Hence, Patusan.

I have remarked upon the prevalence of the benefactor–protégé theme in Conrad's work and shown how this derived from his sources. But it derived also from the importance in his own life of the same situation—his uncle remained his benefactor as long as he lived and was constantly offering advice, criticism, and money, and getting him out of such scrapes as the incident at Marseilles. Perhaps this aspect of his own life attracted Conrad to Lingard, and perhaps also caused him to provide Jim with two benefactors. A. P. Williams, after all, so far as we know, managed without one. To what extent, therefore, Conrad saw himself as Jim it is impossible to say. I have suggested that the concern with betrayal existed in his own mind, but Conrad's life also fell into two halves as great in contrast as those of Jim. Conrad was more successful in each case, but his own life's pattern might have been a further influence.

The contrast between the first part of the novel, set in the sophistication of the Eastern sea-port, with its police courts, hotels, tourists, sea-faring population, and gossip, and the second, set in that native state of Patusan, could not be greater. 'I don't suppose any of you have ever heard of Patusan?'[14] Marlow remarks, and proceeds to give a reasonably detailed account of its history, geography, and Stein's trading connections with it.

There is moreover a sense of fitness in Jim going to a settlement, such a one as some of the *Patna*'s pilgrims must have come from, in order to find the isolation he needed in which to prove himself. But it is a return to the primitive after the orderly sophistication of the Eastern port, and he is in an anomalous position. He is 'appointed to be a trading-clerk, and in a place where there was no trade...'.[15]

Conrad's choice of the Bornean jungle for the scene of Jim's temporary triumph must have depended upon the process of association in Conrad's mind. He himself travelled direct from Singapore to Berau. In Singapore Williams was working as a water-clerk and at Berau there was Jim Lingard, a young man of twenty-five already an important figure at the settlement of

Tandjong Redeb, a friend of the Sultan, an established trader —but cut off from civilization and living in one of the lost, forgotten places in the world. But there were probably other associations which caused Conrad to identify his hero with the more heroic exploits of Brooke, the more heroic traditions of the Empire and the gentleman. Jim's position in Patusan, like Brooke's, was essentially that of the artistocratic ruler, on whom the people depend absolutely, and who displays the values of honour, duty, fidelity, and friendship, in a heroic arena which provides no rewards for his service except the happiness and safety of his dependants. It would seem that Conrad was here returning to his own Polish background:

> His was the outlook of an uprooted nobleman, conscious of his chivalrous past, although now hard-working: an outlook very typical of Polish literature after 1863. The values he wanted to see cherished—honour, duty, fidelity, friendship—were typically romantic and typically chivalrous, and it is only too obvious that we have to look for their origin to Poland, where the life of the whole nation was, for better or for worse, dominated by these very values.[16]

*

Other aspects of Conrad's source material which appear in his novels cannot strictly be related to his conception of life's predicament, though they probably influenced his work through his conception of his art. The form of the first part of *Lord Jim* is based upon the Inquiry. The official Inquiry into the *Patna* incident takes place at a formal and factual level, and metes out official deserts according to the facts. As Conrad says: 'Its object was not the fundamental why, but the superficial how, of this affair.'[17] It was after the facts which 'had been visible, tangible, open to the senses, occupying their place in space and time, requiring for their existence a fourteen-hundred-ton steamer and twenty-seven minutes by the watch...'.[18] The Inquiry into the *Jeddah* incident and Conrad's own involvement in the *Palestine* Inquiry were obviously his source here. Presumably he himself was only too aware of the difference between the findings of the Court of Inquiry into the burning at sea of the *Palestine* and the emotional experience of the incident. He must have been aware that once panic and fear entered into the situation the public account becomes irrelevant—as irrelevant, and perhaps as incongruous, as that of the *Jeddah*: 'I passed my wife through the window of my cabin', 'when the boat was lowered, the pilgrims commenced to throw boxes, pots and pans, and anything they could lay hands on, into the boat', 'the first officer found himself in the water'. These convey nothing of the emotions of fear and panic that must fill and blur such a moment: '...something else besides, something invisible, a directing spirit of perdition that dwelt within, like a malevolent soul in a detestable body' (p. 35). This is the opposite face of the facts—this is the moaning of the engineer that Jim 'could have reproduced like an echo'.[19] Being strongly aware of the limitations of the public Court of Inquiry, Conrad sees fit to carry out a private inquiry into Jim's motives, with Marlow as a kind of jury, which is enclosed within the official Inquiry. The purpose of this is to get at the 'why' of the affair and it is interesting to note that the facts of the *Patna* case in *Lord Jim* are given to the reader step by step during *this* inquiry and not during the public Inquiry.

The method of narration in the first part of the novel is therefore that of the Inquiry and this comes directly from the source.

There is a further influence of the source on the method of narration, for here we have an instance of the means by which an incident from real life reaches an author becoming the method by which he chooses to relate that incident in his fiction. The complex method of narrative in *Lord Jim* is often pointed out, and criticized or justified on critical grounds. The narrator, Marlow, has come in for his share of abstruse interpretations. But he is, after all, only one of Conrad's many seaman narrators of his sea stories. He is the same Marlow in 'Heart of Darkness', but he is related to the narrator in *The Shadow-Line* and 'The Secret Sharer', and appears in a comic, caricatured, debased form in Captain Joseph Mitchell, the O.S.N.'s superintendent in Sulaco in *Nostromo*. Of course, all these men are different in experience, depth of perception, and ability to understand the significance of events they are involved in, but they are all joined by the common bond of the sea, and their voices are all voices of the seaman relating his experiences when he is safely ashore again.

The story of the *Jeddah* and her desertion reached Conrad by means of the gossip of such seaman narrators and Conrad must have heard expressed every possible opinion on the case. As a result, he began his novel with an incident already in his mind as a number of different points of view, as something heard of in different parts of the world, and with different aspects of the story emphasized at different times. And in writing his novel he would recall some of the occasions which made the story initially so interesting and so complex:

'He left—let's see—the very day a steamer with returning pilgrims from the Red Sea put in here with two blades of her propeller gone. Three weeks ago now.' 'Wasn't there something said about the *Patna* case?' I asked, fearing the worst. He gave a start, and looked at me as if I had been a sorcerer. 'Why yes! How do you know? Some of them were talking about it here. There was a captain or two, the manager of Vanlo's engineering shop at the harbour, two or three others, and myself...the rest of us were round the telescope watching that steamer come in; and by and by Vanlo's manager began to talk about the chief of the *Patna*; he had done some repairs for him once...He came to mention her last voyage, and then we all struck in. Some said one thing and some another—not much—what you or any other man might say...Captain O'Brien of the *Sarah W. Granger*...he let drive suddenly with his stick at the floor, and roars out, "Skunks!" Made us all jump..."It's no laughing matter. It's a disgrace to human natur'—that's what it is. I would despise being seen in the same room with one of those men. Yes, sir!"' (pp. 235–6).

One may rediscover the possible topics of seamen's gossip in a particular port at a particular time, but one cannot of course rediscover the actual gatherings and the actual form of the gossip. But it is very likely that when the young seaman Korzeniowski first found himself in Singapore, he might have been part of such a group as this—perhaps even in some ship-chandler's store—watching the *Jeddah* at anchor in the port, and hearing such comments passed upon her officers. So that the incident became an integral part of the story of Williams. For the story of the *Jeddah*, like that of the *Patna*, consisted not only of the incident itself, but of the attitudes and opinions it called forth in others.

*

A study of *The Shadow-Line* and its source in Conrad's first command throws some light on Conrad's attitude to what he calls 'autobiography'. It suggests that Conrad was very much the story-teller, and that he could not avoid using the techniques of the story-teller even when it came to writing autobiography. The selection and high-lighting of relevant detail, the use of exaggeration, of drama and tension, of the dramatic encounter rather than the straightforward narrative, reveal the writer of fiction, and reflect also the seaman's yarn. So that, in *The Mirror of the Sea*, although Conrad keeps close to the facts of his experience, his method of relating them is the method of the writer of fiction, and to this extent he can never be accurately described as a writer of autobiography.

The Shadow-Line is undoubtedly near autobiography, and undoubtedly Conrad was within his rights to alter his biography towards the realm of fiction as much as he wished. In this instance, he retains the basic facts of his experience at that time—his giving up the berth on the *Vidar*, staying at the Sailors' Home, the interview with the Master-Attendant, the journey to Bangkok, the difficulties encountered there, the fever-ridden ship, the difficult journey back through the Gulf of Siam. He is as exact as ever where dates, length of time, and so on are concerned. But the pattern into which the tale falls, the predominance of certain themes, the emphasis upon the supernatural element, are aspects which suggest a creative process. *The Shadow-Line* is not exact autobiography.

We must consider first of all that although Conrad stresses the idea of a test, of a maturing, through the experiences encountered in the incident, he himself, when he was offered the command of the *Otago* in 1888, probably did not see it in this light. No doubt the offer came as a surprise, and no doubt he saw it as an opportunity, but he would see it also as a sailor—a responsibility to be carried through. Only looking back in later years, and against the background of the First World War, would the elements of testing and maturing appear to be present. And this gap of time between the events and the writing of them—there was a gap of almost thirty years—would surely invalidate Conrad's claim that even the conversations were accurate. Is it likely that at such a distance of time precise conversations, the precise thoughts of the master seeing himself in a mirror, would be remembered exactly? Is it likely, also, that the whole incident would fall so neatly into specific patterns, pointing certain themes? That the ship's company should foreshadow so exactly the people of the world—the mad man, the trouble-maker, the good man who carries death with him?

Granted, therefore, that Conrad is moving from the facts of his source to create fiction, in what ways does he move, what changes does he make, and why?

It seems likely that there was some disagreement between Conrad and the Steward of the Sailors' Home in Singapore, and perhaps it was over the command. Whether or not there was a Captain Giles involved we cannot tell, but he is suspiciously like the typical Conradian benefactor. Especially, the whole incident at the beginning is designed to emphasize the theme of the shadow-line as a maturing period, and part of this maturing comes about through confrontations, with various men, which bring an understanding of human nature, and of its malevolence, jealousy, and self-interest. Near the beginning of the story we have the narrator's comment on the captain who takes him to Bangkok: 'He was the first really unsympathetic man I had ever come in contact with. My education was far from being finished',[20] and later 'the good, sympathetic man' (the Legation doctor).[21] The narrator obtains his command under circumstances which reinforce this theme of maturing through encountering human nature:

> I perceived that my imagination had been running in conventional channels, and that my hopes had always been drab stuff. I had envisaged a command as a result of a slow course of promotion in the employ of some highly respectable firm. The reward of faithful service. Well, faithful service was all right. One would naturally give that for one's own sake, for the sake of the ship, for the love of the life of one's choice...
>
> And now, here, I had my command, absolutely in my pocket, in a way undeniable indeed, but most unexpected...and even notwithstanding the existence of some sort of obscure intrigue to keep it away from me... (pp. 43–4).

I have already suggested that the sickness was not quite so bad on the *Otago* as Conrad pictures it, and that I have some doubts about the fate of the medicine box, but the most unusual thing about Conrad's treatment of his source material lies in his transformation of the kindly, harmless Captain Snadden into the mad, malignant old man who was the narrator's predecessor.

In his Author's Note to the tale, Conrad specifically, if equivocally, denies the intrusion of the supernatural: 'I believe that if I attempted to put the strain of the Supernatural on it [his imagination] it would fail deplorably and exhibit an unlovely gap...The world of the living contains enough marvels and mysteries as it is...' (p. ix). Yet we know that the whole incident of the previous captain, which introduces the theme of the supernatural, was an invention on Conrad's part. But in terms of narrative art, it is an excellent device.

The shadow-line is part of a maturing process, and for the narrator that process is bound up with the code and responsibilities of the merchant service imposed on the master of a ship: 'That man had been in all essentials but his age *just such another man as myself* [my italics]. Yet the end of his life was a complete act of treason, the betrayal of a tradition which seemed to me as imperative as any guide on earth could be' (p. 77). And immediately connected with this is the suggestion of evil: 'It appeared that even at sea a man could become the victim of evil spirits. I felt on my face the breath of unknown powers that shape our destinies.'[22] But the idea of the tradition —the tradition of which the narrator is now part—is the strongest theme:

> Deep within the tarnished ormolu frame, in the hot half-light sifted through the awning, I saw my own face propped between my hands. And I stared back at myself with the perfect detachment of distance, rather with curiosity than with any other feeling, except of some sympathy for this latest representative of what for all intents and purposes was a dynasty; continuous not in blood, indeed, but in its experience, in its training, in its conception of duty, and in the blessed simplicity of its traditional point of view on life.
>
> It struck me that this quietly staring man, whom I was watching, both as if he were myself and somebody else, was not exactly a lonely figure. He had his place in a line of men whom he did not know, of whom he had never heard; but who were fashioned by the same influences, whose souls in relation to their humble life's work had no secrets for him (pp. 65–6).

The narrator is almost immediately brought into abrupt contact with that 'line of men whom he did not know' in the person of the late captain, his predecessor:

> 'Where did he die?'
>
> 'In this saloon. Just where you are sitting now,' answered Mr Burns.
>
> I repressed a silly impulse to jump... (p. 69).

The tradition lies also with the ship which is, like the narrator, needing to cross her particular shadow-line:

> 'I suppose she can travel—what?'
>
> ...He said that a ship needed, just like a man, the chance to show the best she could do, and that this ship had never had a chance since he had been on board of her (pp. 68–9).

And so the past history of the ship is brought out as a contrast to her present history under her new captain. She had been kept loafing at sea for inscrutable reasons, kept sweltering at anchor for three weeks in Haiphong, a pestilential hot harbour without air, and then suddenly had been taken out to beat up to Hong Kong against a fierce monsoon. It had taken the determination of Mr Burns to break through this enchantment, face the captain, and turn the ship about. She has the late captain's *curse* upon her: 'If I had my wish, neither the ship nor any of you would ever reach a port. And I hope you won't.'[23]

The narrator's reaction to this is again his recollection of the hereditary nature of his authority:

> I was already the man in command. My sensations could not be like those of any other man on board. In that community I stood, like a king in his country, in a class all by myself. I mean an hereditary king, not a mere elected head of a state. I was brought there to rule by an agency as remote from the people and as inscrutable almost to them as the Grace of God.
>
> And like a member of a dynasty, feeling a semi-mystical bond with the dead, I was profoundly shocked by my immediate predecessor (p. 77).

As ruler of the ship, he soon cuts through the mate's suggestions of his own brave actions in bringing the ship into port to discover the real motive beneath—'He took the ship to a port where he expected to be confirmed in his temporary command...'[24] And he replies with a declaration of intention: 'I am here to take the ship home first of all, and you may be sure that I shall see to it that every one of you on board here does his duty to that end. This is all I have to say—for the present.'[25]

The suggestion of enchantment continues through Mr Burns's delirium, and through the actual delays of sickness, charterers, and calms with which the ship and her master have to contend, down to the final malignant act of the previous captain in selling the ship's quinine supplies. The ship deteriorates till the men 'were the ghosts of themselves' using only 'spiritual strength' and 'the quietness that came over me was like a foretaste of annihilation...The seaman's instinct alone survived whole in my moral dissolution.'[26]

The ordeal, which had been 'maturing and tempering' the narrator's character, ends with the words of Captain Giles, that simple and unabashed repository of knowledge of human nature: '...a man should stand up to his bad luck, to his mistakes, to his conscience, and all that sort of thing. Why—what else would you have to fight against?...A man has got to learn everything...' (p. 165).

Conrad transforms the story of his first command, by these means, to the dimensions of the traditional folk-tale, with the narrator as the traditional folk-hero who is given certain responsibilities, well defined and in a definite tradition, and a task to carry out within the area of those responsibilities. Before him was the state of evil and enchantment which he, by his example, his wisdom, his determination, has to break through. In *The Shadow-Line* all these elements are present—the comparison with the Ancient Mariner, during the calm, is apparent. Even the captain who takes the narrator to Bangkok, in his surliness, is a folk-tale figure, and Captain Ellis is seen specifically as the good fairy: 'I was very much like people in fairy tales...Captain Ellis (a fierce sort of fairy) had produced a command out of a drawer almost as unexpectedly as in a fairy tale' (p. 49). The folk-tale element is obtained deliberately by Conrad through the transformation of the character of the previous captain, the extension of the sickness, and the emphasis upon the calm. But the basis of this folk-tale element is the factual tale, with all its factual detail of people, places, and ships, that was the story of Conrad's first command. Out of this comes the third element of the story—the real training of the narrator through the solitary testing which also brings insight into the petty jealousies, intrigues, and superstitions of human nature, as well as its heroism and steadfastness. The narrator's experience brings him across the lives of so many other men that his experience of human nature is widened from the officer of some Rajah's yacht who had been 'seeing life' and who tomorrow would 'feel worse yet'[27] to the unfailing Ransome who went 'in mortal fear of starting into sudden anger our common enemy it was his hard fate to carry consciously within his faithful breast'.[28]

No doubt his first command was a maturing process for Conrad, but not exactly in the way he describes. Without the heightening of his material it would have been a sea story of not a great deal of interest. But seeing within that experience the possibilities of universal appeal, he developed his autobiography to that end.

The recurrent theme of the test that appears in so many of his Eastern novels, and which was the theme he sought in his source material in order that the mind in such a predicament might be analysed, is present in a different way in 'The Secret Sharer'. Here fantasy plays a much more obvious part than in the other novels, where fidelity to his source material is apparent. But here also three of the most striking aspects of his Eastern experience appear—the *Otago*, the *Jeddah* and the *Cutty Sark* incidents, though all appear only slightly and obliquely. Conrad's own interest is shown in his writing himself into the *Cutty Sark* situation, involving himself in the mate's guilt—much more strongly than Marlow was involved in Jim's—by aiding his escape, and enhancing this involvement by the similarity in appearance between himself and the murderer. This sympathetic identification on Conrad's part with the violent crime on the clipper is one of the most striking aspects of his use of his source material. In this instance we can point to Conrad's sources and indicate where they are present and where they diminish; and Conrad's deeper concerns—the concerns with failure and consequent self-judgement which haunt the story of Brierly and Wallace, with guilt, betrayal, and extenuating circumstances in a particular predicament—take over.

Finally, may I say that, though I do not think that I have laid Conrad's ghost or exorcized him, I hope I have made some inroad into his secrets, and that this study, in allowing us to contemplate Conrad's original materials, lets us appreciate his skill in bringing together material from so many sources, and in building up the complexity of his stories from them with minute and loving care for the truth.

19-2

APPENDICES

APPENDIX A

AN UNPUBLISHED CONRAD LETTER

Capel House
Orlestone
Nr Ashford

14 June 1917

Dear Mr Saunders

You are a terror for tracking people out! It strikes me that if I had done something involving penal servitude I wouldn't have liked to have you after me. However, as I have done nothing of the sort and am not likely to, now, (too old) I can enjoy without misgivings the evidences of your skill, tenacity and acuteness. Many thanks for your letter with the enclosures giving the history of those lively ladies, the daughters of the late lamented Hayes.

Mostly all the inferences and surmises in your letter are correct. I did go to Minlacowie. The farmers around were very nice to me, and I gave their wives (on a never-to-be-forgotten day) a tea-party on board the dear old 'Otago' then lying alongside the God-forsaken jetty there. *The Smile of Fortune* story does belong to the 'Otago Cycle' if I may call it so. The *Secret-Sharer* in the same vol: also does in a way—as far as the Gulf of Siam setting goes. The Swimmer himself was suggested to me by a young fellow who was 2d mate (in the '60) of the *Cutty Sark* clipper and had the misfortune to kill a man on deck. But his skipper had the decency to let him swim ashore on the Java Coast as the ship was passing through Anjer Straits. The story was well remembered in the Merchant Service even in my time.

To a man of letters and a distinguished publicist so experienced as yourself I need not point out that I had to *make* material from my own life's incidents arranged, combined, coloured for artistic purposes. I don't think there's anything reprehensible in that. After all I *am* a writer of fiction; and it is not what actually happened, but the manner of presenting it that settles the literary and even the moral value of my work. My little vol: of autobiography of course is absolutely genuine. The rest is a more or less close approximation to facts and suggestions. What I claim as true are my mental and emotional reactions to life, to men, to their affairs and their passions as I have seen them. I have in that sense kept always true to myself.

Appendix A

I haven't the time to write more at present but pray believe that I appreciate very highly the kind way you are keeping me in mind. In a few days I'll dispatch to you a copy of the new edn of Lord Jim which is about to be published by Dent's.

Believe me sincerely yours

JOSEPH CONRAD

APPENDIX B

THE 'PALESTINE' INQUIRY*

REPORT of a Marine Court of Enquiry held at the Police Court, in Singapore, on the 2nd day of April 1883, by order of His Excellency Sir Frederick Aloysius Weld, K.C.M.G., Governor and Commander-in-Chief of the Colony of the Straits Settlements, for the purpose of investigating into the burning of the British barque 'Palestine' Official Number 12,684, of London, of 427 tons burthen, on a voyage from Falmouth to Bang Kok.

Present:—

Richard Spear O'Connor, Esquire,
Senior Magistrate, President.

Edward Bradberry, Esquire, Deputy Master Attendant, John Blair, Esquire, Master Mariner	Nautical Assessors.

The 'Palestine' was built of wood, at Sunderland, in 1857, and registered 427 tons. On the 29th November 1881 she sailed from Newcastle-upon-Tyne with a cargo of 557 tons of West Hartley coal, bound to Bang Kok, and a crew of 13 hands all told. Arriving in the chops of the English Channel, the vessel encountered a succession of heavy gales, losing sails and springing a leak on the 24th of December 1881, the crew refusing to proceed, the vessel put into Falmouth. The coal was there discharged and stored under cover, with the exception of about 90 tons, and the vessel thoroughly repaired in dock. On the 17th September 1882 the 'Palestine' sailed from Falmouth with a complement of 13 hands all told, and proceeded on her voyage to Bang Kok. The passage was tedious owing to persistent light winds, but nothing unusual occurred until noon of the 11th March, when a strong smell resembling paraffin oil was perceived; at this time the vessel's position was lat. 2 36 S and long. 105 45 E. Banca Strait. Next day smoke was discovered issuing from the coals on the port side of main hatch. Water was thrown over them until the smoke abated, the boats were lowered, water placed in them. On the 13th some coals were thrown overboard, about 4 tons, and more water poured

* Document no. 1810.

down the hold. On the 14th, the hatches being on but not battened down, the decks blew up fore and aft as far as the poop. The boats were then provisioned and the vessel headed for the Sumatra shore. About 3 p.m. the S.S. 'Somerset' came alongside in answer to signals and about 6 p.m. she took the vessel in tow. Shortly afterwards the fire rapidly increased and the master of the 'Palestine' requested the master of the 'Somerset' to tow the barque on shore. This being refused, the tow-rope was slipped and about 11 p.m. the vessel was a mass of fire, and all hands got into the boats, 3 in number. The mate and 4 seamen in one boat, the 2nd mate with three hands in another and the master in the long boat with 3 men. The boats remained by the vessel until 8.30 a.m. on the 15th. She was still above water, but inside appeared a mass of fire. The boats arrived at Mintok at 10 p.m. on the 15th, and the master reported the casualty to the harbour master. The officers and crew came on to Singapore in the British steamer 'Sissie' arriving on 22nd March.

The Court, having carefully inquired into the circumstances attending the burning and abandonment of the British barque 'Palestine' of London, Official Number 12684, —

FINDS, from the evidence adduced, that there were two ventilators fitted in the vessel, and that the main hatch was frequently taken off during the passage, that the coal was put on board in a dry state, and that the vessel was not provided with thermometers for testing the temperature of the hold. After the fire broke out the officers and crew appear to have done all in their power to subdue it, but, with the limited means at their disposal, without success.

The Court considers that the cause of the fire was spontaneous combustion, the passage having been unusually protracted.

The Court is further of opinion that the vessel was not prematurely abandoned and that no blame is attached to the master, officers or crew.

The officers certificates are therefore returned.

(Signed) R. S. O'CONNOR,
Senior Magistrate, President.

(Signed) E. BRADBERRY, } Nautical
JOHN BLAIR, } Assessors

SINGAPORE, 3rd April 1883.

APPENDIX C

THE 'JEDDAH' INQUIRY

REPORT of a Court of Inquiry held at Aden into the cause of the abandonment of the steamship 'JEDDAH'.*

The steamship 'Jeddah', of Singapore, official number 67,990, under British colours, of $993\frac{44}{101}$ tons register, and owned by the Singapore Steamship Company, Limited, Joseph Lucas Clark, master, left Singapore on the 17th July 1880, for Penang.

On arrival at Penang she filled up with pilgrims, making a total complement of 953 as adult passengers, and proceeded on her voyage on the 19th idem for Jeddah direct; she had 600 tons of cargo on board, principally sugar, garron-wood, and general merchandise. Her crew consisted of 50 souls all told, which number included the master, first and second mates, and third engineer, who were Europeans, and with the captain's wife, the only Europeans on board.

The 'Jeddah' appears to have experienced heavy weather for the most part of her voyage. On the 3rd August 1880, the wind increased almost to a hurricane, with high breaking sea.

On this date the boilers started from their fastenings and began to work, and steps were subsequently taken to secure them with wedges.

The weather increased in severity until the 6th August; on that day, about 9.30 p.m., the feed valve of the port boiler broke, and the ship had to be stopped for repairs, and the vessel then, it was considered, commenced to leak considerably, having shipped much water previously. As soon as repairs were executed, at 1.30 p.m., the vessel again proceeded under steam, when the feed valve on the starboard boiler also broke; and after again stopping for repair, the ship proceeded at 8.30 p.m. with one boiler only. All hands and passengers were then working at the pumps and baling. As the water appeared to increase, the bilge injection was utilized and the leak reduced; but as that became choked, and the vessel stopped to clear it, the leak increased, it is stated, so rapidly as to put out the fires. In consequence of the quantity of water in the stoke-hole, and from the temporary wedges and supports to the boilers having washed away, and the boilers working backwards and forwards owing to the rolling of the ship, every connection pipe was carried away, and the engine-rooms became untenable and a wreck.

* Document no. 896.

Sail was apparently set as soon as the engines became useless, but these were blown away, and other sails subsequently set when the wind moderated.

In the meantime pumping and baling was resorted to, and the passengers appear to have given willing assistance after the evening of the 7th August. On that day the master ordered the boats to be got ready, provisioned, armed, and swung out.

Pumping continued on the part of the passengers up to 12 midnight, then apparently some diminution took place. Certain of the crew were then ordered shortly after to man a boat or boats; the bulk of the crew appear to have manned the boats.

At this time the passengers appear to have become partially disorganized, and to have entertained the idea that the boats were going to leave the ship. The master then appears to have decided to hang the starboard lifeboat astern, and to remain in it with his wife and the first engineer and a boat's crew until daylight, being, he states, afraid of his own and his wife's life being attempted if he remained on board. The starboard lifeboat was then about to be lowered, and the captain and his wife and chief engineer got into it. The captain's wife had to pass some 50 feet from the cabin to the boat. When the boat was lowered, the pilgrims commenced to throw boxes, pots and pans, and anything they could lay hands on, into the boat, and pulled the first officer, who was lowering the boat, off the rails; and seeing they could not prevent the lowering of the boat, they attempted to swamp it. The third engineer had in the meantime got into the boat, and the first officer found himself in the water, and was taken into it, and the boat was then cut adrift, and for about a couple of hours the boat's head was kept to the wind and sea, but after that allowed to drive and partially before the wind, until at 10 a.m. on the 8th August, it was sighted by the steamship 'Scindia', and the persons in it rescued and brought to Aden, where they arrived on the 10th August. On arrival at Aden, the master and others rescued reported the foundering of the 'Jeddah' with all on board, and also reported that the second officer and second engineer had been murdered.

After the master left the 'Jeddah', it appears that the passengers tried to prevent the second officer leaving the ship, which he appears to have attempted, by leaving the captain's boats and going over to the port side to the boat to which he was appointed, and which was manned and ready for lowering. Two of the passengers, Lojis, and an Arab, appear also to have got into this boat. On the pilgrims ordering the people to come out of the boats, and on their refusal, some of the pilgrims (it cannot be ascertained who) cut the falls, and it fell into the sea bow first from the fore fall being cut first, and all in it appear to have perished.

Shortly after this, the second engineer, who was awoke out of his sleep a little time before by the second officer, and told to go to his boat, proceeded to his boat, also on the port side. This boat was to have been commanded by the first officer, the Lojis, finding this boat also manned with the second engineer in it, got in, and threw all the men back from her into the ship, and would not allow them to leave. They then appear to have resumed pumping and baling, and continued doing so without intermission, gaining on the leak; and on the following morning, 8th August, finding themselves in smooth water, they sighted land and made for it, having had sail set all night. They hoisted signals of distress, and at 3 p.m., when about 7 or 8 miles from land, the wind died away. At about 4.30 p.m., the steamship 'Antenor', seeing the signals, bore down on the disabled ship; and the master, after ascertaining the state of affairs, sent his chief mate on board, and took charge, and brought the 'Jeddah' in tow to Aden, where both vessels arrived on the afternoon of the 11th August.

The water in the 'Jeddah' was considerably reduced by the exertions of the passengers, under the direction of the chief officer of the 'Antenor', and that officer on first boarding the ship, and seeing the quantity in her, came to the immediate conclusion that the vessel could be saved. Three sailors, one topman, one syrang, eleven firemen, and one clerk, one fireman working his passage, were all the crew on board the 'Jeddah' when brought to Aden, together with the second engineer and supercargo, and 992 passengers—778 men, 147 women, and children 67, not counting infants in arms, were on board.

The above appear to the Court to be, as far as can be ascertained, the circumstances connected with this case; and in reviewing them, and after a patient and careful inquiry into all the details, the Court record the following opinion:—

It appears that the fastenings of the boilers, which are placed athwartships in the 'Jeddah', were defective, and in consequence of the rolling of the ship and the heavy sea, these fastenings gave way, and caused a leak by the breaking of the connecting pipes with the ship's bottom. This leak, though serious in itself, was intensified by the vessel shipping large quantities of water, and the boilers having to be blown off or emptied into the ship's bilge on several occasions instead of into the sea, when repairs were being executed. With the rolling of the ship, the quantity of water in the stoke-hole appeared greater than it actually was, and from the engine and donkey-engine being useless, the vessel having water also in the after-hold through the sluice, the actual condition of affairs was thought more serious than was the case; the ship having a leak, and being in a heavy sea. It appears to the Court that sufficient notice was not at once taken of the movement of the boilers, and every available means adopted to secure them as much as possible, immediately it was ascertained that they had shifted and were working.

The chief engineer of the 'Jeddah' appears to have treated this matter lightly, and is, in the Court's opinion, primarily responsible for his ignorance in not knowing the extent of the risk and danger run by the boilers moving, and not insisting on all available means being employed at once to stay them.

Had more energetic measures been taken at the outset, it appears just probable to the Court that subsequent events might have been averted. When steam power was no longer available on board the 'Jeddah', it appears to the Court that no regular system of reducing the leak was organized by the master. He appears to have come to the conclusion early on the 7th August that the boats would probably be required, and they were prepared and swung out, and the crew engaged in attending to them rather than to the vessel's condition. The firemen, however, appear to have been steadily engaged in working the ash buckets up to midnight of the 7th August.

The master does not appear to have taken his passengers into his confidence or to have endeavoured in the least degree to raise their hopes in any way. On the contrary, it seems he informed them that if they would not pump the vessel would founder, thereby giving no hope. On this point, situated as he was, the Court consider he was wanting in simple judgment, for he had much in his favour to dispel fear and raise the hopes and energies of his passengers, who appeared ready and willing to assist. Land was not far distant, and yet by his act in ordering the boats he led the passengers to believe that the vessel would probably founder, and the boats would be lowered. Although there is conflicting evidence that the master was of this opinion before the Logis had their thoughts averted from the pumping, the master's action after being picked up by the 'Scindia', and brought to Aden, and his report of the 'Jeddah' having foundered, leads the Court to infer that the master considered the vessel would founder whether pumped and baled out or not. The Court consider he was under the impression from his acts that the 'Jeddah' would founder under any circumstances, but, apart from his impressions, his action in ordering the boats to be prepared was an inducement to disturbance, as only about one quarter of the souls on board could have been accommodated in them.

The Court consider that in this the master showed a want of judgment and tact to a most serious extent, and that he caused disorganization and discontent, not to say despair, at a time when none of these feelings should have been engendered.

The master states that on finding the pilgrims would not work the pumps, shortly after midnight on the 7th and 8th August, and that they appeared altered in demeanour and were some of them armed with knives, he feared that his wife's life and his own would be attempted, as he had been led to infer the same from what he had been told, and consequently very shortly after he found that this was the state of affairs, in place of resorting to measures to restore confidence or to organize any system of defence in case of need, for the protection of the lives of himself and the Europeans on board, which he could easily have done by keeping the bridge with the arms on board, he determined on lowering a boat, in which he intended, he states, first to place his wife and to remain in her himself, to hang astern of the ship until daylight. What the master's intentions were after daylight does not appear. He ordered the boat to be manned, and, after having his wife placed in it, he himself got in and others did also. Up to this time it is evident that no violence or even show of force had been made by the pilgrims to anyone on board; it was only when the boat was being lowered and they became aware of what was taking place, that they appear to have resorted to force, and then not such force as they might have utilized, armed with knives as they were. Failing in preventing the lowering of the boat, the pilgrims proceeded to endeavour to swamp her; two pistol shots were fired in the direction of the pilgrims from the boat by the first officer, and these appear to have prevented any further attempts to swamp the boat, which then was cast off and away from the ship. The passengers, finding other boats were manned, they proceeded to endeavour to prevent their leaving the ship, and, in the case of the second officer's boat, cut it adrift when its inmates would not return on board, and unceremoniously ejected those who had got into the third boat with the second engineer.

The Court consider that the action of the pilgrims tends to prove that they never intended to harm the master and his officers had they remained in the 'Jeddah', that their demeanour is accounted for by the evidence that they had made up their minds that they should not be deserted by the only persons capable of protecting and helping them in the circumstances in which they were placed, and consequently they would prevent to the utmost the master or his officers leaving the ship. It is in the Court's opinion more than probable that the master was misled in regard to the real intentions of the pilgrims, but he has himself to blame for not making more certain of these intentions, or waiting for some more clear proof of these intentions than took place. It is to be regretted that the principal witness, Lezed Omar, on this point could not be examined, as he had left Aden for Jeddah the day after his arrival, and before the steamship 'Jeddah' was towed in.

There is no evidence before the Court to show that the life of the captain's wife was in danger by reason of any threats made by the pilgrims, and this man, Lezed Omar, alone appears to be the authority of this report, and he is stated to have been in dread himself and much frightened for his own safety.

Doubtless the master on hearing this report, as well as imperfectly understanding the threats actually made by the pilgrims, viz., 'that they would not allow any one to leave the ship, and would prevent them to the extent of violence if necessary,' the fact of the pilgrims having armed themselves to ascertain extent to carry out this threat if need arose, aided by the officious ill-advice of his chief officer, entirely forgot his first duty as a shipmaster, and proceeded to be one of the first instead of the last to leave his disabled vessel to her fate. This last act roused the pilgrims to violence in attempting to swamp his boat, and such the Court consider might naturally have been expected from any body of human beings, even Europeans, situated as the pilgrims were.

With every consideration for the master under the trying circumstances in which he and his crew found themselves placed, the Court is reluctantly compelled to state that they consider that Captain Clark has shown a painful want of nerve as well as the most ordinary judgment, and has allowed his feelings to master the sense of duty it is the pride of every British shipmaster to vaunt, and they consider that in the instances mentioned he has been guilty of gross misconduct in being indirectly the cause of the deaths of the second mate and ten natives, seven crew and three passengers, and in abandoning his disabled ship with nearly 1,000 souls on board to their fate, when by ordinary display of firmness, combined with very little tact in dealing with natives, with whom he is no stranger, he could have ensured their co-operation and gratitude, and saved considerable loss to his owners. The Court must here also remark on the want of anxiety shown by the master for the fate of the 'Jeddah', in not doing all in his power to induce the 'Scindia' to search for her, as there is little doubt but that a proper statement of facts and little persuasion would have induced the master of the 'Scindia' under the circumstances to steam for an hour or so to windward, when the 'Jeddah' would certainly have been sighted.

The Court feel compelled to mark their sense of the master, Joseph Lucas Clark's, conduct by ordering, subject to the confirmation of the Bombay Government, that his certificate of competency as master be suspended for a period of three years.

Before concluding, the Court consider it necessary to place on record their disapprobation of the conduct of the first officer of the 'Jeddah', Mr Williams, who may be said to have more than aided and abetted the master in the abandonment of his vessel. The Court consider it very probable that, but for Mr Williams's officious behaviour and unseamanlike conduct, the master would (by the first mate's own showing) have probably done his duty by remaining on the ship.

Had there been any evidence, except the first mate's own statement, on this point, the Court would have felt constrained to have put him on his trial also, they cannot therefore refrain from remarking that they consider that in this instance he has shown himself unfitted for his position as first mate on a crowded pilgrim vessel.

The Court have to regret that, owing to the positive report made of the 'Jeddah' having foundered, no steps were taken to detain or record the evidence of the master and officers of the steamship 'Scindia', as to the reasons and causes for their not searching for the steamship 'Jeddah' after picking up her master and others. The examination of these witnesses would have completed the evidence which otherwise is not as complete as it might, and very desirable that it should be in this case—the most extraordinary instance known to the Court of the abandonment of a disabled and leaking ship at sea by the master and Europeans, and almost all the crew, with close on 1,000 souls on board when no immediate danger existed of her foundering. The Court consider that it is due to the master of the 'Antenor' to place on record their opinion of the contrast of his conduct to that of Captain Clark, and consider him worthy, with his chief officer, Mr Campbell, of great commendation for their action, not only for rescuing those on board the 'Jeddah' from a perilous position and shipwreck, but also for saving a valuable ship and her cargo from loss.

In conclusion the Court consider it is not out of place to remark, that in their estimation nearly 1,000 souls on board a vessel of the tonnage of the 'Jeddah' was a greater number than should be allowed by any regulation, especially for a long sea voyage, as taken by the 'Jeddah', and at a season when bad weather might naturally have been expected.

(Signed) G. R. GOODFELLOW,
Resident and Sessions Judge.

Aden, *20th August 1880.*

I concur.
(Signed) W. K. THYNNE,
Assessor.

Confirmed.
(Signed) JAMES FERGUSSON,
Governor of Bombay.

Appendix C

The Mercantile Shipping Act, in the case of a Board of Trade certificate, only requires the confirmation of the Local Government with reference to the regularity of the proceedings. Had I been advised that any option rested with it with reference to the details, I should have declined to confirm them, as I think the sentence inadequate to the offence committed by the master of the 'Jeddah' as described by the Court.

Assuming that his abandonment of his ship, without necessity, and with the probable loss of an enormous number of helpless people for whose safety he was responsible, was the result rather of cowardice and want of resource than of inhumanity, his subsequent conduct in not doing his utmost to procure them succour showed that latter quality. But in either point of view, he has, in my judgment, shown himself entirely unfit to be entrusted with the charge of life and property at sea.

(Signed) J. F.

ASSESSOR'S REPORT on the abandonment of the steamship 'JEDDAH', of Singapore.

I consider the chief engineer of the 'Jeddah' very much to blame for not taking the most active measures to secure the boilers when he first saw them move on the 3rd of August, more especially as the vessel was labouring heavily. When the matter was reported to the master is doubtful, but from the chief engineer's own statement, my opinion is that the engineer did not report to the master the moving of the boilers until the following day; the reason given by the engineer, viz., that the pipes in connection with the boiler were copper and could stand any strain caused by the moving of the boilers, the movement first observed being three-eighths of an inch, but which gradually increased to about two inches, before the boilers became totally useless by all the important pipes breaking, including the donkey engine steam-pipe. Before this happened, the vessel leaked a good deal in the engine-room, and as long as the engines could be worked the leak could be kept down. Had the chief engineer exercised a little judgment, he surely would have known that the movement of the boilers (which was of a jerky nature) was a most dangerous thing, and likely to become more and more dangerous with every heavy roll of the ship, and was a matter which required his most vigilant care from the first. I cannot understand how the engineer could make himself believe that the movement of the boilers (huge masses, each weighing probably not less than 30 tons when filled with water) was a matter of no consequence at first, merely because the movement was only three-eighths of an inch. Common sense might have taught him that the movement was likely to increase with every roll of the ship.

On the 6th August the engines and steam pumps became useless, the ship leaking, but not to any alarming extent. The bilge injection when working being able to keep the leak down; pumps were manned and baling started without any attempt being made to organise the Hadjees into working gangs, with regular reliefs, or replenishing the supply of buckets, by making canvas ones.

At noon of the 7th August, the ship's position was said to be in latitude 11° 55′ north, and longitude 51° 55′ east, 'Abdul Kuri' bearing north-east ½ east, true distant about 28 miles. With this position, the bearing of Cape Guardafui would be nearly due west, distant about 35 miles. Shortly after the position of the ship had been ascertained, the order was given to get the boats made ready, which was done before sunset, and crews told off, the engineers and officers were informed what boats they were to go in should the boats leave the ship. Before midnight some of the passengers, it was said, had been heard to say they would kill the captain and his wife. This was reported to the captain. Again it [was] stated that the passengers would use force to prevent the captain from leaving the ship; some of the passengers were observed about midnight to be armed with their knives, stated to be any number, from 20 up to 300. The second engineer went to bed at midnight; he did not see any man armed. The captain was warned by the first mate to be careful how he went about the decks, as the passengers might kill him. Up to the time the captain left the ship he was not molested, until he went into the starboard lifeboat, at 2.30 a.m. The first and second mates were at the lowering of this boat. The second mate left at once, called the second engineer, and got into his own boat on the port (*i.e.* weather) side, which was all ready for lowering. As the boat was being lowered the falls were cut by the Hadjees, which caused one end of the boat to fall first, and it is supposed threw the crew out, who were drowned.

Nothing was ever seen of this boat. The Hadjees did what they could to destroy her, they also did what they could to destroy the starboard lifeboat, and I believe knocked the first mate overboard. The distance from the captain's cabin to the starboard lifeboat is stated to be about 40 feet; the captain's wife was passed through one of the windows of the cabin, and either walked along or was carried and put into the boat without being molested, the first mate taking a prominent part in this proceeding.

The first mate of the 'Jeddah', according to his own statement, is greatly to blame in doing what he could to demoralize the master, by advising him to leave the ship, telling him his life was in danger, also his wife's life; that he, the master, was sure to be killed if he remained on board; and that he, the first mate, did thrust the master into the boat. The mate worked on the fears of the master for the safety of his wife, and by so doing hurried the master into leaving the ship.

From noon of the 7th until the 'Jeddah' was picked up by the 'Antenor' she was on the port tack under short canvass, blowing hard from the south, steering west, every hour bringing the vessel nearer to a weather shore, where smooth water might be expected. When the master left the ship at 2.30 a.m. on the 8th August, he must have been distant from Cape Guardafui about 10 miles, judging from the position of the vessel at noon of the 7th of August, viz., latitude 11° 55′ north, and longitude 51° 55′ east; and her approximate position at 4.30 p.m. of the 8th August, viz., latitude 12° north, and longitude 51° 6′ east, when the 'Antenor' steered for her and picked her up.

When the 'Scindia' picked up the starboard lifeboat the 'Jeddah' would be distant about 22 miles, bearing from the 'Scindia' about south-south-west.

The 'Jeddah' having been towed into Aden harbour on the 11th instant, with the water reduced nearly two feet in the after-hold, proved there was nothing hopeless in the state of the ship when abandoned.

1. I am of opinion the master was not compelled to leave the 'Jeddah'.

2. That the master left the 'Jeddah' against the will of his passengers.

3. That no disturbance took place until it became known that the master was leaving the ship, and that such disturbance was confined to damaging the boats and occupants when lowering and when lowered by throwing at and into the boats anything which first came to hand, and by cutting the boats' falls.

4. That by leaving the ship the master was the means of causing the loss of 11 lives, and the ship to be abandoned by the major portion of her crew, thereby greatly increasing the danger of the vessel being lost with all on board had she been leaking very badly. The master concluded she had foundered about three hours after he left her, as he was unable to see her at daylight.

5. The master of the 'Jeddah' when picked up by the 'Scindia', was guilty of great cruelty in not representing matters in such a way to the master of the 'Scindia' as would have induced him to steam dead to windward, or in such a direction as might have been considered best to look for the 'Jeddah', more especially as the master before leaving had no expectation of her foundering soon.

6. A vessel with upwards of 1,000 souls on board is a charge of great responsibility, and makes it more binding if possible on the master to remain on board to the very last, and by so doing tend to inspire his crew

and passengers with courage and determination to save the ship if possible, and by so doing, their lives and property.

I am of opinion had the master's wife not been on board the master would not have deserted his ship.

I am of opinion had the master received proper assistance and advice from his first mate, he, the master, would not have left the ship.

I am of opinion had the master not left the 'Jeddah' no lives would have been lost.

I am further of opinion that the first mate should not be permitted to go in the ship again.

The master of the 'Antenor' states he passed Cape Guardafui about 3.30 p.m., 3′ distant, and steered N. 62° W., true, until he sighted the 'Jeddah' at 4.30, Cape Guardafui being distant about 14 miles, bearing S. 60° west. This bearing is wrong, and should be, according to the course steered, about south 46° east.

Given under my hand at Aden, on this the 20th day of August 1880.

(Signed) W. K. THYNNE, Assessor,

Port Officer, Aden.

*Captain Clark's Report**

CAPTAIN CLARK, lately of the S.S. *Jeddah*, has furnished us with the following statement signed by him of the particulars of the abandonment of that vessel.

'I left Penang on 20th July with a crew of 50 men, 5 European officers and 953 adult pilgrims bound to Jeddah. The weather was heavy and threatening, strong head winds and high sea up to the "1½ degree channel", for two days only we had fine weather. After this (29th July) the weather became very heavy the wind increasing almost to hurricane force at times with a very high cross sea, the ship rolling, pitching and straining heavily. The gale continued with unabating fury and the ship labouring and straining so heavily caused the boilers to break adrift from their fastenings on the 6th August. Steps were immediately taken to secure the boilers, but the weather was so bad that all the toms put in were broken up and every connection with the boilers broken. The water rose in the ship very rapidly and the steam pumping power was rendered useless. The deck pumps were all at work and the Hadjis and firemen were bailing the water out of the engine room in buckets. Notwithstanding, the water gained about an inch per hour, and on the 7th, the water still increasing,

* Published in the *Straits Times Overland Journal*, 8 September 1880.

all the boats were ordered to be prepared and provisioned. On the night of the 7th there was a great difference in the demeanour of the pilgrims, they armed themselves with knives and clubs. About 400 men were clustered all around my cabin on deck and I was informed it was their deliberate intention to murder my wife. I satisfied myself assuredly on this point from the various conversations of the Hadjis and their demeanour left no doubt in my mind as to their intention. At midnight they refused to take the pumps, saying that they would sooner die than pump. I passed my wife through the window of my cabin and got one of the officers to put her in one of the boats. Immediately after this, when starting to lower the boat, a general rush was made by the pilgrims and I was pushed into the boat during which I received several serious blows. The boat was manned by the Chief Engineer with a boat's crew. The boat went down with a rush, the Chief Mate who was in the ship, was hurled overboard and every effort was made to sink my boat. The Hadjis cut us away from the ship. There was a heavy sea on. The third Engineer jumped or was thrown into the boat during the excitement and attack. I picked up the first officer and took him into my boat. This is all I know personally. It transpired in evidence at the Court of Inquiry that the second mate and 11 others—Hadjis and Crew—who were in another boat, were similarly attacked and the boat cut away, the boat went down and all were drowned. I kept my boat's head hove to sea during the remainder of the night and in the morning I saw no signs of the *Jeddah*. My boat was picked up about 10 a.m. by the *Scindia* and taken to Aden.'

(Sd.) J. L. CLARK.

*Letter from Chief Engineer Baldwin of the 'Jeddah'**

The following is a copy of a private letter, dated Jeddah 16th September, received by a resident here from Mr Baldwin, who was Chief Engineer of the vessel when she was abandoned:—

'I little thought when the *Jeddah* left Singapore, that the run would terminate so unfortunately. In fact everything went so well for the three weeks we were under steam that I had begun to congratulate myself on the evident decrease in the consumption, and the continued easy working of the engines. But pride goeth before a fall. And it was a considerable shock my pride got one morning when we were within eighty miles of the African coast, the feed check valve chests gave way one after the other. The cast iron brackets supporting the port boiler broke in pieces allowing

* Published in the *Straits Times Overland Journal*, 2 October 1880.

the boiler to come down two inches on to the fore and after beams, breaking the pipe communicating from the donkey and main boilers to the donkey engine and breaking the bolts holding the main blow down cock to the ship's bottom, causing a leak which in the course of the next twenty four hours let in water enough to lift the plates and bearers in stoke hole and engine-room, and which water with every roll of the ship surged into the furnaces, and returned in streams from the tube doors of the boiler to leeward. I kept the bilge injection open as long as we could get a turn out of the engines, but when the last valve chest gave way, and no means remained for pumping water into the boilers, and our store room flooded, and all but knocked to pieces, and six feet of water to navigate about in and the three of us half drowned, and knocked up for want of sleep, I was at last compelled to own we could do no more and set the firemen to draw water in ashbuckets up the ventilator. I had had the carpenter down trying to stay the boilers from shifting, but the weight of the boilers and superheater and water, combined with the impetus of the rolling of the ship, crushed the wooden blocks like so much dry tinder, and allowed the boilers a travel of about one and a half inches. For myself and the other engineers, I believe we were perfectly justified in acting as we did. Poor Scott in the hurry had got in the wrong boat, from which he was hauled by the Hadjis, and I believe would have been knocked under but for the interposition of Ali the supercargo. Had there been more Europeans left on board when the Captain and Syed Omar left the ship, there would have been more scrimages, and but one Ali. However the whole affair was bad enough to make me decide to have no more to do with the *Jeddah*, and so I told the Agent in Aden, who telegraphed for another Chief, and last Tuesday, Mr J. C. Anderson arrived here with Capt. Craig and the mates. The Agent offered to continue my pay if I would give a hand for a few days which I have done fixing new angle iron brackets under the boilers, and assisting generally. I leave this to-morrow or next day for home. The *Jeddah* is also going to London, and the Agent has offered me a free passage, but I prefer paying my way in another steamer. And so will finish other two years of seagoing, the one dark feature in which is the drowning of our second mate and fourteen others while attempting to lower their boat.'

APPENDIX D

LINGARD'S JOURNEYS ON THE 'COERAN' AND 'WEST INDIAN'

Extracted from the Shipping in Harbour columns of Singapore newspapers

	Coeran			*West Indian*
1864				
Dep.	Craig	Macassar	June	
Arr.	Lingard	Macassar	Nov.	
	(Lingard marries)			
Dep.	Lingard	Borneo	Dec.	
1865				
Arr.	Craig	Borneo	March	
Arr.	Lingard	Sourabaya	July	
Dep.	Lingard	Borneo	Aug.	
	(No mention of next arr.)			
Dep.	Craig	Borneo	Dec.	
1866				
Arr.	Lingard	Brow	May	
	(Lingard buys Craig out)			
Dep.	Lingard	Sourabaya Borneo	July	
Arr.	Lingard	Borneo	Nov.	
Dep.	Hanisch	Labuan	Nov.	
1867				
Arr.	Hanisch	Brow	June	
Dep.	Hanisch	Borneo	July	
1868				
Arr.	Hanisch	Brow	Mar.	
Dep.	Hanisch	Brow	April	
1869				
Arr.	Partridge	Borneo	June	
Dep.	Lingard	Bulungan	July	

Lingard on the 'Coeran' and 'West Indian'

	Coeran					*West Indian*			
1870									
	Arr.	Lingard	Borneo	Mar.					
	Dep.	Lingard	Borneo	April					
	Arr.	Lingard	Brow	Aug.					
	Dep.	Lingard	Borneo	Sept.					
1871					1871				
	Arr.	Ewing	Borneo	Mar.					
	Dep.	Lingard	Borneo	April		(Buys the *West Indian*, April)			
	Arr.	Moss	Coti	July					
	(No mention of next departure)								
						Arr.	Lingard	Macassar	Dec.
1872					1872				
	Arr.	Palmer	Macassar	June					
	Dep.	Merry	Brow	Aug.		Arr.	Lingard	Brow	Aug.
						Dep.	Lingard	Brow	Sept.
1873					1873				
						Arr.	Merry	Borneo	Feb.
						Dep.	Merry	Brow	Feb.
						Arr.	Merry	Borneo	Aug.
						Dep.	Lingard	Brow	Sept.
	Arr.	Avery	Borneo	Oct.					
	(In port till sold)								
1874					1874				
	Sold, February					Arr.	Lingard	Borneo	Feb.
						(No mention of departure)			
						Arr.	Mackay	Borneo	Aug.
						Dep.	Mackay	Brow	Oct.
						Arr.	Donald	Brow	Nov.
						(Repairing)			
						(No mention of departure)			
					1875				
						Arr.	Mackay	Brow	April
						(Ship sold and rebought, June–Aug.)			
						Dep.	Lingard	Borneo	Aug.
						Arr.	Lingard	Bulungan	Dec.

Appendix D

Coeran	*West Indian*			
	1876			
	Dep.	Lingard	Samarang	Jan.
	Arr.	Lingard	Macassar	July
		(No mention of departure)		
	Arr.	Lingard	Brow	Dec.
	1877			
	Arr.	Lingard	Brow	May
	Dep.	Lingard	Brow	May
	Arr.	Lingard	Borneo	Aug.
	Dep.	Lingard	Borneo	Oct.
	1878			
	Arr.	Lingard	Brow	Jan.
	Dep.	Lingard	Macassar	Jan.
	Arr.	Lingard	Borneo	July
		(Up for sale, Aug.)		
	Dep.	Lingard	East Coast	Sept.
	Arr.	Hugill	Borneo Coti	Dec.
			In Singapore Regatta)	
	1879			
	Dep.	Lingard	Macassar	Jan.
	Arr.	Lingard	Macassar	May
		(Up for sale from 22 July and Lingard's name dropped)		

APPENDIX E*

JOSEPH CONRAD: SINGAPORE JOURNALIST'S REMINISCENCES

Two Interesting Letters

Mr W. G. St Clair, former editor of the *Singapore Free Press*, contributes the following to the *Ceylon Observer*:

...While Joseph Conrad was, from about thirty-five to thirty-seven years ago, a mate in the Mercantile Marine in Eastern waters, chiefly in and about the Java and Banda Seas, and of necessity often at Singapore, I was also at Singapore, occupied with the duties of my editorial profession. And although Conrad would have known of my existence, I had no opportunity of knowing [of] his. And so we never met all that time, as our lines did not cross...But the year after I had retired from my work in Singapore, early in March 1917, I happened to pick up, from the magazine table in one of the smoking-rooms of the Sports Club in St James's square, the new *English Review* for that month. I was at once struck by the opening of a new story by Joseph Conrad *The Shadow-Line* with Singapore as the scene. But when the Master-Attendant's Office was mentioned and an interview with that official, whose real name was given—I well remember him as a tall bigboned Ulsterman, rough to look at, but an honest good fellow withal—I felt at once that Conrad and I were just then together on familiar common ground. And there were other points and persons indicated or implied that so interested me that I wrote to the publishers of that Review, to say how greatly I was attracted to the opening of the story from my own actual knowledge of the places and persons introduced. I thought that Conrad would like to know that at length one reader of his new work was familiar, so many years ago, with the scene in which he laid the beginnings of *The Shadow-Line*. I also mentioned others whom Joseph Conrad must have known and had dealings with, such as Bradbury, the Assistant Master-Attendant at Singapore...

Another personage I referred to in my letter to Dent's was one whose name is familiar to readers of Conrad. That is Captain Lingard, the type of the adventurer-skipper of those seas in the old days, now quite extinct. Curiously I met Captain Lingard before Conrad had ever heard of him. It was on my way out to Singapore at the beginning of 1887, in the then

* Abridged from *Malay Mail*, Tuesday, 2 September 1924.

brand new China Mutual steamer—*Tsinan*, on her maiden voyage from Glasgow to Hongkong. The only passengers were Mr Edwin Mackintosh, chairman of the Hongkong Chamber of Commerce (a director of the Blue Funnel line and of the China Mutual) his family, an inspecting engineer of the company and myself. At Penang, two extra passengers came on board, Captain Lingard and his niece. He and I soon made acquaintance, and I was told a good deal about himself and his wanderings through the Dutch Archipelago. He mentioned that he was popularly known among the Malay, Bugis, and Javanese sea-going people, mostly pirates, when a chance offered, as 'Raja Laut', the 'Sultan of the Seas'. When I told him that on the voyage out I had picked up about 800 Malay words from Swettenham's *Vocabulary*, he at once held an examination of a searching character, and when I promptly solved his nautical queries as to the Malay equivalents for scores of sea terms, I was passed with much credit.

Lingard, who was a personage of almost mythical renown, a sort of ubiquitous sea-hero, perhaps at times a sort of terror to evildoers, all over the Eastern waters from Singapore to Torres Straits, and from Timor to Mindanao, was a well-set-up man of perhaps fifty-two when I saw him. Alert, decisive in his movements, just above middle height, with grizzled hair, moustache and beard, cut short after naval style, he had two kenspeckle peculiarities. One of these was the texture of skin of his face, well tanned and wrinkled but with many small areas of smooth almost glossy cuticle, giving his features a hard-bitten weather-beaten impression of a remarkable character. Another was the exceptional definiteness of the 'arcus senilis' that surrounded and encroached upon the corner of his eye. In that Lingard presented to me the most strongly marked case of this recognised token of advancing age, in his case evidently rather premature.

I suggested to Dent and Sons that possibly Joseph Conrad, whose address I did not know, might like to see my letter, and so I enclosed my card for Conrad, writing thereon my long tenure of the Editorship of the *Singapore Free Press*...a few days later I received the following letter from Joseph Conrad:

Capel House,
Orlestone,
nr. Ashford.
March 31, 1917.

Dear Mr St Clair,

Dent communicated to me your letter and enclosed your card, for which much thanks.

Yes, I remember Bradbury. It was he who let me off port-dues when I put into Singapore in distress with *all* my crew unfit for duty (1888). It is a very difficult thing to shove everybody into a tale even as autobiographical as *The Shadow-Line* is. My Captain Giles was a man called Patterson, a dear, thick, dreary creature with an enormous reputation for knowledge of the Sulu Sea. The 'Home' Steward's name (in my time) I don't remember. He was a meagre wizened creature, always bemoaning his fate, and did try to do me an unfriendly turn for some reason or other.

I 'belonged' to Singapore for about a year, being chief mate of a steamer owned by Syed Mohsin bin Ali (Craig, master) and trading mostly to Borneo and Celebes somewhat out of the usual beats of local steamers owned by Chinamen.

As you may guess we had no social shore connections. You know it isn't very practicable for a seaman. The only man I chummed with was Brooksbanks, then chief officer of the s.s. *Celestial* and later, as I've heard, Manager of the Dock at Tan-Jong Pagar. I've heard of course a lot about the men you mention. Old Lingard was before my time but I knew slightly both his nephews, Jim and Jos, of whom the latter was then officer on board the King of Siam's yacht.

In Bangkok when I took command, I hardly ever left the ship except to go to my charterers (Messrs Jucker, Sigg and Co.) and with the chief mate sick I was really too busy ever to *hear* much about shore people. Mr Gould, Consul-General and then Chargé d'Affaires in the absence of Sir E. Satow, was very kind to me during the troubled times I had in port.

Naturally, like everybody else, I was a diligent reader of the excellent and always interesting *Singapore Free Press* then under your direction. I keep my regard for that paper to this day. It was certainly the newspaper of the East between Rangoon and Hong-Kong...

Believe me,
Yours Faithfully,
JOSEPH CONRAD.

A few points in the above letter may be further explained....The Capt. Patterson who appears as Capt. Giles in the story, I remember as a stout ungainly man often to be seen at Motion's, the chronometer and compass-regulating business in Battery Road. The steward of the Sailors' Home, originally Balestier's house, was a retired sergeant of artillery, who combined the supervision of the Sailors' Home with the job of instructor to the old Rifle Volunteers, disbanded about the time Conrad came to the East. His name was Phillips, really a very well-meaning person, whose evangelical activities were mainly devoted to Malay missions. He certainly did much work in translating hymns and portions of the New Testament into Malay. Perhaps his indigestion was strong upon him when he clashed with Conrad...

I think it is a remarkable thing that I should have seen and spoken to the man whom Conrad has made his chief hero of Eastern life in these tropical waters, and yet Conrad should have only known him by hearsay. But as long as Conrad's earlier stories of Eastern seas are read, the name of Captain Lingard will abide as a striking permanent figure in fiction.

The reference to the King of Siam's yacht, the *Maha Chakkhri*, also partly a cruiser and flagship of the Siamese navy, reminds me that that and the other Siamese Government ships were largely officered by Danes ...The firm who were the charterers of the unlucky vessel...Jucker, Sigg and Co., are Danish...

APPENDIX F

PART OF A LETTER FROM THE CHIEF MATE OF THE 'OTAGO'*

...would not be very long amongs us. his last wish was to tell you it as lightly as possible because he said that it would come to hard on you He told me to look after the Vessel as well as I could He left his effects in my care which I will send you as soon the Vessel arrives in the Colones. And if it should happen that I should come to Port Adelaide I will tell you almost every word he said in his last hour The Ring to be delivered to the eldest and the Watch to the second sone. The Capt dictated me a Letter 2 days before he died to send to you I enclose this with my Letter

Yours truly CHAS BORN
Chief Mate

* The remainder of this letter, written by Charles Born, chief mate of the *Otago*, to Captain Snadden's wife, has not survived. I have retained the spelling and punctuation of the original.

APPENDIX G

CONRAD'S 'OTAGO': A CASE OF MISTAKEN IDENTITY

Conrad's love for the only sea-going vessel he commanded finds rich expression in *The Mirror of the Sea*:

> Thus I well remember a three days' run got out of a little barque of 400 tons somewhere between the islands of St Paul and Amsterdam and Cape Otway on the Australian coast...the little vessel...would go on running in a smooth, glassy hollow...There was such fascination in her pluck, nimbleness, the continual exhibition of unfailing seaworthiness, in the semblance of courage and endurance, that I could not give up the delight of watching her... (p. 75).
>
> ...a less than five-hundred-ton barque, my first command, now gone from the face of the earth, but sure of a tenderly remembered existence as long as I live (p. 19).

The only photograph of the *Otago* to have been published appears to be that in Jocelyn Baines's biography of Conrad, and this photograph has been accepted as being of Conrad's *Otago*. However, the photograph in Baines's book is not of the *Otago* which Conrad commanded, but of another and larger ship of the same name.

A leading authority on shipping, Mr A. D. Edwardes, of Glenunga, South Australia, provided me with a photograph of a ship which he claimed was Conrad's *Otago*. Mr Edwardes wrote:

> My collection of photographs contains three photographs of the *Otago*, none of which is particularly good. I have a copy negative of a photo depicting the barque alongside at Melbourne. This is perhaps the best extant and I shall enclose a print for you (letter dated 6 May 1963).

This photograph presented a problem, since it was clearly not of the ship which Baines claimed was Conrad's first command. Baines's photograph had been supplied by the National Maritime Museum at Greenwich, and I sent a copy of my photograph to them, pointing out the difficulty. The Custodian of Manuscripts replied, admitting that there had been a mistake and that

> ...Jocelyn Baines was supplied with a photograph of another vessel also called the *Otago* which was launched in 1869. The vessels are of course different, Conrad's was a barque and that in Baines's book is a ship rigged (letter dated 16 May 1963).

A ship rigged is a vessel with three (or more) masts, square rigged on all; a barque is a vessel with three (or more) masts, square rigged on all except the aftermost mast, which is fore and aft rigged. It is in the matter of rigging that the ship in my photograph differs most obviously from that in Baines's, but it is also a smaller ship. Clearly the photograph supplied to me by Mr Edwardes is of the 'little barque', Conrad's *Otago*. (See Plate 12.)

Conrad gives few details of the *Otago*, and those he gives are not accurate. She was not quite the four hundred tons he makes her, and when he wrote in 1906 that she was 'gone now from the face of the earth' he was mistaken. It has been possible, however, to discover something of 'her age and her history' and Conrad probably knew a good deal of it.

She was built in Glasgow in 1869 by A. Stephen and Sons; her tonnage was 367 tons gross and 346 tons nett; and her measurements were 147 ft. by 26 ft. by 14 ft. She was registered in Adelaide, but her owners were not Henry Simpson and Sons as has been stated. It was not until 1889 that, according to the Registrar of British Ships, Customs House, Adelaide, this firm took her over entirely. Until that date several people, of whom only one was a Simpson, had shares in her.

Conrad would not know what happened to the *Otago* after he gave up his command and left Australia in 1889. She continued to be used as a trading vessel until she was converted into a coal hulk in 1903, according to Lloyd's Register. Huddart Parker Ltd, of North Melbourne, informed me that she was used by them as a coal hulk in Hobart, Tasmania, until 1931, when she was sold to a Captain H. Dodge for £1, and that she was now, they believed, rotting on the banks of the Derwent river, Hobart. An article in the *Royal Australian Historical Society Journal and Proceedings*, XXXIX, Part 5, 1953, pp. 251–2, by R. W. Glassford, describes her situation rather differently: 'Captain Dodge had her beached in her present site with her bows almost in an apple orchard and within the shadows of Mount Direction.' The teak steering-wheel of the *Otago* was presented to Sir David Bone to mark the twenty-fifth anniversary of Conrad's death, to be preserved in the sloop *Wellington*, head-quarters of the Honourable Master Mariners' Company.

The *Otago* has now 'gone from the face of the earth' since she was destroyed by fire in August 1957. A photograph of the water-logged remains was published in the *National Geographic Magazine*, 124, no. 3, September 1963 (Plate 13).

APPENDIX H

A. T. SAUNDERS'S LETTER TO 'NAUTICAL MAGAZINE'*

Sir,

In your issue of February, 1921, is 'A Seaman's Tribute' to Joseph Conrad (Korzeniowski), by F. G. Cooper, which I read with interest, for not only do I intensely admire and delight in Conrad's writings, but I well knew three ships in which he sailed, 'Loch Etive', 'Torrens' and the iron barque 'Otago', 345 tons, built at Glasgow, November, 1869, by Stephen, her first voyage being from Glasgow to Adelaide, where she arrived 31/10/1869.

I was in the office of the 'Otago's' Port Adelaide agents then; her captain, Angus Cameron, joined the Union Steamship Company of New Zealand and died about five years ago, having been local marine superintendent for years. I knew the 'Otago' ever after this, and for twenty-five years knew Captain John Snadden who died in the Gulf of Siam on board the 'Otago', from heart disease, 8th December, 1887, and whom Captain Joseph Conrad Korzeniowski succeeded. Several friendly letters have passed between Joseph Conrad and myself re the 'Otago' and his command of her, and I write this letter in justice to my old friend Captain Snadden and to Joseph Conrad. Clearly Captain Snadden and Conrad never met, therefore Captain Conrad depended on what the officers of the 'Otago' told him and what they said was untrue.

The account of Captain Snadden in the 'Shadowline' is absurd, but I do not blame Joseph Conrad for it. Captain Snadden was not an uncommunicative man; he was rather loquacious and never kept his ship loafing at sea. He had been employed by the owners of the 'Otago', Henry Simpson & Son, Adelaide (to whom Joseph Conrad sent his kind regards through me, but the firm was defunct and its members dead) for over twenty years.

I sent Captain Conrad's good wishes to the widow of the owner of the 'Otago' and she replied: 'Your letter giving Joseph Conrad's message and address reached me yesterday—Thank you very much for it—We all remember with pleasure Capt Korzenowski's [sic] visits to us at Woodville. The boys used to enjoy them as much as my husband and I did.'

Yours etc.,

(Signed) A. T. SAUNDERS

* June 1921, p. 567.

REFERENCES

The numbers are those in the text. Page references to the works of Joseph Conrad are to the 1921 Heinemann Collected Edition unless otherwise stated.

I. INTRODUCTION: THE CONDITIONS OF CONRAD'S ACTIVE LIFE (pp. 1–15)

1 *A Personal Record* (London: Dent, 1946), p. 87.
2 Author's Note to *The Shadow-Line*, p. xii.
3 G. Jean-Aubry, *Joseph Conrad, Life & Letters* (London, 1927).
4 Jocelyn Baines, *Joseph Conrad, A Critical Biography* (London, 1959).
5 *The Mirror of the Sea* (London: Dent, 1946), p. 3.
6 See J. D. Gordan, *Joseph Conrad, The Making of a Novelist* (Cambridge, Mass., 1940), ch. II, and *Life & Letters*, chapters V and VI.
7 Letter of 1 November 1906, *The Selected Letters of Henry James*, ed. Leon Edel (New York, 1955), p. 157.
8 Introduction to *Letters from Joseph Conrad (1895–1924)* (Indianapolis, 1928).
9 Author's Note to *Within the Tides*, pp. vii–viii.
10 Letter of June 1896, *Letters from Joseph Conrad*, p. 59.
11 *Lord Jim*, p. 13.
12 *The Shadow-Line*, p. 21.
13 *The Mirror of the Sea*, pp. 121–3.
14 Letter of 27 March 1917, *Life & Letters*, II, 186.
15 *The Shadow-Line*, p. 77.
16 *Ibid.* p. 133.
17 Gordan, p. 35.
18 So far as Conrad's Eastern novels and stories are concerned, the most interesting studies have been Florence Clemens's article, 'Conrad's Favorite Bedside Book', *South Atlantic Quarterly*, XXXVII (1939), 305–15; chapter II of J. D. Gordan's book, *Joseph Conrad, The Making of a Novelist*, pp. 28–74, and his article 'The Rajah Brooke and Joseph Conrad', *SP*, XXXV (1938), 613–34.
19 Ford Madox Ford, *Joseph Conrad, A Personal Remembrance* (London, 1924), pp. 231–2.
20 Author's Note to *The Secret Agent* (London: Dent, 1947), p. x.
21 Ford, p. 232.
22 *A Personal Record*, pp. 74–6.

23 Author's Note to *Victory* (London: Dent, 1946), p. xii.
24 Author's Note to *Lord Jim*, p. vii.
25 Author's Note to *Typhoon*, p. vii.
26 *The Mirror of the Sea*, pp. 133–4.
27 Robert Payne, *The White Rajahs of Sarawak* (London, 1960), p. 171.
28 *The Mirror of the Sea*, pp. 56–7.
29 *Ibid.* p. 59.
30 Author's Note to *Typhoon*, p. viii.
31 Letter of 24 May 1912, *Life & Letters*, II, 139.
32 Author's Note to *Tales of Unrest* (London: Dent, 1947), p. vii.
33 Author's Note to *Within the Tides*, pp. viii–ix.

2. BIOGRAPHY: THE EASTERN SEAS (pp. 16–37)

1 Author's Note to 'Youth', pp. xi–xii.
2 Letter of 20 January 1882, *Life & Letters*, I, 68.
3 'Youth', p. 6.
4 *Ibid.* p. 40.
5 *Ibid.* p. 43.
6 *Ibid.* p. 44.
7 'Youth', p. 44.
8 *The Shadow-Line*, p. 11.
9 *Ibid.* p. 10.
10 Ashley MS, 4787, British Museum.
11 J. H. Drysdale, 'Awakening Old Memories', *One Hundred Years of Singapore* (London, 1921), II, 540.
12 *Lord Jim*, p. 236.
13 Baines, p. 73.
14 *Life & Letters*, I, 79–86.
15 *Ibid.* I, 83.
16 Letter of 19 January 1922 (*ibid.* II, 264).
17 Baines, p. 85.
18 *A Personal Record*, pp. 68–9.
19 'Youth', p. 47.
20 *Lord Jim*, p. 13.
21 *Life & Letters*, I, 95.
22 *Ibid.* I, 94.
23 *The Shadow-Line*, p. 5.
24 *Ibid.*
25 *Life & Letters*, I, 98.
26 *'Twixt Land and Sea* (London: Dent, 1947), p. 6.
27 *Life & Letters*, I, 116.
28 Baines, p. 100.
29 Information supplied by State Library of Victoria, Melbourne.
30 *Life & Letters*, I, 116.
31 *Life & Letters*, I, 120; Baines, p. 105.
32 *Life & Letters*, I, 117; Baines, pp. 100–1.

References

3. THAT SCANDAL OF THE EASTERN SEAS (pp. 41–64)

1 *Lord Jim*, p. 10.
2 *Ibid.* p. 14.
3 *Ibid.* p. 15.
4 *Ibid.* p. 17.
5 *Ibid.* p. 22.
6 *Ibid.* p. 31.
7 *Ibid.* p. 102.
8 *Ibid.* p. 105.
9 *Ibid.* pp. 163–4.
10 *Ibid.* p. 165.
11 *Ibid.* p. 10.
12 Author's Note to *Typhoon*, p. viii.
13 'Joseph Conrad in Polish Eyes', *The Art of Joseph Conrad: A Critical Symposium*, ed. R. W. Stallman (Ann Arbor, 1960), p. 43.
14 'On Lord Jim (an excerpt)', *ibid.* p. 140.
15 *Lord Jim*, p. 26.
16 *The Times Literary Supplement*, 6 September 1923; Gordan, pp. 60 and 61; Baines, p. 252.
17 'Youth', p. 4.
18 *Ibid.* p. 20.
19 *Ibid.* p. 10.
20 *Ibid.* p. 16.
21 'As regards the value of the property salved, it appears that the *Jeddah* was insured for £30,000' (*Straits Times Overland Journal*, 22 October 1881).
22 Gordan, p. 61.
23 *Lord Jim*, p. 43.
24 *Ibid.* p. 44.
25 *Ibid.* p. 15.
26 *Ibid.*
27 *Ibid.* p. 17.
28 *Ibid.* p. 32.
29 'Youth', p. 27.
30 *Lord Jim*, p. 102.
31 *Ibid.* p. 120.
32 *Lord Jim* MS, p. 162 (Rosenbach), quoted from Gordan, p. 165, since the Rosenbach Museum does not provide microfilms of MSS.
33 *Lord Jim*, p. 102.
34 Report on the Action for Salvage brought against the *Jeddah*, *Straits Times Overland Journal*, 22 October 1881.
35 *Ibid.*
36 *Ibid.* The newspaper was torn and difficult to read at this point.
37 *Ibid.*
38 *Lord Jim*, p. 168.
39 'Youth', p. 38.
40 *Lord Jim*, p. 44.
41 *Ibid.* p. 42.
42 *Lord Jim*, p. 185.
43 Author's Note to *Lord Jim*, p. viii.

4. THE FLESH AND BLOOD INDIVIDUAL (pp. 65–86)

1 *The Times Literary Supplement*, 6 September 1923.
2 Gordan, p. 63.
3 Baines, p. 253.
4 *Lord Jim*, p. 190.
5 *Ibid.* p. 179.

6 This is according to his Application for Renewal of his Master's Certificate.

7 *Lord Jim*, p. 144.

8 *Ibid.* p. 127.

9 *Ibid.* p. 196.

10 The report of the Legislative Council debate appeared in the *Straits Times Overland Journal*, 20 September 1880, reprinted from the *Singapore Daily Times*, 16 September 1880.

11 *Lord Jim*, p. 80.

12 *Ibid.*

13 *Ibid.* p. 91.

14 *Ibid.* p. 161.

15 *Ibid.* pp. 188–9.

16 *Ibid.* p. 3.

17 *Lord Jim* MS, p. 308 (Rosenbach), quoted by Gordan, p. 168.

18 Gordan, p. 169.

19 *Lord Jim*, p. 144.

20 *Ibid.* p. 146.

21 *Ibid.* pp. 80–1.

22 *Ibid.* p. 159.

23 Baines, p. 1.

24 Ford, p. 57.

25 *Lord Jim*, p. 225.

26 *Ibid.* p. 286.

27 *Ibid.* p. 287.

28 *Lord Jim* MS, p. 1 (Harvard).

29 *Lord Jim*, p. 90.

30 *Ibid.* p. 94.

31 *Ibid.* p. 241.

32 *Ibid.* pp. 47–8.

33 Williams's Application for Certified Copy of Certificate of Mate.

34 *Life & Letters*, I, 97.

35 *Lord Jim*, p. 237.

36 *Ibid.*

37 Author's Note to *Lord Jim*, p. x.

5. THE RAJAH LAUT (pp. 89–118)

1 *Almayer's Folly*, p. 6.

2 *Life & Letters*, I, 97.

3 Gordan, pp. 35–45.

4 The newspapers consulted were the *Straits Times*, the *Singapore Daily Times*, the *Singapore Free Press*, the *Straits Times Overland Journal*, and the *Straits Budget*.

5 *An Outcast of the Islands* (London: Dent, 1923), pp. 189–90.

6 *Almayer's Folly*, p. 6.

7 Gordan, p. 38.

8 *Een Halve Eeuw Paketvaart, 1891–1941* (Amsterdam, 1941), p. 292, n. 1. 'Over „Olmeyer" schrijft M. G. Van Der Burg in zijn rapport over dienst 8a in 1893, dat hij toen reeds 13 jaren in Beraoe woonde en...'

9 'Conrad's River', *Columbia University Forum*, V, no. 1 (Winter, 1962), 34.

10 F. W. Burbidge, *The Gardens of the Sun: or a Naturalist's Journal on the Mountains and in the Forests and Swamps of Borneo and the Sulu Archipelago* (London: John Murray, 1880), p. 19. The date of this book precludes the influence of Conrad.

11 John Dill Ross, *Sixty Years' Life and Adventure in the Far East* (London, 1912), I, 82.

12 Roland St J. Braddell, 'The Merry Past', *One Hundred Years of Singapore*, II, 518.

13 John Dill Ross, I, 81.

14 *Almayer's Folly*, p. 33.

15 John Dill Ross, I, 82.

16 'The Merry Past', *One Hundred Years of Singapore*, II, 503.

17 The *Singapore and Straits Directory*, 1885, appendices, p. 175.

18 *Almayer's Folly*, p. 30.

19 Reference here is to an edition published by Ernest Benn (London, 1951). The passage beginning 'Seeing him go away beyond his reach' to 'the image of that man' does not appear in the Dent Edition of 1946.

20 *Een Halve Eeuw Paketvaart, 1891–1941*, p. 292, n. 1: '„feitelijk het hoofd van het landschap" and: „De sultans raadplegen hem in alle aangelegenheden".'

21 'A Familiar Preface' to *A Personal Record*, p. xv.

6. AN EASTERN RIVER (pp. 119–38)

1 *Lord Jim*, p. 399.

2 Gordan, pp. 35–45 and 51.

3 *Lord Jim*, p. 408.

4 The *Eastern Archipelago Pilot*, 1st ed. (London, 1893), II, 340.

5 *Almayer's Folly*, p. 161.

6 *An Outcast of the Islands*, p. 112.

7 The *Eastern Archipelago Pilot*, 6th ed. (London, 1949), II, 468–9.

8 *Ibid.* II, 470.

9 *Ibid.* 1st ed. II, 340.

10 *Ibid.*

11 Quoted by Captain Sir Edward Belcher, R.N., C.B., *Narrative of the Voyage of H.M.S. Samarang during the years 1843–46* (London, 1848), I, 279.

12 *Ibid.*

13 *Ibid.* I, 214–15.

14 *Ibid.*

15 *Almayer's Folly*, p. 8.

16 Belcher, I, 241–2.

17 *Ibid.* II, 167–8.

18 The *Eastern Archipelago Pilot*, 1st ed. II, 340.

19 *Almayer's Folly*, p. 7.

20 *Ibid.* p. 16.

21 The *Eastern Archipelago Pilot*, 1st ed. II, 340.

22 *Lord Jim*, p. 317.
23 *Ibid.* p. 412.
24 *Ibid.* p. 384.
25 *Ibid.* p. 269.
26 *Ibid.* p. 270.
27 *An Outcast of the Islands*, p. 64.
28 *Ibid.* p. 33.
29 *Ibid.* p. 34.
30 Gordan, p. 64.
31 *Ibid.* p. 66.
32 *Ibid.* p. 71.
33 *Lord Jim*, p. 334.
34 Public Record Office, F.O. 12/86.
35 *Almayer's Folly*, p. 151.

7. UNDOUBTED SOURCES: DULL, WISE BOOKS (pp. 139–70)

1 'The End of the Tether', p. 204.
2 'The Trail of the Book-Worm: Mr Joseph Conrad at Home and Abroad', *Singapore Free Press*, 1 September 1898.
3 Letter of 13 December 1898, *Joseph Conrad. Letters to William Blackwood and David J. Meldrum*, p. 34.
4 Captain Rodney Mundy, *Narrative of Events in Borneo and Celebes down to the Occupation of Labuan* (London, 1848).
5 Captain the Hon. Henry Keppel's *Expedition to Borneo of H.M.S. Dido for the Suppression of Piracy* (London, 1846), and *Visit to the Indian Archipelago in H.M. Ship Maeander* (London, 1853).
6 Spenser St John, F.R.G.S., F.E.S., *Life in the Forests of the Far East; or Travels in Northern Borneo* (London, 1863).
7 *Memoirs of a Malayan Family* written by themselves and transcribed by W. Marsden, F.R.S. (London, 1830).
8 J. D. Gordan, 'The Rajah Brooke and Joseph Conrad', and Florence Clemens, 'Conrad's Favorite Bedside Book'.
9 Alfred Russel Wallace, *The Malay Archipelago* (London, 1894).
10 Major Fred. McNair, *Perak and the Malays: 'Sārong' and 'Krīs'* (London, 1878).
11 Sherard Osborn, *My Journal in Malayan Waters* (London, 1860).
12 Frank S. Marryat, *Borneo and the Indian Archipelago* (London, 1848).
13 Richard Curle, 'Joseph Conrad: Ten Years Later', *Virginia Quarterly Review*, x (1934), 431.
14 Clemens, p. 309.
15 *Ibid.* p. 310.
16 *Ibid.*
17 *Ibid.* p. 312.
18 *Ibid.* p. 313.
19 Wallace, p. 259.
20 *Lord Jim*, p. 248.
21 Wallace, p. 36 n.
22 *Lord Jim*, p. 279.
23 Reprinted in the *Straits Times*. See chapter 5, p. 104.

24 *Tales of Hearsay and Last Essays* (London: Dent, 1928), p. 91.
25 Gordan, p. 354 n. 256.
26 Baines, p. 254.
27 McNair, p. 283.
28 *Lord Jim*, p. 359.
29 *Ibid.* p. 324.
30 *Ibid.* p. 312.
31 McNair, p. 380.
32 *Lord Jim*, pp. 324–5.
33 Wallace, p. 360.
34 *Lord Jim*, p. 421.
35 *Ibid.* p. 316.
36 *Ibid.* p. 317.
37 Gordan, p. 354, n. 253.
38 *Lord Jim*, p. 443.
39 *Ibid.* p. 444.
40 Belcher, I, 214.
41 *Lord Jim*, p. 445.
42 Belcher, I, 218.
43 *Ibid.* I, 219.
44 *Lord Jim*, p. 455.
45 Carl Bock, *The Head-Hunters of Borneo: A Narrative of Travel up the Mahakhan and down the Barito, also Journeyings in Sumatra* (London, 1882), p. 22. I would not want to press this as a source.
46 *Lord Jim*, p. 319.
47 *Ibid.* p. 320.
48 *Almayer's Folly*, p. 20.
49 *Ibid.* p. 67.
50 *Ibid.*
51 *Ibid.* pp. 61–2.
52 *Ibid.* p. 99.
53 Wallace, p. 127–8.
54 *Almayer's Folly*, p. 44.
55 *Ibid.*
56 *Ibid.* p. 72.
57 *Ibid.* p. 106.
58 *Ibid.* p. 147.
59 Osborn, p. 69.
60 *Ibid.* p. 36.
61 *An Outcast of the Islands*, p. 52.
62 St John, II, 196.

8. AN EASTERN PORT: SINGAPORE (pp. 173–94)

1 Letter of 24 April 1922, *Conrad to a Friend*, ed. Richard Curle (New York, 1928), pp. 113–14.
2 Gordan, p. 50.
3 *Lord Jim*, p. 12.
4 *Ibid.* p. 32.
5 *The Shadow-Line*, p. 2.
6 'The End of the Tether', p. 204.
7 *Ibid.* p. 219.
8 *The Shadow-Line*, p. 33.
9 *Ibid.*
10 'The End of the Tether', p. 219.
11 *Ibid.* p. 219.
12 *Ibid.*
13 G. P. Owen, 'Shikar', *One Hundred Years of Singapore*, ed. W. Makepeace, G. E. Brooke, R. St J. Braddell (London, 1921), II, 374.
14 *Ibid.* II, 369.
15 F. J. Hallifax, 'Municipal Government', *One Hundred Years of Singapore*, I, 328.
16 'The End of the Tether', p. 220.

17 'The End of the Tether', p. 221.
18 *Ibid.* p. 254.
19 *Ibid.* p. 229.
20 *Ibid.*
21 *Ibid.* p. 231.
22 *Ibid.* p. 232.
23 R. St J. Braddell, 'The Merry Past', *One Hundred Years of Singapore*, II, 486.
24 'The End of the Tether', p. 232.
25 *Almayer's Folly*, p. 50.
26 *The Shadow-Line*, p. 8.
27 *Lord Jim*, p. 80.
28 *The Shadow-Line*, p. 45.
29 *Ibid.* p. 48.
30 *Ibid.* p. 47.
31 *Lord Jim*, p. 50.
32 *Ibid.* p. 93.
33 *Ibid.* p. 95.
34 *Ibid.* p. 93.
35 'The End of the Tether', pp. 223–4.
36 *Lord Jim*, p. 46.
37 Braddell, *One Hundred Years of Singapore*, II, 495.
38 'The End of the Tether', p. 228.
39 *Ibid.* p. 236.
40 *Ibid.* pp. 235–6.
41 *One Hundred Years of Singapore*, I, 584–6.
42 'The End of the Tether', p. 235.
43 *Ibid.* p. 238.
44 Keppel, *A Sailor's Life under Four Sovereigns* (London, 1899).
45 *Ibid.* I, 263.
46 Sherard Osborn, *My Journal in Malayan Waters* (London, 1860).
47 *Ibid.* p. 11.
48 Braddell, *One Hundred Years of Singapore*, II, 474.
49 'The End of the Tether', p. 240.
50 Mrs Florence Caddy, *To Siam and Malaya* (London, 1889).
51 *Ibid.* p. 78.
52 *Ibid.* p. 82.
53 *Ibid.* p. 201.
54 *Ibid.* p. 222.

9. THE DEPUTY NEPTUNE AND THE ARAB SHIPOWNER (pp. 195–207)

1 *The Shadow-Line*, p. 33.
2 *Ibid.* p. 34.
3 *Ibid.* p. 35.
4 *Ibid.* p. 40.
5 *Ibid.* p. 35.
6 *Lord Jim*, p. 45.
7 *Ibid.* p. 46.
8 *The Shadow-Line*, p. 163.
9 'The End of the Tether', p. 243.
10 *Ibid.* p. 244.
11 *Ibid.* p. 245.
12 Secret and Confidential Despatches to the Secretary of State for the Colonies, 26 December 1887.
13 'The End of the Tether', p. 244.

14 *Ibid.* p. 221.
15 *Ibid.* p. 227.
16 *Ibid.* p. 228.
17 *Ibid.* p. 238.
18 *Ibid.* p. 244.
19 *Ibid.* p. 247.
20 *Ibid.* p. 251.
21 *Ibid.* p. 209.
22 Letter of 27 March 1917, *Life & Letters*, II, 186.
23 'The End of the Tether', p. 210.
24 *Ibid.* p. 254.
25 *Ibid.* p. 246.
26 Charles Burton Buckley, *An Anecdotal History of Singapore*, II, 565.
27 J. H. Drysdale, 'Awakening of Old Memories', *One Hundred Years of Singapore*, II, 541.

10. FIRST COMMAND (pp. 211–17)

1 *Life & Letters*, II, 181.
2 *Ibid.* II, 182.
3 *Ibid.* I, 104. 'From comparison between these two stories [*The Shadow-Line* and "Falk"] and documents in our possession we can reconstruct the events which followed accurately.' See also Baines, p. 94 and footnote.
4 Author's Note to *The Shadow-Line*, pp. x–xii.
5 *Singapore and Straits Directory*, 1884.
6 Baines, p. 92 n.
7 *The Shadow-Line*, p. 58.
8 *Ibid.* p. 57.
9 *Ibid.* p. 58.

11. CONRAD'S PREDECESSOR ON THE 'OTAGO' (pp. 218–27)

1 *The Shadow-Line*, p. 101.
2 *Life & Letters*, I, 105.

12. THE DELAY IN BANGKOK (pp. 228–45)

1 *The Shadow-Line*, p. 81.
2 *Life & Letters*, I, 109.
3 *Ibid.* I, 105–6.
4 *The Shadow-Line*, p. 80.
5 *Ibid.* p. 82.
6 Baines, p. 94.
7 *The Shadow-Line*, p. 85.
8 *Ibid.* p. 79.
9 *Ibid.* p. 101.
10 Keating Collection, Yale.
11 'Falk', p. 169.
12 *Life & Letters*, I, 107.
13 'Falk' MS, p. 26.
14 'Falk', p. 219.
15 *Ibid.* p. 222.
16 *Ibid.* p. 221.
17 *Life & Letters*, I, 108.
18 'Falk', p. 206.
19 *Ibid.*
20 *Ibid.* p. 216.
21 *Ibid.* pp. 215–16.
22 *Typhoon*, p. 8.
23 'Falk', p. 206.
24 *Life & Letters*, I, 108.
25 Baines, pp. 94–5.
26 'Falk', p. 207.

27 Author's Note to *Victory*, p. viii.
28 'Falk', pp. 203–4.
29 *Ibid.* p. 179.
30 E. A. Brown, *Indiscreet Memories* (London, 1934).

13. THE GULF OF SIAM (pp. 246–9)

1 *Life & Letters*, I, 110.
2 Baines, p. 95.
3 *The Shadow-Line*, p. 163.

14. 'THE SECRET SHARER': THE BASIC FACT OF THE TALE (pp. 253–69)

1 Basil Lubbock, *The Log of the Cutty Sark* (Glasgow, 1925), pp. 191–7.
2 'The Secret Sharer', p. 101.
3 *Ibid.* p. 142.
4 *Lord Jim*, p. 4.
5 *Ibid.* p. 96.
6 'The Secret Sharer', p. 106.
7 This information was obtained from his certificates, copies of which are in my possession.
8 Lubbock, p. 196.
9 *Ibid.*
10 *The Shadow-Line*, p. 64.
11 *Ibid.* p. 79.
12 *Lord Jim*, p. 71.

15. JUSTICE TO THE VISIBLE UNIVERSE (pp. 270–91)

1 MS of *Rescue* (Ashley MS, 4787, British Museum), p. 61.
2 Author's Note to *The Nigger of the 'Narcissus'*, pp. vii and xiii.
3 *Youth and Gaspar Ruiz* (Dent: London and Toronto, 1920), p. 167.
4 Humphry House, *The Dickens World* (Oxford University Press, 1960), p. 12.
5 Letter of 29 February 1908, *Life & Letters*, II, 68.
6 *Lord Jim*, p. 113.
7 *Ibid.* p. 60.
8 *Ibid.* p. 198.
9 *The Shadow-Line*, pp. 132–3.
10 *Lord Jim*, p. 185.
11 *Ibid.* p. 300.
12 *Ibid.* p. 227.
13 *Ibid.*
14 *Ibid.* p. 267.
15 *Ibid.* p. 289.
16 Zdzisław Najder, *Conrad's Polish Background, Letters to and from Polish Friends* (Oxford University Press, 1964), p. 31.
17 *Lord Jim*, p. 67.
18 *Ibid.* p. 35.
19 *Ibid.*
20 *The Shadow-Line*, p. 58.
21 *Ibid.* p. 99.
22 *Ibid.* p. 77.
23 *Ibid.* p. 75.
24 *Ibid.* p. 78.
25 *Ibid.* p. 79.
26 *Ibid.* p. 136.
27 *Ibid.* p. 17.
28 *Ibid.* p. 167.

1 Conrad at twenty-six.

2 A. P. Williams at Porthleven Parsonage, 1868.

3 A. P. Williams and his wife.

4 A. P. Williams at McAlister's.

5 Jim Lingard.

6(*a*) Tandjong Redeb.

6(*b*) The *Rajah Laut*.

7 Nakhoda Trong.

N° 27.

Master Attendants Office
Singapore 19th January/88

S. B 1/88.
No

Sir,

I have the honor to acknowledge the receipt of your telegram "can you engage Master to take "Otago" from Bangkok to Melbourne "salary £14 a month to come here "by first Steamer and sail at once to which I replied " Master engaged proceed "Hecate".

The person I have engaged is Mr. Conrad Korzeniowski, who, holds a Certificate of Competency as Master from the Board of Trade. He bears a good Character from the several Vessels, he has sailed out of this Port.

I have agreed with him that his wages at £14. per month to count from date of arrival at Bangkok.

H. B. M. Consul General.
Bangkok.

Bangkok. Ship to provide him. with food and all necessary articles for the navigation of the vessel. His passage from Singapore to Bangkok to be paid by the ship; also on his arrival at Melbourne if his services be dispensed with, the owner to provide him with a cabin passage back to Singapore.

I consider the above terms are cheap, reasonable, and trust will meet with your approval.

I have the honor to be
Sir
Your Obedient Servant

Henry Ellis
Master Attendant S.S.

8, 9 Letter from Henry Ellis to the Consul at Bangkok.

10, 11 Captain Snadden's photograp and last letter.

Barque Otago Dec 6th 87.

My dear Wife & Children

The Worry through Simson Agency has at last effected my heart so much, that I am compelled to resign shortly to nature great destruct. I regret I have not foreseen this before. I can only commend you and my Children to the care of him who has watched over you so often in my absence. It may linger on a little longer but finnally in a few hours or days I mus say good bye to all remember me to all my friends My business matter are in the hands of J. P. Hodg, as

Agent Port Adelaide and should
you require further Advice
consult D. Bews Esq J. Taylor and
A T Taylor to who I wished to be
at the last moment kindly remembered
Capt and Mrs Hay also. I your last
Letter you spoke of Mort as being
in the Hospital. I trust the opporation
on her ears will be succesfull. I am
unable at present to write this
myself but I kindly got the Chief
Mate Mr Chas Born to do so for
me he has been very kind during
my illness for over a week this
Gentleman will have care of all
my effects which he will see carefully
send to you packed up. Stewart

and Mr Jackson has been also very
kind to all which Gentleman I sinciely
thanks. No doubt they world will
jump on you now, as it has been
in all cases nearly. Should any
Lawyer be required you be wise
and consult C. H Deshwood Igle
chambers Adelaide wishing you
all and more a short farewell
I am yours in Christ
John Snadden.

12 Two photographs of the *Otago*.

13 The water-logged remains of the *Otago*.

14(*a*) Post Office and Cavenagh Bridge, Singapore, looking east *c.* 1890:

A. The Post Office; B. The Harbour Office; C. Cavenagh Bridge; D. Building in which Emmerson's Tiffin-Rooms, McAlister's and Motion's were situated; E. The Esplanade.

14(*b*) James Motion's shop. See D above.

Index

Index